COLLECTOR'S GUIDE TO
WALLACE NUTTING PICTURES
IDENTIFICATION & VALUES

Michael Ivankovich

COLLECTOR BOOKS
A Division of Schroeder Publishing Co., Inc.

The current values in this book should be used only as a guide. They are not intended to set prices, which vary from one section of the country to another. Auction prices as well as dealer prices vary greatly and are affected by condition as well as demand. Neither the author nor the publisher assumes responsibility for any losses that might be incurred as a result of consulting this guide.

Searching for a Publisher?

We are always looking for knowledgeable people considered to be experts within their fields. If you feel that there is a real need for a book on your collectible subject and have a large comprehensive collection, contact Collector Books.

On the cover:
The Coming Out of Rosa...14 x 17...$418.00 (6/94).

Cover design: Beth Summers
Book design: Michelle Dowling

COLLECTOR BOOKS
P.O. Box 3009
Paducah, Kentucky 42003–3009

Michael Ivankovich
P.O. Box 2458
Doylestown, PA 18901

Copyright © 1997 by Michael Ivankovich
Values updated 1999

Contents

Other Wallace Nutting reference books available from Michael Ivankovich

P.O. Box 2458 * Doylestown, PA 18901
(add $3.75 P&H for 1st book ordered, $1.25 for each additional book)

Wallace Nutting Expansible Catalog...featuring nearly 1,000 Wallace Nutting Pictures...160 pgs...$14.95

The Alphabetical and Numerical Index to Wallace Nutting Pictures, by Michael Ivankovich...Listing over 10,000 Wallace Nutting picture titles and including the location of most titles...310 pgs...$16.95

Wallace Nutting, by Louis MacKeil...Includes information on Nutting's personal background and picture & furniture business...48 pgs $8.95

The Guide to Wallace Nutting-Like Photographers of the Early 20th Century, by Michael Ivankovich...including David Davidson, Fred Thompson, Sawyer, Higgins & more...64 pgs...$11.95

The Guide to Wallace Nutting Furniture, by Michael Ivankovich...the #1 book on Nutting's Reproduction Furniture...160 pgs $14.95

The Wallace Nutting General Catalog, Supreme Edition,...a great visual reference reprint of Nutting's 1930 Reproduction Furniture Catalog...168 pgs........$13.95

Wallace Nutting: A Great American Idea...a useful visual reference reprint of the 1923 Reproduction Furniture Catalog covering Nutting's Script Branded Furniture...36 pgs $11.95

Wallace Nutting Windsor Furniture...a useful visual reference reprint of Nutting's 1918 Windsor Reproduction Furniture Catalog; Nutting's most complete Windsor Catalog...48 pgs $11.95

Wallace Nutting Gallery

You can also visit Mr. Ivankovich's Wallace Nutting gallery on the Internet at www.wnutting.com. This Wallace Nutting web site features information on upcoming Nutting auctions and events, a frequently updated "pictures for sale" page, Nutting collecting tips, Q&A's and trivia, help in obtaining a value on your Nutting pictures, and much more.

An Introduction to Wallace Nutting Pictures

Wallace Nutting was America's foremost photographer. Between 1900 and his death in 1941, he sold literally millions of hand-colored pictures. His work achieved such enormous popularity that hardly an American middle-class household was without one during the first quarter of the twentieth century.

Beginning in 1897, Wallace Nutting took nearly 50,000 pictures. Most failed to meet his high standards and were destroyed. Of the 10,000 that he did keep, most were sold in limited numbers, while others were not sold commercially at all. Wallace Nutting would simply take photos for use in his lectures, research, or for his friends, and those particular pictures would never be hand-colored or sold to the general public.

By most estimates, only 2,000 different titles were sold commercially. Some of these titles were extremely successful and sold in very large numbers. Titles like The Swimming Pool, Larkspur, A Barre Brook, An Afternoon Tea, and Honeymoon Drive were so popular that tens-of-thousands of each picture were sold.

*Wallace Nutting,
1861 – 1941.*

Other titles were introduced commercially, failed to generate any significant sales, and were withdrawn. For example, titles like The Belles of San Gabriel, Southbury Water, and Mohonk House from Spring Path appear in the 1912 Picture Catalog but do not appear in the 1915 Expansible Catalog, indicating a low level of sales in the 1912 – 15 period.

Literally millions of these hand-colored platinotype pictures were sold. They were beautiful, inexpensive, and provided many people with the opportunity to decorate the walls of their homes at a very reasonable price.

As with many other things, however, people tended to tire of them after 20 – 30 years. Many were thrown away, others were stored in attics and basements. Only within the past 30 years, as they have been recycled through auctions and estate sales, have they regained much of their previous popularity.

In the 1960s Wallace Nutting pictures could sometimes be purchased for as little as $.50 or $1.00 each or, for all practical purposes, for the price of the frame. Older collectors remember the days when an auctioneer would hold up

Apple blossoms were some of Wallace Nutting's favorite views.

five Wallace Nutting pictures and say "What'll you give me on this frame lot?"

By the early 1970s, prices had increased to the $10 – $50 level. Some people assembled fabulous collections during this period. Collections of several hundred pictures were not uncommon. Gordon Chamberlain assembled a collection of nearly 1,000 pictures, all framed and hanging in one house; Lou MacKeil's collection was approximately 800 pictures; several other collections contained in excess of 500 pictures.

By the 1980s, Wallace Nutting collecting had caught on and prices began to escalate. In fact, prices more than doubled in some categories between 1986 and 1988 alone. In the second edition price guide published in 1986, I had predicted that "In a few years, quality Wallace Nutting pictures will no longer be readily available. They will occasionally turn up, but prices of several hundred dollars will probably seem reasonable, not high." It would appear that I may have been correct because Nutting collectors today are constantly bemoaning the fact that they rarely find anything but "junk" or over-priced pictures at antique shows, flea markets, and even at Brimfield, the world's largest antique event.

And, as we near the year 2000, prices remain strong, especially for the best pictures in the most unusual categories. The Nutting market has become more sophisticated than before, and collectors have developed a better eye for rarer and higher quality pictures. Although more common pictures with water stains, poor coloring, or other imperfections still continue to sell, the better pictures, the "4's" & "5's" are bringing more than ever because today's collector has developed a better understanding of the differences between a poor, average, and great picture.

Why? What's behind all this interest in Wallace Nutting?

First and foremost was the formation of the Wallace Nutting Collector's Club. Founded by Justine and George Monro in 1973, this club

Justine & George Monro, founders of the W. Nutting Collectors Club.

served as the initial gathering place for collectors to buy, sell, and trade Wallace Nutting pictures. More importantly, it still serves as an important source of information on Wallace Nutting. For more than 20 years the Wallace Nutting Collectors Club has gathered and shared Wallace Nutting research material with collectors all over the country. This has not only heightened awareness and educated people about Wallace Nutting, but began to create a demand for his pictures as well. Although Justine Monro passed away several years ago, George Monro still serves as club president, and the Wallace Nutting Collectors Club boasts nearly 400 members throughout the United States and Canada. (You can write to the author for details on how to join the Wallace Nutting Collectors Club).

The second reason for this increased interest in Wallace Nutting was the publication of several books relating to Wallace Nutting pictures. Four important books were written concerning the who-what-where-how much questions most frequently asked by most collectors.

Who Was Wallace Nutting? The late Louis MacKeil covered this in his 1982 book *Wallace Nutting*. This biographical-type book covered such topics as Wallace Nutting, the Man; Wallace Nutting's Picture Business; Wallace Nutting's Furniture Reproduction Business; and Books Written by Wallace Nutting. This easy-to-read book covered all key parts of his life and provided collectors with a fundamental understanding of who Wallace Nutting was.

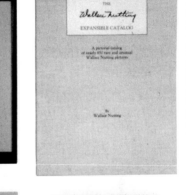

What Do His Pictures Look Like? In the absence of seeing huge collections in person, the publication of Wallace Nutting's 1915 salesman's picture catalog, the *Wallace Nutting Expansible Catalog*, enabled collectors to visually observe nearly 900 pictures that had actually been sold...and that were still available to collect.

Where Was My Picture Taken? The 1988 release of The Alphabetical and Numerical Index to Wallace Nutting Pictures covered that question. Serious collectors take Wallace Nutting much further than simply buying a picture and hanging it upon their wall. They want to know where it was taken...is it an early or late picture?...what is its Studio #?...does it appear in any other Wallace Nutting books? The Alphabetical/Numerical Index answered all these questions...and more...for collectors.

Assorted Wallace Nutting picture reference books.

How Much Is My Picture Worth? Beginning with the first edition *Price Guide to Wallace Nutting Pictures* in 1984, the second edition in 1986, the third edition in 1989, and the fourth edition in 1991, now this *Collector's Guide to Wallace Nutting Pictures* answers this very important question. By showing collectors and dealers what key characteristics to look for...what is common and what is rare...what the difference is between a good, better, and best picture...this guide will help collectors to gauge the approximate value of any Wallace Nutting picture.

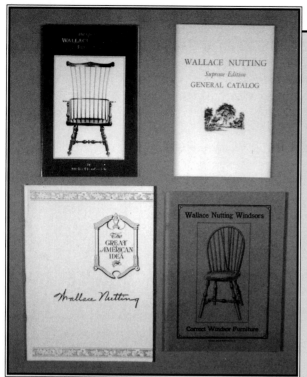

Assorted Wallace Nutting furniture reference books.

Four additional books are also available on Wallace Nutting bench-made reproduction furniture. The most important book is *The Guide to Wallace Nutting Furniture*. Although this book focuses primarily upon Wallace Nutting's furniture reproduction business, it also covers important information on Wallace Nutting pictures and books. And more importantly, this book further stimulated interest in Wallace Nutting pictures simply because of the synergy of the Wallace Nutting name.

The net effect of these Wallace Nutting reference books has been to create a more informed, better educated group of collectors. As in other fields of collecting, the more knowledgeable collectors become, the more dedicated they are to their specialized field of collecting.

The third key factor in this expanding popularity of Wallace Nutting pictures has been their increased visibility throughout the antique trade. Nearly every trade paper and magazine in the country has carried several articles on Wallace Nutting over the past few years. This has served to open the doors of Wallace Nutting collecting to new collectors who wouldn't normally have had the opportunity to read about the subject.

This increased awareness has led many dealers to now actively add Wallace Nutting pictures to their inventory. Both dealers and auction houses also now actively advertise Wallace Nutting pictures in the trade papers. And, several dozen dealers are now even specializing in them, establishing strong followings at various shows and markets around the country.

Antique trade papers with published articles on Wallace Nutting.

This specialization in Wallace Nutting has even carried into the auction field. In March 1988 the first all-Wallace Nutting auction was held in Lee, Massachusetts. Nearly 1,000 pictures from the Gordon Chamberlain collection were offered in a two-day sale, with strong prices indicating a high level of interest in Wallace Nutting.

This was followed six months later by the Michael Ivankovich auction in Framingham, Massachusetts. This auction represented the first all-Wallace Nutting consignment auction, with nearly 500 lots of Wallace Nutting pictures, books, and furniture, consigned by 25 collectors and dealers...all offered in a one-day auction. More than 300 people attended this sale and the high level of enthusiasm generated at the early Nutting auctions has led to 25 more all-Wallace Nutting auctions between 1988 – 1996, with three to four Michael Ivankovich Wallace Nutting specialty auctions taking place each year throughout the New England and Mid-Atlantic states.

These Wallace Nutting auctions have now become the primary national market place for Wallace Nutting pictures. They provide the opportunity for collectors and dealers to compete for a wide variety of Wallace Nutting pictures, ranging from the more common untitled exterior scenes… to the best and rarest pictures in the country…all sold in one location, at one single auction.

A Wallace Nutting specialty auction.

For collectors and dealers, these auctions allow individuals to see more Wallace Nutting pictures in one day than they will see anywhere else. And only by seeing 300 – 500 pictures, all laid out side-by-side, can collectors really begin to examine and learn the subtle differences between average, good, and great pictures. Many collectors have told us that they have stopped wasting their weekends combing the flea markets and antique shows looking for pictures and instead plan two to three trips per year to attend our Wallace Nutting auction weekends.

These auctions also give sellers of Wallace Nutting pictures an excellent means of reaching the top collectors in the country. Whether a private individual selling out an entire collection of rare and unusual pictures, a collector weeding out lower-end pictures in order to trade up, or a dealer liquidating unsold Wallace

Nutting inventory, these auctions attract collectors and enthusiasts from around the country who all have one thing in common…a love for Wallace Nutting pictures. And when you have 100+ Nutting collectors in the same room, the Wallace Nutting market will help to determine fair market value for whatever is being sold on that particular weekend.

But most importantly of all, the popularity of Wallace Nutting pictures can be attributed to their universal appeal. Young people love them because they show our country as it once was…the way they have never seen it. Older people love them because of the memories of simpler times past…no skyscrapers…no telephone poles…no super highways…no pollution.

Unblemished country roads were another of Nutting's favorite views.

The objective of this book is not to set prices, but to report prices. A good price guide does not and should not set prices. Rather the market place should set prices by what people are willing to pay for particular pieces.

Many people will be amazed at the prices they see in this *Collector's Guide to Wallace Nutting Pictures*. Some will think "I've never seen prices like these at my local auction. These prices are way too high." Not so. You should be aware that prices will generally vary by region of the country. Some regions have a much higher level of interest in Wallace Nutting than others, and therefore prices are generally the highest where the interest is the greatest. Most prices reported in Chapter 12 represent prices actually paid.

Others may think "I saw a picture go much higher at my local auction. Therefore some of these prices are too low." In some cases, this may be true. However, you must remember the nature of auctions: some items sell for considerably more than their true worth, many items sell for their approximate value, and some items are downright bargains (which are then frequently purchased and marked-up by knowledgeable dealers). That's the nature of auctions.

Secondly, prices included here are representative of what is being paid around the country. The price of all Wallace Nutting pictures sold throughout the country obviously cannot be included here. After the publication of the second edition price guide, I had a dealer from New York write me a nasty letter, and then follow it up with a loud phone call, accusing me of "ruining her Nutting business." It seems that she had regularly been charging, and getting, higher prices than I had reported in the price guide. She became upset when a customer questioned her prices as being out of line, using the price guide by "that guy in Pennsylvania" as a reference.

A Virginia Reel, interior scene, Framingham, MA, 14" x 17", 4, $225.00 – 325.00.

I tried to explain to her that if she was able to get higher prices than I reported, great. But just because she was able to get a certain price in the Hudson River valley, that didn't mean the same price structure held up in the Delaware River valley or the Tennessee River valley.

My point here is that regional prices do exist. Although we have seen a definite trend toward nationally recognized price levels since the introduction of the first edition *Price Guide to Wallace Nutting Pictures*, prices will still vary around the country, depending upon the local level of interest in Wallace Nutting, and the current economic climate there. In some regions, the higher levels in the price chart will apply; in others, the lower levels may apply for the same picture.

The prices and price ranges listed in this book are intended to help the reader establish a fair and approximate range of values for various Wallace Nutting pictures. It will be helpful to all levels of collectors or dealers in differentiating excellent pictures from average pictures, and rare pictures from common pictures.

The pricing chart in Chapter 3 is a unique guide that can be used in establishing a "ballpark" value on any Wallace Nutting picture. It provides useful rules of thumb and will be of value to both the person buying or selling a particular picture.

Chapter 12 includes the actual sale price, or in some instances, the asking price, on several thousand pictures. This list has been compiled from many sources and represents current prices that have either been:

* Paid at auction (primarily Michael Ivankovich Antiques auctions of 1994 – 1996, but also in many regional auction houses as well).

* Paid at the retail level (including prices reported from antiques shows, flea markets, and direct mail sales).

* Observed by us during our research and travels to antique shops, group shops, flea markets, antique shows, Brimfield, the Wallace Nutting Collectors Club Convention, etc. These were prices and pictures that we actually observed, we saw the condition, and we felt the asking price to be fair, realistic, and consistent with the current market.

Wallace Nutting pictures at auction.

The titles in Chapter 12 represent a comprehensive cross-section of pictures that have come into the market place. Those titles that appear several times are generally indicative of more common pictures. This collector's guide also includes an expanded numerical grading system to help you better correlate condition with price, as well as the approximate date of sale, to help you determine the recency of any particular sale.

One final word of caution. Just because the $5,000 level has nearly been reached at auction, and that the $1,000 level has been surpassed on numerous occasions, not all Wallace Nutting pictures are worth $1,000. Nor will they ever be worth that much.

One of the biggest problems with record prices is that they attract a great deal of public attention, especially from dealers and collectors. Dealers read a portion of an article, figure their picture is special, and raise the price from $100 to $500. And

The Guardian Mother still holds the Wallace Nutting auction record for a single picture, selling for $4,950 in 1989. This picture had the only Guardian Mother label that collectors had ever seen.

the picture sits…and sits…and sits. I've seen so many common overpriced pictures lately that I can't imagine anyone ever buying them.

Or what's worse, dealers will raise the price of a $100 picture to $275, and then drop the price to $200 for the first semi-serious buyer who comes along. Who's getting the bargain, the buyer…or the seller?

We have seen literally thousands of inflated and unrealistic prices set by uninformed dealers in our travels. Just remember, only the rarest pictures, in the absolute best condition, will sell at top prices. Everything else is worth proportionately less. And, as the Wallace Nutting market has become more sophisticated and mature, condition has become increasingly important.

Nutting Collecting Tip: Only the rarest pictures, in the best condition, will sell at top prices. Everything else is worth proportionately less and should be valued accordingly.

But regardless of price, whether paying $50 for a small untitled exterior or $1,500 for a cow scene, Wallace Nutting pictures are a pleasure to collect. They are colorful, beautiful, and historical. They can be purchased at antique shops or antique shows, at garage sales or flea markets, at auctions or through the mail. And bargains are still out there, if you look hard enough.

Keep looking, because Wallace Nutting pictures have finally come of age.

Wallace Nutting Collecting Tips

* Read as much as you can on the subject of Wallace Nutting. Observe and study as many pictures as possible in order to learn the difference between average, good, and great pictures.

* Join the Wallace Nutting Collectors Club. For a very modest investment ($17/year in 1996), you will receive two semi-annual club newsletters, the opportunity to attend the annual club convention, the mailing list of club members, and invaluable contacts throughout the Wallace Nutting collecting community.

* Attend a Wallace Nutting Specialty auction. This will give you the opportunity to see and compare 300 to 500 Wallace Nutting pictures, all laid out side-by-side, in one location. Only when you see so many pictures together will you really begin to understand the Wallace Nutting Numerical Grading System and the differences between average, good, and great pictures.

* As with all other forms of antiques and collectibles…buy the best quality that you can afford. In the past, average pictures have increased in value at an average pace. Great pictures have appreciated at a much greater rate.

* Remember that only the rarest pictures, in the best condition, should be valued at top prices. Everything else will be worth proportionately less and should be valued accordingly.

* But most importantly: buy what you like…because you like it…not because you think it will increase in value. Remember that all markets, whether it be antiques, commodities, real estate, etc., have peaks and valleys. Don't let anyone guarantee that a picture will increase in value. There are no guarantees in the antique business.

Wallace Nutting and The Picture Process

Chapter 1

Wallace Nutting was born in 1861, in Rockbottom, Massachusetts. Upon his father's death during the Civil War in 1864, he moved to Maine to live with his grandparents. After working on his grandfather's farm and attending high school there, he entered Exeter Academy in 1880. From 1883 to 1886 he attended Harvard University and from 1886 to 1888 he attended the Hartford Theological Seminary and the Union Theological Seminary in New York.

In 1889, Wallace Nutting was ordained as a Congregational Minister at the Park Congregational Church in St. Paul, Minnesota. There was no doubt that he always wanted to be a minister as he was frequently quoted as saying "I would rather preach than anything else on earth."

Wallace Nutting, circa 1936.

And preach he did. Never willing to accept second best, Wallace Nutting worked tirelessly at writing the perfect sermon. He would work for many days writing each sermon, and would be tired long afterward.

Perhaps he worked too hard. Some sources reported that he suffered from vertigo. Others say that he suffered a nervous breakdown resulting from the energy he expended preaching. Regardless of the cause, Wallace Nutting retired from the ministry in 1904.

Prior to his retirement, while living in Providence, Rhode Island, his wife Mariet (Griswold) had urged him to take long bicycle rides into the countryside to help him relax. As his health began to fail, he took more trips than ever. Never a man to sit still for too long, Wallace Nutting learned that he could enjoy his trips even more if he took his camera along. Traveling at first by bicycle or carriage, and later by car, he soon found that he had a knack for taking pictures.

He attempted to sell his first few pictures to a local merchant, and they sold very quickly. Using his profits to buy better cameras and equipment, he took more pictures, sold them, and his business began to grow. At age 43, he started upon a brand new career.

As the next several years went by, he began touring the New England countryside while on vacation, either by carriage, car, or train, taking photographs of rural America. Nutting was one of the first to recognize that the American scene was rapidly changing. Industrialization was altering the way America looked and our pure and picturesque country would never look the same again. He seemed to feel it his divine calling to record the beauty of America for future generations.

A Wallace Nutting touring car, circa 1915.

Wallace Nutting opened his first studio in New York City in 1904. After a prolonged illness, he decided he needed the fresh air of the country. In 1905 he opened a larger studio in Southbury, Connecticut and purchased a new home which he named Nuttinghame. As his business continued to expand, he quickly grew into several other buildings.

Nutting developed a keen eye for composition and he mastered the technical skills of printing high quality pictures on a special platinum paper. He enhanced the beauty of his pictures by having them hand colored by a small group of colorists he employed in his studio. He placed some of his pictures in several smaller art and gift shops where they began to readily sell. He then used his early profits to purchase better equipment and to expand the scope of his operations.

Starting first in Vermont, and then eventually traveling throughout the rest of New England, Nutting would photograph country lanes, streams, orchards, lakes, and mountains. Wallace Nutting would take the photograph, assign a title, and instruct his colorists how it should be colored. Each picture that met Nutting's high standards of color, composition, and taste would be affixed to its matting and signed by his employees with the Wallace Nutting name. Those pictures that did not meet his strict standards were destroyed.

Beginning first with outdoor scenes in New England, Nutting eventually traveled throughout the United States and Europe, taking photographs in 26 states and 16 foreign countries between 1900 and 1935. Overall, he took more than 50,000 pictures, 10,000 of which he felt met his high standards. The balance were destroyed.

It was around 1905 that Nutting began taking his first interior pictures. Supposedly one day while it was raining outside, Mrs. Nutting suggested that he take a more personable picture indoors. So he set up a colonial scene in his Southbury home, had an employee dress up in a colonial fashion, and took several different pictures. These sold relatively easily which encouraged him to expand further into this area.

In 1907, he opened a branch office in Toronto, Canada. Nutting took a number of pictures in Canada and hoped to market them effectively there. This expansion proved to be too costly and was soon closed.

With the business doing very well around 1911 – 12, he opted to sell it...and *Nuttinghame.* As luck would have it, after *Nuttinghame* was sold, the buyer of the picture business backed out and Nutting was left with the picture business, but no home.

As a result, he packed up and moved to Framingham, MA, where he purchased another house, this time named *Nuttingholme.* Starting with a group of 20 employees he brought from Southbury, Framingham is where the business really blossomed, growing to over 200 employees.

The China Cupboard, a typical Wallace Nutting scene.

Between 1900 and his death in 1941, Nutting sold literally millions of his hand-colored photographs. Sold throughout the first quarter of the twentieth century, well before the invention of color photography, these pictures initially cost only pennies. His picture market was primarily those middle and lower-middle class households which could not afford finer forms of art. Because of their low price, Wallace Nutting pictures were purchased in large numbers. By 1925, hardly an American middle-class household was without one. They were purchased as gifts for weddings, showers, Christmas, birthdays, and just about any other reason imaginable.

The height of Wallace Nutting picture popularity was 1915 – 25. During this time Nutting employed nearly 100 colorists, along with another 100 employees who acted as framers, matters, dark room staff, salesmen, management, and assorted administrative office personnel.

Nuttingholme, Framingham, MA, circa 1935.

Let there be no mistake about it...Wallace Nutting pictures were big business. Shortly before World War I, the business was grossing as much as $1,000 a day.

The Picture Process

Wallace Nutting would always take his own photographs. He had a keen sense for composition and taste, and excelled at finding beautiful locations to shoot. He would personally determine the angle, lighting, and position, and would take the actual photograph himself.

Upon returning to the studio, each picture would be given a title. Some titles were created by Nutting, and others were created by his staff. Some titles were entirely unique. Others were very similar to other titles in existence. Frequently Nutting would find the appropriate location, shoot a picture from several different angles, give each picture a different title, and see which title would sell best.

The title would then be inserted into the master studio number book. With literally thousands of loose pictures floating around the studio at any given time, the studio number was written on the back of most pictures to help in their later identification.

Wallace Nutting colorists and employees, circa 1930.

Glass negatives were used to print pictures onto sheets of platinum paper, which led to his pictures being called platinotypes. Nutting liked the platinum paper because he felt it held the colors better and gave a more favorable overall appearance to the picture. After World War I began, Nutting lost his source of platinum paper and was forced to find a substitute paper. Although slightly inferior to the platinum paper, few collectors can detect the difference.

After assigning a title, Wallace Nutting would have a sample picture colored. He would describe in detail how the picture should look, and usually the head colorist (supervisor of colorists) would color the first picture to Nutting's specifications. Once approved by Wallace Nutting, the "model" picture became the one that all of the other colorists would strive to follow when coloring subsequent pictures.

Once the model picture was approved, the other colorists would hand color either a single picture or an entire proof sheet of the same picture, following the model as closely as possible. The larger the picture, the fewer pictures to a sheet. Each colorist would apply all colors on a sheet, until finished.

Model picture, with colorist coloring instructions.

Prior to painting, the uncolored picture would first be coated with a thin layer of amyl acetate (more commonly called banana oil), because Nutting found that the banana oil helped the water colors adhere to the platinotype better and longer. The colors used by the colorists were produced by the Winsor and Newton Company and were imported directly from England. There were many colors which came in both tubes and cubes. The colorists used their own porcelain trays and mixed their own colors to the specification of the model picture.

Once colored, the entire sheet would be given to the head colorist who made the determination of which pictures met the Nutting standards. Those that did not were discarded. Those that did meet the Nutting standards were sent to be mounted on the appropriately sized matboard.

An authentic colorist's porcelain paint tray.

Usually the picture was mounted on a light tan matboard having a slight indentation around the entire picture. However, other matting styles were tried over the years. Frequently mats with a black border around the picture are found. This was used occasionally in the 1930s at the suggestion of a Wallace Nutting salesman, but never really caught on for a variety of reasons. Overall, the public preferred the indented mats. Occasionally you may also find a linen mat as well.

Once mounted, the entire matted picture was returned to the head colorist or another designated individual who signed the Wallace Nutting name. Employing many different colorists and head colorists over a 35+ year period, many different Wallace Nutting signatures are found today. The earliest signatures were signed in pencil but, as the business grew, pen & ink signatures were used. Pencil signatures are rarer and generally considered somewhat more desirable by collectors.

Once signed, the picture was sent to the framing department. The Wallace Nutting Studio used a variety of frame types, each designed to make the picture as visually pleasing as possible. Generally Nutting preferred dark mahogany frames and always suggested that the frame be narrow in proportion to the picture. Volume purchasers such as large department stores usually purchased their pictures in bulk and unframed, offering framing services as well as a wide variety of frames to their customers.

Some individuals even reframed their own pictures to suit their personal tastes and preferences. As a result, you will find a wide variety of different frames on Wallace Nutting pictures today.

One thing to keep in mind is that although Wallace Nutting is credited with creating approximately 10,000 different titles, literally millions of Wallace Nutting pictures were sold. Customers were able to order titles in a wide variety of sizes, with pictures ranging from 2" x 3" to 20" x 40", and sometimes larger by special order.

To simplify the ordering process, the Nutting Studio used a special letter code to differentiate sizes.

Periodically Wallace Nutting would issue special picture catalogs which were either loaned or given to customers. These catalogs visually displayed hundreds of subjects that helped those customers in ordering pictures.

To further help customers order, the Nutting Studio recommended particular sets of bestsellers. These were what Nutting perceived as his best selling pictures and those that would presum-

The following sizes were both signed and titled:

Code	Picture Size	Mat Size		Code	Picture Size	Mat Size
A	5 x 7	11 x 14		F	14 x 17	22 x 28
Q	4 x 10	11 x 17		T	12 x 20	22 x 30
S	6 x 10	13 x 17		G	16 x 20	26 x 30
C	8 x 10	14 x 17		H	20 x 24	29 x 36
O	5 x 14	13 x 22		J	20 x 28	29 x 40
P	7½ x 14	15 x 22		J	20 x 30	29 x 40
E	11 x 14	18 x 22		W	20 x 40	30 x 52

These sizes were signed, but not titled because the title could not be tastefully displayed on such a small mat:

Code	Picture Size	Mat Size		Code	Picture Size	Mat Size
R	4 x 6	10 x 12		D	2½ x 5	7 x 9
K	3 x 6⅝	8 x 12		B	2 x 3	5 x 7
D	3¼ x 4	7 x 9				

ably sell the fastest in the customer's store. Although these pictures could be ordered individually, they were most typically ordered in sets.

Wallace Nutting Collecting Tips

* Wallace Nutting retired from the ministry at age 43, in 1904, to begin a new career as a photographer.

* Nutting worked in Southbury, CT, from 1905 to 1912.

* His Southbury home was called Nuttinghame.

* Most of his Southbury pictures were signed in pencil.

* Nutting worked in Framingham, MA, from 1912 until his death in 1941.

* His Framingham home was called Nuttingholme.

* Most Framingham pictures were signed in pen.

* It was generally the head colorist who approved pictures for sale and signed the Wallace Nutting name.

* Nutting's most popular pictures were sold in many different picture and mat sizes.

When first sold, all Wallace Nutting pictures sold for the same amount, from as little as $.25 – $.35 per picture in 1910, to $2.00 – $3.00 per picture in the 1930s. However, it wasn't until the 1970s that values began to widen as collectors started pursuing Wallace Nutting rarities.

Understanding the Main Determinants of Value

Several basic concepts must be understood about the prices and values of Wallace Nutting pictures. As with all other antiques, prices are very subjective. A dealer can charge what he or she feels the market will bear. Some dealers price things low in order to turn them over quickly. Other dealers ask top dollar and are willing to sit on an item until they get their price. If it doesn't sell at their price, it will simply go back up on their wall. In either case, you must pay the price or pass up the picture.

The price of Wallace Nutting pictures also depends upon several other factors.

Subject Matter…What is the topic or theme of the picture? Is it common or rare? How many people are interested in owning that same picture?
Condition…Is the picture in poor or excellent condition? What is the mat like? Is the frame attractive or unattractive? How difficult will it be to find the same picture in the same condition?
Size…How big is the picture itself? The matting? The frame?

Each of these items must be considered in arriving at the final estimated value.

An Airing at the Haven, a triple rarity: foreign, man, and child, 13" x 16", 4.5, $600.00 – 850.00.

A picture in very poor condition, therefore value is minimal.

A picture in excellent condition. Subject matter, condition, and size are all important in determining value.

Subject Matter of Wallace Nutting Pictures

There are several primary categories of Wallace Nutting pictures.

Exterior Scenes

Exterior scenes are what most people associate with Wallace Nutting and they comprise the largest segment of his pictures. These include pictures of apple blossoms, birches, country lanes, streams, rivers, ponds or lakes, and fall scenes.

Wallace Nutting worked out of Framingham, Massachusetts, and sold a large percentage of his pictures in New England. Winters were very long and cold and people generally desired pleasant, optimistic signs of the warmer weather ahead. As a result, these nice warm-weather pictures were the most popular and sold the best. Being an observant businessman, Nutting produced what the public would buy. This accounts for the very large percentage (85%) of exterior pictures that may be found.

A Birch Hilltop, a common exterior scene, 14" x 17", 4, $125.00 – 175.00.

Since they were so popular then, and since so many were produced, they are fairly common today. The fact that they are more common and readily available is the reason for their relatively lower price when compared to other rarer Wallace Nutting pictures.

Interior Scenes

These were pictures taken inside old colonial homes and usually featured women in long dresses and bonnets. Some were done in primitive settings, others in more formal surroundings. They included period furniture and were quite charming.

Although these were popular, they were not nearly as popular as the exte-

The Swimming Pool — probably the most common W. Nutting picture, 11" x 14", 4, $100.00 – 150.00.

The Quilting Party, 16" x 20", 4.5, $250.00 – 375.00.

rior scenes, accounting for only approximately 10% of all Wallace Nutting pictures. Thus, the law of supply and demand holds true here. Since fewer were originally done, fewer are available today. With so few available, demand has pushed the prices of some to 2 – 3 times higher then comparable exterior scenes.

Nutting Collecting Tip: All things being equal, i.e. size and condition, many interior scenes are worth approximately 2 – 3 times as much as exterior scenes.

A Knickerbocker Fireplace, 14" x 17", 4.5, $325.00 – 375.00.

Foreign & Miscellaneous Unusual Topics

This third category somewhat overlaps the exterior and interior categories, and includes many sub-categories as well. But this is the most desirable area for the serious or advanced collector. It is also the category least understood by beginning collectors.

Collectors usually begin buying exterior scenes because of their lower prices, and then progress to buying interior scenes. But once the collector becomes hooked on Wallace Nutting collecting, the real search begins for rare and unusual pictures.

A Bit of Paradise,
13" x 16", 4, $150.00 – 200.00.

Wallace Nutting collectors are like any other collector; they are always looking for rare and unusual items to add to their collection. They travel long distances, scour flea markets and antique shows, and pay whatever it takes to acquire a special picture.

Few serious collectors will go too far out of their way to purchase an exterior scene. They are too common and easy to obtain. Even interior scenes must be something very unusual before the serious collector becomes motivated to buy. But once you have a rare and unusual picture in your hands, you have something very desirable to all levels of Wallace Nutting collectors.

Some of the unusual topics would include foreign scenes, seascapes, pictures with animals, exteriors with people, pictures with children, pictures with men, floral arrangements, and snow scenes.

All unusual topics combined account for only approximately 5% of all Wallace Nutting pictures.

Dutch Maids,
14" x 17", 4.5,
$400.00 – 600.00.

I'll cover more on this topic later.

Condition

Once you have determined the subject matter of your picture, the next step in determining the value is to assess its condition because condition is the most important determinant of value. Over the past five years, condition has become increasingly important to collectors. After 25 catalog auctions, and having had the opportunity to observe literally thousands of Nutting pictures together, astute collectors have developed a better eye for differentiating between good, better, and best pictures. Conversely, some pictures in average/below average condition aren't bringing the prices they did five years ago because today's collectors have become more discriminating.

Nutting Collecting Tip: Condition is the most important determinant of value. The rarest picture in poor condition has minimal value; a common exterior in excellent condition is still a very desirable piece.

There are several important characteristics to look for in determining condition.

The Picture Itself

Many pictures are nearly 100 years old and, as time has passed, their condition has deteriorated. Some hung on walls that received years of direct sunlight, causing the colors to fade or mats to darken. Others were stored in damp basements where condensation formed and caused spots, foxxing, water stains, or other blemishes to occur.

Secondly, each picture was individually hand colored, not colored by machine. Whenever something is manually produced in large numbers, some items are inevitably going to look better than others.

The condition of the picture is extremely important when determining value.

Finally, although quality standards were set, some hand-tinted pictures were almost masterpieces while others barely met the minimum standards. Wallace Nutting also sold the business at one time, so different minimum standards were in place at various times between 1905 and 1941.

It should therefore be understood that the quality of pictures can vary widely. Experience is your best guide. The more pictures you see, the better you will be able to differentiate between an average and an excellent piece.

Nutting Collecting Tip: A damaged or badly-colored platinotype picture cannot be repaired and will have minimal value to most collectors.

Matting

The matting is the off-white backing that the picture is mounted upon and which generally contains the title and signature. This is really the most susceptible to damage. All too often, as pictures were stored in basements or attics,

The condition of the matting is very important when determining value.

water would get on the matting because of basement floods or attic leaks. Once a matting becomes water stained, it is almost impossible to remove.

Severe water stains are very unsightly and definitely detract from the beauty and value of a picture. Although some people will still buy a picture with a water-stained mat, many collectors will shy away from it unless the picture itself is very rare and of high quality.

Nutting Collecting Tip: A water-stained mat decreases the value of a picture, sometimes by as much as 25% – 50% or more, depending upon the size, location, and severity of the stain.

Another problem with matting is yellowing from the sun. It was not uncommon for a picture to hang in direct sunlight for many years. A yellowed mat is usually accompanied by a faded picture, thus significantly reducing the value.

Spotting or foxxing on the mat is another problem. Not as severe as water stains, spots form because of age, dampness, fungus growth, the type of backing used, or any of several other reasons. They can sometimes be removed but this should only be attempted by a qualified, experienced individual.

It goes without saying that a torn or creased mat will significantly reduce the value of a picture.

Sometimes mat damage may be camouflaged by an overmat. There is nothing wrong with this because the picture itself is the most important part and, if overmatting will enhance the beauty of a picture, fine. But just be aware that an overmat is probably a sign of a damaged mat and is no substitute for a mat in excellent condition. It will also reduce the value of the picture.

Nutting Collecting Tip: Overmatted pictures may be worth more than 50% less than pictures with clean, original mats.

Sometimes you will see a picture with a black border instead of an indented mat. Stories that the black border represents pictures done after Wallace Nutting's death are not true. These are also not reproductions. Rather, this was just another style that Wallace Nutting tried to market in the 1930s. Most black-bordered pictures are brightly colored (vs. only partial or muted coloring on most early pictures). Frequently original labels can be found on the back of these pictures. Some people love these black bordered pictures; others do not.

Nutting Collecting Tip: Pictures & mats with the black borders date from the 1930s and are somewhat less desirable to collectors than those without it.

Frame

The frame is very important to the overall beauty of a picture. Although the solid brown wooden frame is the most common and desirable type, Wallace Nutting framed many of the pictures he sold, with the Wallace Nutting Expansible Catalog showing approximately 20 different types of frames that Nutting was selling in 1915 alone. And some of his large customers (e.g., some department stores) preferred to buy their pictures unframed. They would then frame them according to their customer's tastes, charge extra for the framing, and presumably save shipping charges as well. This accounts for the wide variety of frames you may see.

Only when you have seen a Wallace Nutting picture in a perfect frame do you realize the importance of the frame to the overall picture. Chipped, pitted, painted, or unsightly frames can spoil an otherwise perfect picture.

The condition of the frame is important when determining value, but less important than the picture or matting.

Although frames are replaceable (whereas the picture and original mat are not), the cost of replacing a frame can turn a good buy into a bad buy.

Miscellaneous Items

There are several other things you can look for in determining value.

Original Paper Backing

Some collectors view an original paper backing the same way toy collectors view the original box. That is, extremely important. Most collectors, however, take the position that the original backing is not nearly as important as the condition and cleanliness of the picture. In my opinion, there is nothing wrong with removing the original paper backing if the picture and matting needs cleaning. I would much rather have a re-backed picture in clean condition than a dirty picture retaining its original paper backing. In the end, it becomes a matter of personal preference.

Copyright Label

After several of his pictures were copied by other companies, Nutting began putting a copyright label on the paper backing of the picture. One label read:

> *This subject is copyrighted. Original features added by hand. All negatives made by me are owned by me. Use of my name is unauthorized. All rights reserved. No._____ Wallace Nutting.*

This use of this label not only clearly identified his pictures as Wallace Nutting pictures, but also differentiated his hand-colored pictures from his machine-produced process print pictures which were identified by a separate label.

An original copyright label dating from the 1930s can add 10 – 25% to the value of a picture.

Nutting Collecting Tip: A copyright label can sometimes add 10% – 25% to the value of a picture.

Original Wavy Glass
Old glass with visible imperfections can also add to the overall look of the picture. It's not absolutely necessary for an excellent picture, but it may represent the difference between an excellent picture and a mint condition piece.

THIS PICTURE IS ONE OF A LARGE SERIES MADE AT THE
WENTWORTH-GARDNER HOUSE, ONE OF THE
Wallace Nutting Colonial Chain of Picture Houses
restored and furnished in period by him as fine examples of the best in architecture, and may be visited by the public.
WENTWORTH - GARDNER HOUSE -1760- with an unrivalled hall, remarkable panels, carvings and fireplaces, and Chippendale Furniture - 56 Gardner St., Portsmouth N. H.
CUTLER - BARTLET HOUSE - 1782 - A noble specimen of brick work, with Hepplewhite Furniture.- 32 Green St., Newburyport, Mass.
HAZEN GARRISON HOUSE – about 1680 - A beautiful little brick manor, with leaded casements, wooden latches and hinges. Rare early furniture in pine and oak. 6-8 Groveland Ave., Haverhill, Mass.
BROADHEARTH - IRON WORKS HOUSE about 1640 - Remarkable for its huge chimney stack, cavernous fireplaces, picturesque overhang and Gothic roof. Furnished with unique pieces - 137 Central St., Saugus Centre, Mass.
None of these houses are museums, but each exhibits a beautiful early American home.

A label from a Wentworth-Gardner House picture.

Between 1915 and 1918 Nutting purchased, restored, and furnished five historic New England homes. Each was located in a different town and each offered a different architectural and furnishing style. These houses included Webb House (Hospitality Hall), Wethersfield, CT; Wentworth-Gardner House, Portsmouth, NH; Cutler-Bartlett House, Newburyport, MA; Hazen-Garrison House, Haverhill, MA; and Broadhearth (Saugus Iron Works),Saugus, MA.

In addition to opening these houses to the general public for a small admission fee, Nutting also shot many different colonial interior scenes in each location. Often times these were identified with a large Wallace Nutting Colonial Chain of Picture Houses label. Because many of these labels were applied nearly 80 years ago, many have been lost as the brittle paper backings have fallen off pictures. As a result, these labels can sometimes add a premium value to a picture.

Nutting Collecting Tip: A Colonial Chain of Picture Houses label can sometimes add 10% – 25% to the value of a picture.

Overall Size of Pictures

After analyzing the subject matter and condition of the picture, the third key to determining value is size. With only a few exceptions, assuming that the quality is comparable, the larger the picture, the greater the value. A larger exterior is usually more valuable than a smaller exterior; a larger interior is usually more valuable than a smaller interior.

There are two sizes to consider; the picture size and the mat size. Some people lend particular importance to the size of the picture itself, others do not. I personally feel

Condition Guide

Poor/Fair Condition	Good/Excellent Condition
Picture	**Picture**
Faded Coloring	Sharp & Clear Detail
Torn Picture/Bent Corner	Nice Coloring
Poor Tinting	Almost Looks Like a Color Photograph
Foxxing/White Spots	No White Spots or Blemishes
Mat	**Mat**
Water Stains	No Stains or Spotting
Spotting/Foxxing	No Fading or Discoloration
Torn Mat	Sharp Indentation Around Picture
Yellowing	No Rippling or Curling
Frame	**Frame**
Chipped	Original Brown or Gold
Painted/Pitted	No Chipped Paint or Pitting
Damage/Flaking	Tasteful, with Proper Proportions
Miscellaneous	**Miscellaneous**
Dirt Under Glass	Original Copyright Label
Scratched Glass	Old Glass
Broken Glass	Original Paper Backing

that the mat size is the primary determinant of value because most collectors are concerned about how much wall space a picture will occupy. However, a disproportion between picture and mat could indicate that a mat has been cropped down to eliminate water stains or other damage.

There are two basic exceptions to this size rule. The first has to do with miniatures. These are small, framed pictures that first appeared in the 1930s. The frames are approximately 4" x 5", the pictures 2" x 3", and they frequently have a black border surrounding the pictures. These miniatures are especially desirable to most collectors and command prices in the range of larger 7" x 9" or 8" x10" pictures.

The second exception may come as somewhat of a surprise. We have consistently seen at auction that the very large pictures, i.e., 20" x 30", 20" x 40", 30" x 52", etc, just don't command a very high price. Although I would not consider these larger pictures rare, I would call them unusual. And, because they are unusual, and considering all the work that went into coloring them, you would expect that they would bring a value consistent with their scarcity and the amount of work that went into them.

To the contrary, we have seen that these large pictures seem to consistently bring prices comparable to a 14" x 17" picture.

The problem with larger pictures seems to lie in two areas: subject matter and size. Nearly all large pictures I have seen are exterior scenes, and common exteriors at that: The Swimming Pool, Slack Water, Water Maples, Flowering

Time, Dream & Reality, Enticing Waters, etc. (Very few large pictures were interior, foreign, or miscellaneous unusual scenes.) As a result, relatively few people seem interested in making such a large, but common, picture the focal point of their collection.

The second problem has to do with size. Relatively few people today have sufficient wall space to accommodate such a large picture. Smaller pictures can be placed pretty much anywhere in an apartment or home but, if you don't have room for such a large picture, you can't hang it.

When you consider their relative rarity, and all the fine handwork that went into each picture, I would think that such large pictures might be undervalued today. But based upon the prices we have consistently seen at auction, the demand just doesn't seem to be there for such large pictures.

Wallace Nutting Collecting Tips

* Exterior scenes…are the most common pictures and are generally purchased by beginning collectors because of their lower price.

* Interior scenes…are very desirable and are sought after by all levels of collectors.

* Foreign and miscellaneous unusual scenes…are usually the most desirable and generally bring the highest prices from serious collectors.

* Condition is the most important determinant of value. All pictures in good condition have value, regardless of subject matter. In poor condition, even the rarest picture may have minimal value.

* With only a few exceptions: the larger the picture, the greater the value.

* Many items make up the overall picture: the picture itself, the matting, the frame, the glass, etc. A blemish to any of these tends to reduce the overall value.

* When you see an overmat, assume there is some type of damage to the original matting. Although some people overmatted perfectly good mats because of personal tastes or preferences, assume that the original matting is either stained, torn, creased, discolored, or cropped down…unless you see for yourself that it is in acceptable condition.

* Black borders date from the 1930s. Frequently black-bordered pictures will have an original copyright label on the back as well.

* Although original paper backings are nice to have…most date from the 1920s or earlier and have become so brittle that they have either fallen off or been removed.

* In my opinion it is acceptable to remove an original backing to clean a dirty or otherwise blemished picture. I would personally prefer a clean picture with a new backing to a dirty picture with an original backing.

* If you see a picture with a new backing and soiled matting…unless you are an experienced cleaner or restorer, you should probably assume that the blemish cannot be removed. (Otherwise, why would the last individual not have removed the blemish prior to replacing the new backing?)

General Guide to Pricing Wallace Nutting Pictures

The following chart is a unique guide which provides a range of values that you might expect to pay for Wallace Nutting pictures. It provides some useful rules of thumb and can be a valuable aid in establishing an approximate value so that you don't pay too much or sell for too little. It is not meant to be an absolute statement of value and should not be taken as such.

Several further points should be considered.

* These values are estimated retail prices, i.e., what you might expect to fairly pay for a picture. If you are expecting to sell a picture, you can assume a dealer will pay somewhat less (usually 50% of the listed price).

* The higher range should be reserved for pictures in excellent condition (4.0 – 5.0), i.e., those possessing most or all of the characteristics listed in the good-excellent condition category on page 27.

* The lower range is for pictures possessing only some of the characteristics listed in the good to excellent range (3.0 – 3.75). Pictures in poor condition (2.5 or less) would generally fall below the lower range.

* Although these prices are indicative of the current market, prices tend to fluctuate in different parts of the country. Prices may be higher or lower, depending on where you live.

The Price Guide may look complicated, but it's really easy to use. For example:

An Old Parlor Corner, an interior scene, 14" x 17", in above average 4.0 condition (i.e., clean mat, nicely framed, excellent detail and coloring in the picture.) Go to the 14" x 17" interior column, which shows a over-all 3.0 – 5.0 price range of $125 – $350. Since all key characteristics are in above-average to excellent condition, the 4.0 rating would fall within the upper portion of the range, or approximately $250 – $350. If the picture was rated a 4.5 – 5.0, if would fall within the higher end of that range, or approximately $300 – $350.

On the other hand if the picture had nice coloring and excellent detail, but also some water staining and a damaged frame, the value would drop to the lower range, or $125 – $250.

A rating of less than 3.0 would drop the value below the lower end of the range, or less than $125, depending upon the extent of damage.

An Old Parlor Corner.

Wallace Nutting Price Guide to Exterior and Interior Pictures

Mat Size	Exterior Scenes Overall 3.0 – 5.0 Range	Interior Scenes Overall 3.0 – 5.0 Range
4x5	$35.00 – $85.00	$50.00 – $125.00
5x7	$20.00 – $55.00	$40.00 – $85.00
7x9	$35.00 – $80.00	$50.00 – $135.00
7x11	$40.00 – $90.00	$50.00 – $145.00
8x10	$40.00 – $90.00	$50.00 – $150.00
8x12	$45.00 – $95.00	$50.00 – $155.00
10x12	$45.00 – $150.00	$75.00 – $225.00
11x14	$60.00 – $175.00	$75.00 – $275.00
11x17	$75.00 – $185.00	$95.00 – $300.00
13x16	$75.00 – $235.00	$110.00 – $325.00
14x17	$75.00 – $235.00	$125.00 – $350.00
13x22	$110.00 – $250.00	$125.00 – $350.00
15x22	$110.00 – $275.00	$125.00 – $350.00
16x20	$120.00 – $275.00	$125.00 – $375.00
18x22	$125.00 – $275.00	$125.00 – $375.00
18x22 (or larger)	$100.00 – $255.00	$150.00 – $425.00

Some Observations Regarding Prices within this Price Guide

The following represent some observations regarding the price ranges included above in this collector's guide as compared to the last 4th edition price guide which was published in 1991.

* The overall ranges for each picture size are broader than they previously were. This would seem to confirm that when compared to 5 – 6 years ago…
  a) Collectors are paying more for the better pictures (4.0 – 5.0), and
  b) Collectors are paying less for the average pictures rated below a 4.0.

* Collectors are undoubtedly much more conscious of condition than they were in the 1989 – 91 time period.

* Overall, the difference between the pricing of interior and exterior scenes does not appear to be quite as wide as it was several years ago.

* Larger exterior pictures (larger than 18" x 22") seem to be valued at approximately the same range as the 14" x 17" size.

* When taken as a group, exterior scenes graded 4.0 – 5.0 sold for prices approximately 48% higher than pictures graded 3.0 – 3.75.

* When taken as a group, interior scenes graded 4.0 – 5.0 sold for prices approximately 56% higher than pictures graded 3.0 – 3.75.

* Collectors have minimal interest in pictures with ratings below a 3 and the value for such pictures will fall below the low end of the range.

Pricing of Pictures in the Miscellaneous Unusual Topic Category

The price guide beginning on page 105 covers price ranges on exterior and interior pictures. As I mentioned earlier, however, the rarest Wallace Nutting pictures are those that fall under the miscellaneous unusual topic category. They are also the most desirable for the serious collector. Comparatively few were made and most existing ones seem to be in private collections. As a result, few are readily available for sale today. This is also the area that has seen the most dramatic price increases, and the area where most price records have been set.

Nutting Collecting Tip: Rare pictures in the foreign and miscellaneous unusual categories have seen the most dramatic increase in pricing.

Pricing these is very difficult. Since there are increasingly fewer rare, top quality pictures readily available, demand has pushed prices much higher than they were just a few years ago.

Nutting Collecting Tip: With only a few exceptions, a picture falling under the miscellaneous unusual topic category is worth at least as much as a comparable interior (i.e., same size and condition).

So, the starting point for valuing this category is the interior column on the previous page.

Foreign Scenes

Although Wallace Nutting was best known for his New England exterior pictures and colonial interior scenes, he also took pictures in 16 foreign countries during his three trips abroad (1904, 1915, and 1925), including Algeria, Ireland, Canada, Italy, Egypt, Palestine, England, Scotland, France, Spain, Germany, Switzerland, Greece, Syria, Holland, and Turkey.

The Donjon, Cheneneau — France, rare castle, 13" x 16", 4.5, $500.00 – 750.00.

Considering that he published two books on foreign countries (England Beautiful and Ireland Beautiful), it shouldn't be too surprising that you will find more pictures from these two countries than any other. Certain pictures from Holland and Italy were also good sellers for Nutting. Apparently during this 1910 – 1925 period, when the cost of a trans-Atlantic cruise was beyond the means of most people, and the day of commercial aviation had not yet arrived, one way people were able to fantasize about far-away lands was through books…and pictures, frequently Wallace Nutting pictures. Generally his bestselling foreign pictures were cottages, cathedrals, windmills, and other tranquil foreign settings.

Reinstein, — Germany, rare castle, 13" x 16", 4, sold several years ago for $875.00.

As a result, titles like Larkspur, A Garden of Larkspur, Hollyhock Cottage, Nethercote, Litchfield Minster, The Mills at the Turn, and The Pergola, Amalfi, among others, were quite popular and many copies were sold. Therefore, they are generally easier to find today with prices falling below some of the other rarer foreign scenes that you may find.

Overall I have seen very few hand-colored pictures from the remaining countries listed above. Most of Nutting's pictures from the Mediterranean were taken very early in his picture-taking career, generally 1904 on his "Cruise of the 800" trip. Relatively few were sold commercially and quite frequently, pictures from these countries were never colored.

Somewhat surprisingly, few pictures from Canada will be found, despite the fact that he briefly opened a branch studio in Toronto in 1907. (It closed shortly thereafter because it proved to be unprofitable.) The Canadian titles you may occasionally find will be A Nova Scotia Idyl, The Bay Road, Evangeline Lane, and Evangeline Bough. Rarely will you find other titles from Canada.

Because of the extremely wide range of titles within the foreign category, pricing of these pictures has become increasingly complex. The more common titles should not be valued too high because they are relatively easy to locate. Those rarer titles in the best condition can command much stronger prices, as shown in the Foreign Section of Chapter 11. You can refer to page 98 for a listing of the top 25 foreign picture prices.

Pictures with Animals

Overall, Wallace Nutting didn't sell many pictures with animals. Considering that much of America's population at this time was rural, it shouldn't be too surprising that people living in the country weren't too interested in having a picture of someone else's animals hanging upon their walls. Although they may have been somewhat more appealing to city dwellers, relatively few pictures with animals were sold.

Sheep although uncommon, are not rare. Certain titles such as A Warm Spring Day, On the Slope, and Not One of the 400 offered a very tranquil, peaceful setting that proved to be very popular with the general public. Other sheep pictures did not sell as well back then and command considerably higher prices today.

According to scarcity and desirability to collectors, I would rank animal pictures as follows (from most common to most rare): sheep, cats, cows, dogs, horses, chickens.

Dog-On-It, a rare dog picture has sold in the $1,000.00 – 1,500.00 range on several occasions.

A Warm Spring Day, the most common sheep picture, 13" x 22", 4.5, $325.00 – 375.00.

Seascapes

These are uncommon and have become harder to locate as they have been assembled into private collections. Very few different seascapes scenes were actively marketed by Wallace Nutting, perhaps only 20 – 25. The most common titles you may see are Sea Ledges, Swirling Seas, and A Maine Coast Sky.

Sea Ledges, a common seascape, 10" x 6", 4, $275.00 – 350.00.

Swirling Seas, another common seascape, 13" x 16", 4, $275.00 – 350.00.

Exteriors with People

Many of these are uncommon and generally quite desirable. Usually they involve people walking or sitting on porches. Some of the more common titles are The Sallying of Sally, All in a Garden Fair, and The Going Forth of Betty.

> **Nutting Collecting Tip:** Most exteriors with people have at least the same value as a comparable interior scene. Some may be worth up to 150% – 250% more than a comparable interior.

Unfortunately, rarity determines value and it is difficult to be more specific in such a limited space. You will not go too far wrong by valuing such a picture as a comparable interior.

> **Nutting Collecting Tip:** With few exceptions, the more people in a picture, the more unusual the scene.

Resting at the Old Stoop, 14" x 17", 4, $275.00 – 325.00.

At the Side Door, featured the Hoyt sisters, who also posed for the John Phillip Sousa Band, 13" x 16", 4, $325.00 – 425.00.

Children

Pictures with children are extremely desirable, generally quite rare, and every collector would love to have some in their collection. Just as rural residents were not interested in having pictures of someone else's animals hanging upon their walls, I think that most people were not interested in hanging a picture of someone else's child in their home. As a result, although Nutting did actively try to market pictures with children, they failed to sell in any significant numbers.

Going to the Doctor, 12" x 16", 3, sold at auction for $1,100.00 in June 1996.

One exception to this rule about children is Rosa. One of Nutting's bestselling pictures of all time was The Coming Out of Rosa. This picture, with a little girl standing upon a flower-covered front porch holding her mother's hand, was extremely popular and sold in large numbers. This picture still holds an attraction for collectors today, being voted as the most popular Wallace Nutting picture by collectors at a previous Wallace Nutting Collector's Club Convention. A picture called Posing, with Rosa sitting in a child's chair on the porch beside her mother, was also very popular and sold well. (This picture was always untitled.)

The Coming Out of Rosa, probably the most popular Wallace Nutting picture ever produced.

However, other pictures also containing Rosa (The Going In of Rosa, Watching for Papa, Childhood Wiles, Rosa and a Bud, and Wavering Footsteps) failed to sell in any considerable numbers and are considered rare today.

Considered to be the most highly sought-after child picture by many collectors, The Guardian Mother sold at our April 1989 auction for $4950 and still holds the auction record for a Wallace Nutting picture.

Floral Arrangements

As business was declining during the 1930 Depression years, Wallace Nutting was looking for other subject areas into which he could expand. In an attempt to cater to the growing Women's Garden Club movement, one such area that he tested was floral scenes. These were close-up pictures of vases or bowls of flowers, usually arranged by Mrs. Nutting. They are rare and don't look anything like a typical Wallace Nutting picture.

As florals were all done in the 1930s, they are generally more brightly colored (since platinum paper was not used at this time), frequently have a black border surrounding the picture, and are commonly framed within a gold frame. It is also not uncommon to find the original copyright label on the back of these pictures.

A Dahlia Jar, copyright label on back, 16" x 20", 4, $500.00 – 1,000.00.

There are approximately 30 – 40 different floral scenes, and at one time they were even included in a special Floral Catalog that Wallace Nutting had produced to help sell these pictures. Sizes vary from miniature 4" x 5" to larger 16" x 20" sizes. Floral scenes were frequently sold close-framed. However, with the Depression on at this time, relatively few were sold.

Men

Although Nutting actively tried to market interior scenes with men, relatively few were sold. As a result, pictures including men are rare. Especially desirable are men in red jackets and Uncle Sam (an older man with an Uncle Sam-like beard). You will find relatively few untitled pictures with men. Rather, most seem to be in the 13" x 16" or 14" x 17" sizes.

Pictures with men have been bringing strong prices when in excellent condition.

A Basket of Gourds, 16" x 20", 4, $1,000.00 – 1,500.00.

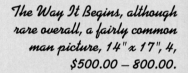

The Way It Begins, although rare overall, a fairly common man picture, 14" x 17", 4, $500.00 – 800.00.

Drying Apples, although rare overall, a fairly common man picture, 13" x 16", 4, $500.00 – 800.00.

Snow Scenes

These are very rare and very desirable. The last thing New Englanders wanted to be reminded of was snow, so therefore, very few snow scenes were purchased. As a result, they are quite rare today. Most snow scenes seem to be in the smaller 7" x 9" – 8" x 10" size and are untitled. If you are lucky enough to find a larger titled picture, congratulations. Within reason, you can name your own price.

Church, Framingham Center, MA, still located on Framingham Center Town Green, beside the former site of Nuttingholme, 7" x 9" (untitled), 4, $250.00 – 350.00.

Snow-covered country road, 7" x 9" (untitled), 4, $250.00 – 350.00.

Miscellaneous Pictures

This is really a catch-all for pictures not already covered elsewhere. An experienced collector can identify an unusual picture immediately. Scenes from New York, Florida, Virginia, Pennsylvania, and California come to mind. Because these states were generally photographed much later than the New England states (i.e., New England, 1900 – 20; other states usually after 1920), there were fewer productive years within which to sell these pictures. Also, the earlier New England pictures were sold within the peak period of hand-colored platinotype pictures; pictures from these other states were not introduced commercially until the popularity of hand-colored platinotypes began to decline. As a result, fewer pictures from outside of the New England states were sold; hence, their rarity.

Depending on the topic, they may be valued anywhere from the base exterior price to the upper limit for miscellaneous unusual topics. Only experience will dictate the accurate price.

The Wayside Inn, Sudbury, MA, a basic architectural view with no people, 13" x 16", 4, $200.00 – 325.00.

Oak Spandrel Ceiling, Kenmore, rare close-up black and white architectural view of a single ceiling tile. Personally signed and titled by Wallace Nutting. Probably one of a kind.

Wallace Nutting Collecting Tips

* Only the rarest pictures, in the best condition, will be valued at the highest end of the range. Limited damage or blemishes will drop the value to the lower end of the price range, and major damage or blemishes could drop the value below the lower end of the range.

* The better the condition, the higher the price you should expect to pay (or receive) for any given picture.

* It is usually very difficult to sell pictures in poor condition.

* Prices vary in different parts of the country.

* With few exceptions, miscellaneous unusual scenes are typically worth at least as much as a comparable Interior.

* Pictures falling under the miscellaneous unusual topic category are generally the most sought-after by serious collectors, and usually command the highest prices.

* When selling a picture, you can expect that a dealer will offer approximately 50% of the retail value.

* Certain common foreign scenes such as Larkspur, A Garden of Larkspur, Hollyhock Cottage, Nethercote, Litchfield Minster, etc. are very common and should be valued somewhere between the basic exterior and interior range.

* There is a wide range in the pricing of foreign and miscellaneous unusual categories and experience will be your best guide in determining proper pricing.

Understanding Wallace Nutting Signatures and Dating Wallace Nutting Pictures

A proper understanding of the Wallace Nutting signature process can not only help you to authenticate a Wallace Nutting picture, but it can help you to date it as well. Authenticating a legitimate Wallace Nutting signature is probably the most difficult part of Wallace Nutting collecting because as we've already

One of the most common Wallace Nutting signatures, circa 1915 – 25.

discussed, Wallace Nutting rarely signed pictures himself.

It can be safely assumed that Nutting signed some of his earliest pictures, before he hired employees and as his business was growing. We also know that he signed some later pictures as gifts to friends or favors to associates. And throughout the years he undoubtedly signed some pictures in the Studio. But for all practical purposes, Nutting probably signed perhaps no more than several thousand pictures out of his overall output of literally millions of pictures.

Rather, it was his colorists, or more specifically, his head colorists, who signed the Wallace Nutting name. As a result, when you buy a Wallace Nutting picture, you are buying a picture with the Wallace Nutting name on it, not a picture signed by Wallace Nutting himself.

If you remember the picture process described in Chapter 1, after the picture was colored and mounted on the matboard, it was returned to the head colorist who actually signed the Wallace Nutting name. And considering that Wallace Nutting was in business full-time between 1905 and 1941, and he had a part-time business between 1900 and 1904, he obviously had many different people signing his name over the 40+ years period. This accounts for the many different Wallace Nutting signatures that will be found on his pictures today.

And with so many different authentic signatures, this is the easiest thing for a forger to fake. As a result, differentiating between authentic and fake Wallace Nutting signatures is the hardest thing for a new collector to master.

I will be the first to admit that even I cannot authenticate each and every signature I see. In nearly every instance, I can determine which signatures are authentic, and which are fakes. But every once in a while a picture comes along that I just don't know whether its real or not. There are a few signatures that look like they might be 70 – 90

Is it or isn't it authentic? (It isn't, it's a fake.)

years old, yet aren't recognizable as a signature I have previously seen. When shown to a group of very experienced collectors, more often than not there is a lack of unanimous agreement regarding its authenticity. Which means that no one knows for sure.

The biggest problem that we are faced with as an auction company is that we guarantee every Wallace Nutting that we sell in our auctions. Our auction catalog contains a two-page written guarantee which outlines what we do and do not guarantee. Our current auction catalogs guarantee that unless clearly stated otherwise, every Wallace Nutting picture that we sell through a Michael Ivankovich Auction Company auction contains an authentic and legitimate signature. If we are not 100% certain that the signature is authentic, we will say so in the auction catalog. And in the absence of any statement to the contrary, our customers can assume the signature is authentic.

So when you see a picture in one of our auctions, you are guaranteed that, in our opinion, the signature is authentic. Outside of our auctions, however, all too often it's Let the Buyer Beware.

The good news is that most fake Wallace Nutting signatures are relatively easy to detect…once you know what to look for.

This is the first in-depth attempt at visually exploring legitimate Wallace Nutting signatures that we are aware of. We ask that you take this Chapter for what it is intended to be: a first-time effort, not the final end-all product.

Basically, we have divided Wallace Nutting signatures into three distinct time periods — Early Southbury, 1904 – 1910; Late Southbury – Early Framingham, 1911 – 1930; Late Framingham, 1930 – 1941.

Each period has certain characteristics which we will try to explore. But before we explore many of the different colorist's signatures, let take a brief look at Wallace Nutting's own signature.

Wallace Nutting's Personal Signature

Wallace Nutting's personal signature, circa 1936, from a Wallace Nutting Biography book.

Prior to the days of desktop publishing, e-mail, Federal Express, UPS, Priority Mail, AT&T Long Distance Service, Sprint, MCI, and all the other modern means of communication, Wallace Nutting had little alternative but to correspond via the U.S. Mail. And since Wallace Nutting was relatively famous, especially in his later life, he corresponded with many individuals, many of whom kept copies of his letters.

Wallace Nutting also actively promoted most of the books that he wrote, especially by attending book signings where he would often sign his books when requested.

And we know that he signed various pictures over the years.

So between his letters, books, and pictures, there is a pretty good sampling of his handwriting and signatures available for comparison. And it is pretty obvious once you have reviewed his signature and correspondence that Nutting's handwriting was not what you would call neat. So when you consider Nutting's relatively poor handwriting, and the large volume of signatures that

were needed as his business grew, it becomes obvious that he needed someone to sign his name to his pictures.

This page contains a sampling of various examples of Wallace Nutting's personal signature. You should understand that Nutting's handwriting obviously
changed over a 40-year period. When he started the Southbury business, he
was 44. He died in Framingham in 1941 at the age of 80. Everyone will have
different handwriting between the ages of 44 and 80, especially when working
in a rushed business atmosphere, and Wallace Nutting was no exception.

*Wallace Nutting's personal signa-
ture, circa 1921, from the Furniture
of the Pilgrim Century book. Note
that the signature is neater and more
readable than the 1936 signature.*

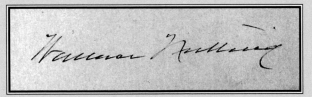

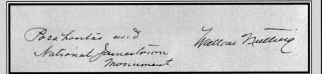

*Wallace Nutting's personal signa-
ture, circa 1930, from the England
Beautiful book.*

*Wallace Nutting's personal signa-
ture. Picture signed and titled by
Wallace Nutting, circa 1930s.*

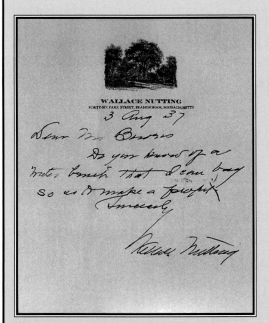

Wallace Nutting letter, dated 1917.

Wallace Nutting letter, circa 1937.

Now knowing what Nutting's personal signature looked like, let's move on to
some of the signatures of his colorists.

Early Southbury Signatures...1904 – 1910

It can be safely assumed that Nutting signed most of his earlier pictures, especially during his beginning years. Volume was small, he was still testing the commercial possibilities for his pictures, and he had no employees until around 1904.

Once he opened the Nuttinghame Studio in Southbury, and as volume grew, he began to hire various employees to help in the day-to-day activities associated with the business. At this point, Nutting turned over the picture signing responsibility to several of his trusted employees.

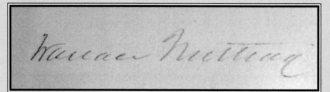

Many people think that this early pencil signature was Wallace Nutting's personal signature. Although similar, it is not.

At first, these employees were trained to copy Wallace Nutting's personal signature, especially with the distinctive formation of the final "g" in "Nutting," which had a tail curving to the right instead of the left. Many people today mistakenly think that any early signature with that right-curving tail is Wallace Nutting's own signature. Unfortunately, that is a pretty dangerous assumption to make. Since the colorists signed so many pictures, and Nutting signed so few pictures, the probability is that Nutting did not sign it. Plus, who can confirm with 100% certainty that Nutting always finished the "g" with the tail curing right rather than left?

The earliest signatures were typically signed in pencil. I have generally used the date of 1910 as the transition year from pencil-to-pen signatures. This doesn't mean that a pen was never used before 1910. Nor does it mean that a pencil was never used after 1910. However, I think that we can safely say that most pencil signatures would date a picture at 1910 or earlier.

How else can an early Southbury signature be identified and dated?

  * If the signature is in pencil, it is probably early Southbury.

  * If the picture has a white, reversed-out block copyright, it is probably early Southbury. Some of the earliest pictures contained a longer copyright marking, e.g. "Copyright 1904, by Wallace Nutting" vs. a much more concise "©WN'16." This longer copyright was phased out by 1905.

  * Often times the subject matter will identify the picture as early Southbury. For example, certain titles that appeared in the 1904 or 1908 picture catalog, but which were not sold in later years, can be assumed to be early Southbury.

Here are some examples of early Southbury pencil signatures. Remember that these signatures are representative, but not all inclusive, of the signatures used during this period.

A variety of early Southbury pencil signatures, circa 1905 – 1910. Please note that these are only some representative examples of authentic Wallace Nutting signatures. These are not all the different signatures from this period.

A variety of early Southbury, pencil signatures, circa 1905 – 1910. Please note that these are only some representative examples of authentic Wallace Nutting signatures. These are not all the different signatures from this period.

Late Southbury – Early Framingham Signatures...1910 – 1930

The years 1910 – 30 marked the peak period for Wallace Nutting pictures. His business was employing 200 people at this time, 100 of whom were colorists. His picture sales were at an all-time high, more signature signers were needed to keep up with production, and you will find a wider variety of authentic signatures during this period than any other.

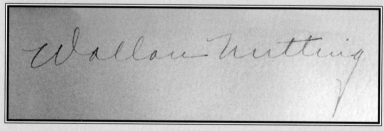

A common pen signature, circa 1915 – 25.

The signatures from this period were typically signed in pen. The most distinctive signature from this period having a bold and flowing appearance.

How else can a late Southbury – early Framingham signature be identified?

* If the signature is in pen, and there is no black border around the picture, it is probably late Southbury – early Framingham.

* The signature was often bold and flowing in appearance. This is not to say that bold and flowing signatures were never used in the other periods, but rather the bold and flowing signatures were more typical of the second period than the first or third period.

* The subject matter and location of a picture can help to date the picture. For example, interior scenes from Nutting's Colonial Chain of Houses will rarely have a pencil signature because they weren't photographed until after 1915, when Nutting purchased the first home within the chain.

* Pictures from Pennsylvania, New York, or Virginia were rarely signed in pencil, because most of these were taken after he left Southbury and stopped using the pencil signature.

The more concise ©W.N.1916-type copy-right typically dates a picture in the late Southbury-early Framingham period (second period).

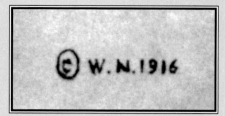

* The more concise copyright © WN'16 are also indicative of this period.

* The color tone can also be indicative of the period. Pictures with more subdued color are typically from the Southbury – early Framingham period. Later Framingham pictures usually were more brightly colored than the earlier years.

Here are some examples of late Southbury – early Framingham pen signatures. Remember that these signatures are representative, but not all inclusive, of the signatures used during this period.

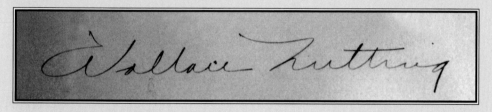

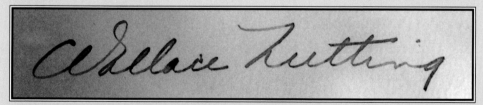

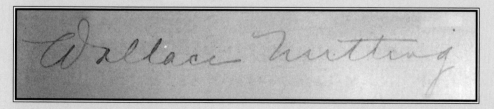

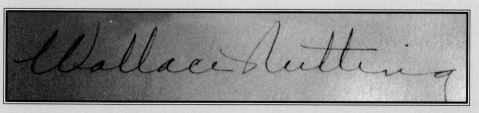

A variety of late Southbury-early Framingham pen signatures, circa 1910 – 1930. Please note that these are only some representative examples of authentic Wallace Nutting signatures. These are not all the different signatures from this period.

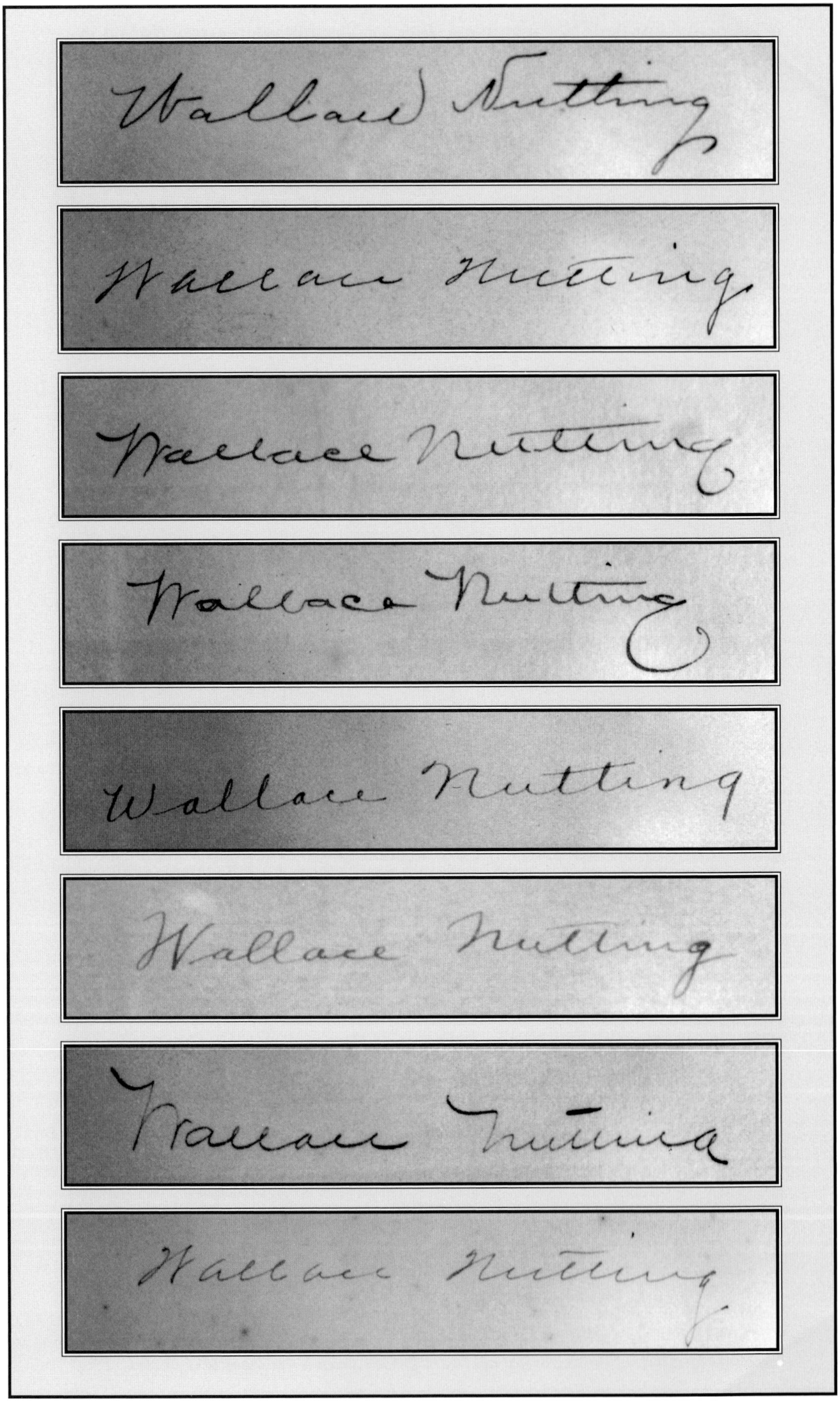
Wallace Nutting
Wallace Nutting
Wallace Nutting
Wallace Nutting
Wallace Nutting
Wallace Nutting
Wallace Nutting
Wallace Nutting

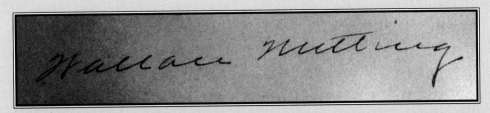

A variety of late Southbury-early Framingham pen signatures, circa 1910 – 1930. Please note that these are only some representative examples of authentic Wallace Nutting signatures. These are not all the different signatures from this period.

Late Framingham...1930 – 41

A typical late Framingham signature, with a black bordered picture.

By this time, Nutting was taking relatively few new pictures for commercial distribution. As interest in his pictures was fading, and with literally thousands of negatives already on hand, he relied primarily on selling images that he already had in inventory.

Generally, 1930s signatures will be found on pictures having these characteristics:

* A black border, with a very colorful picture, will often times be found.

* Signatures on black border pictures were typically smaller and more concise than the early bold and flowing signature. Presumably the bold and flowing signature might have competed with the black border.

* If the picture had an indented matting, without the black border, but having a much more brightly colored picture, it is probably from this period.

* If the picture has a copyright label on the back, it is probably from this period.

Subject matter can also help to identify the type of signature used. For example, floral arrangements and garden scenes were only introduced in the 1930s. Certain of these pictures were matted and signed, other were close-framed and signed directly on the picture itself. Sometimes the picture was signed in pencil, other times it was signed in pen.

Here are some examples of late Framingham pen signatures. Remember that these are representative, but not all inclusive, of the signatures used during this period.

A variety of late Framingham pen signatures, circa 1910 – 1930. Please note that these are only some representative examples of authentic Wallace Nutting signatures. These are not all the different signatures from this period.

Rarity of Pencil vs. Pen Signatures

Many collectors fail to understand the difference in rarity between the pencil and pen signatures. Although there are a few exceptions, the general rule of thumb is that pencil signatures were used until 1910, and after 1910 pen signatures were almost exclusively used.

This means that pencil signatures must be rarer than pen signatures because:

a) Pencil signatures were used for only 10 years (1900 – 1910) when production was at its lowest.

b) Pen signatures were used for more than 30 years (1910 – 1941) when production was at its highest.

Those 30+ peak-production years of pen signatures would indicate that perhaps 90% of all Wallace Nutting signatures were signed in pen, while perhaps only 10% were signed in pencil.

So with all other factors being the same, i.e., subject matter, condition, and size…a picture with a pencil signature is rarer, and should probably be valued higher, than a comparable pen signature. However, if any of these three factors are not the same, the type of signature used should become the least important factor in determining value.

Wallace Nutting Collecting Tips

* The signature on a Wallace Nutting picture can help you to both authenticate and date the picture.

* Most signatures were signed by the head colorist rather than Wallace Nutting himself.

* A pencil signature usually represents pictures taken during the early Southbury period (1900 – 1910).

* A pen signature, without a black picture border, more often than not will be from the late Southbury – early Framingham period (1910 – 1930).

* A pen signature with a black picture border, will date the picture during the late Framingham period (1930 – 1941).

* Pencil signatures are significantly rarer than pen signatures.

* A variety of factors including the picture coloration, matting type, frame style, signature, type of copyright, subject matter, and location of picture can all be used to date a Wallace Nutting picture.

Chapter 5

Wallace Nutting Memorabilia

Most people have heard about Wallace Nutting's hand-colored pictures...many people are aware of the nearly 20 books that Wallace Nutting authored...and an increasing number of collectors are developing an understanding about Wallace Nutting's bench-made reproduction furniture. But as the demand for each of these areas has increased over the past several years, and as the prices of certain Wallace Nutting items have moved beyond what some individuals are willing to pay, an increasing number of Wallace Nutting collectors have started searching out Wallace Nutting memorabilia.

What constitutes Wallace Nutting memorabilia? Quite simply, anything related to Wallace Nutting that is:

1) not a hand-colored or b&w platinotype picture
2) not one of the 20+ different books that he published or contributed to
3) not his reproduction furniture...

...would be classified as Wallace Nutting memorabilia.

Although most serious Wallace Nutting collectors will recognize Wallace Nutting memorabilia when they see it, many are surprised at the wide variety of Wallace Nutting memorabilia that is still readily available to collect. For the purposes of this book, we have identified 19 different categories of Wallace Nutting memorabilia.

Picture Books

These are undoubtedly the rarest and most desirable form of Wallace Nutting memorabilia, and we are aware of only three different picture books that were ever produced by Nutting:

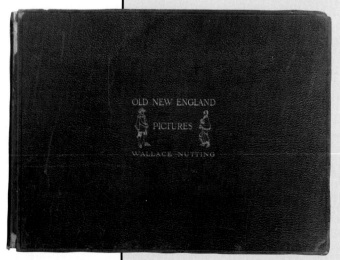

Old New England Pictures, sold at auction for $10,175.00.

a) ***Old New England Pictures***...this 1913 publication consisted of 64 pages, with 32 pages of copy devoted to the joy of living in old New England homes and 32 different pages of mounted, signed, and titled hand-colored photographs. If broken up, a copy of Old New England Pictures would yield 32 individual, ready-to-frame, mostly rare, pictures. Hence, its extremely high value. (We sold one copy of Old New England Pictures, in excellent condition, for $10,175 in 1993. This represents the Wallace Nutting auction record for any single Wallace Nutting item.) Collectors generally agree that there are only approximately 12 – 14 copies of this book still in existence, as several copies had been broken up and sold as individual pictures over the years.

b) **Up at the Vilas Farm**…this 23 page book, originally produced in 1912 consisted of 22 pages of hand-colored photographs taken at the estate of Nutting's friend, Charles Nathaniel Vilas of Alstead, NH. The twenty-third and final page contained a poem. Nutting apparently made several presentation copies of this book for Mr. Vilas. We sold a copy of this book at auction in 1991 for $3,185, and we are aware of only two other complete Vilas Farms books still in existence (both of which are publicly owned). We also know of at least one other copy which had been broken up with the pictures sold individually many years ago.

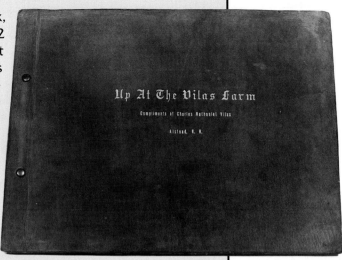

Up at the Vilas Farm, sold at auction for $3,185.00.

c) **Pilgrimage Prints**…this 25 page book is basically a photographic album of black and white platinotypes taken on Nutting's 1904 Cruise of the 800 throughout the Mediterranean Sea region. Although Nutting apparently made several presentation copies of this book, at least one other copy of Pilgrimage Prints had been broken up and sold individually over the years. The copy that we sold in 1995 for $6350 is the only remaining copy that is presently known to us.

Wallace Nutting picture books generally represent the rarest and most sought-after of all Wallace Nutting memorabilia. They are also the most expensive to collect.

Pilgrimage Prints, sold at auction for $6,375.00.

Picture Catalogs

As Wallace Nutting's pictures became increasingly popular, he began developing catalogs of his pictures that could be used by his traveling salesmen, or mailed to larger customers such as department stores or gift shops to help in their picture ordering process. The customers could then actually preview the book, see the wide variety of new and existing Nutting titles that were available for sale, and order their new inventory with ease.

We are aware of nine different picture catalogs, which increased in size as Nutting's business and picture inventory grew:

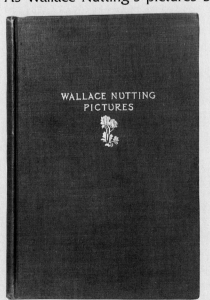

1912 Picture Catalog, $150.00 – 200.00.

1904 Picture Catalog.

a) 1904 (soft cover)...very rare. First edition (never reprinted).

b) 1908 (soft cover)...very rare. Although marked 3rd Edition, we have not yet seen a second edition (never reprinted).

c) 1910 (soft cover)...very rare (never reprinted).

d) 1912 (both soft cover and hard cover)...uncommon, but not rare (never reprinted).

e) 1912 Christmas Catalog (soft cover)...very rare. This was a limited 12-page supplement to the original 1912 catalog (never reprinted).

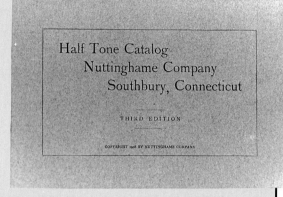

1908 Picture Catalog, $150.00 – 200.00

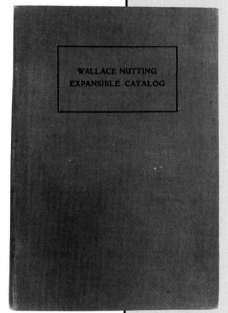

1915 Wallace Nutting Expansible Catalog, Nutting's most complete picture catalog, $100.00 – 150.00.

f) 1915 (hard cover only)...uncommon, but not rare. This catalog is commonly called the Expansible Catalog because the original hard covers were detachable via 2 – 3 butterfly clips, which allowed updated pages showing new and no-longer-available pictures to be inserted into or removed from the catalog without reprinting the entire book. (The Wallace Nutting Expansible Catalog has been reprinted and is available to collectors.)

g) 1917...Wallace Nutting Chain of Colonial Houses supplement (soft cover)...This limited 32 page catalog included a representative selection of pictures taken in Nutting's five historical houses (very rare).

h) Later Updates...Throughout the years, Nutting occasionally issued updates, continuing into the 1930s with certain very limited updated pages showing many of the new floral and other scenes that he was selling. (Most of these are quite rare.)

i) 1937 Recovery Edition...This was Nutting's final picture catalog (soft cover, very rare).

Furniture Catalogs

Although Nutting issued his last major picture catalog in 1915, his first furniture catalog wasn't released until 1918, and he continued issuing them periodically for the next 20 years.

a) 1918…Windsor Chair Catalog…shows more than 160 different Windsor forms that Nutting was reproducing. An original copy is very rare (this has been reprinted and is available to collectors).

b) 1922…Wallace Nutting: A Great American Idea…shows approximately 43 different furniture designs that the Wallace Nutting Furniture Company was reproducing during 1922 – 24. Note that this was during the period that Wallace Nutting had temporarily sold his business to another company. (He repurchased the business in 1924.) An original copy is very rare (this has been reprinted and is available to collectors).

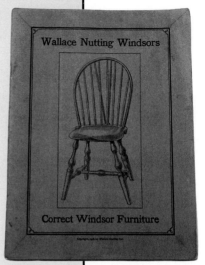

Windsor Catalog (1918), Nutting's first reproduction furniture catalog, $75.00 – 150.00.

c) 1926…This catalog expanded beyond Nutting's preferred Pilgrim Century Furniture designs into the more popular formal styles (Chippendale, Hepplewhite, Sheraton, etc). An original copy is unusual, but not rare. (This catalog had been reprinted in the late 1960s but is out-of-print today.)

d) 1927 – 28…This catalog was slightly larger than the 1926 catalog, including several new and different forms that Nutting had introduced. An original copy is unusual, but not rare. (This catalog has never been reprinted.)

Assorted furniture catalogs, 1926 – 1937, $75.00 – 150.00 each.

e) 1927…Furniture, Rugs, and Iron: Revised Edition…This catalog is very rare and has never been reprinted.

f) 1930…The Wallace Nutting General Catalog, Supreme Edition…This was Nutting's largest furniture catalog, printed at what many consider to be the peak period of Nutting's reproduction furniture business. This catalog is fairly common, and has also been reproduced and is available to collectors.

g) 1937…The Wallace Nutting Furniture Catalog, Final Edition…This was Nutting's last furniture catalog. It contained few new furniture designs, and was somewhat smaller than the 1930 Supreme Edition due to styles and designs that had been eliminated. This 1937 final edition catalog also contained numerous price reductions which reflected the tough economic times Nutting faced during the 1930s. (This catalog is fairly common and has never been reprinted.)

Other Catalogs

In addition to Nutting's picture and furniture catalogs, there are several other catalogs that fall under this Wallace Nutting memorabilia umbrella:

Early American Ironwork Catalog, $150.00 – 200.00.

a) Early American Ironwork Catalog…This was a sales catalog used to describe Nutting's reproduction ironwork made at the Saugus Iron Works under the supervision of Edward Guy. Published in 1919, this catalog is rare and difficult to locate.

b) 1941 Parke-Bernet Auction Catalog…This was the auction catalog from the sale of Wallace Nutting's remaining collection of authentic early American antiques, shortly after his death in 1941. It is not uncommon to find the actual sale prices handwritten into these catalogs.

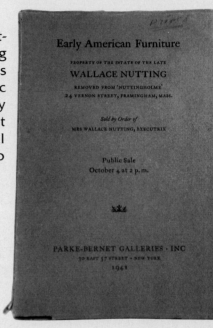

1941 Parke-Bernet Auction Catalog of Wallace Nutting's antiques, sold at auction shortly after his death in 1941, $75.00 – 100.00.

c) The Wannamaker Catalog of the Wallace Nutting Collection…After Nutting had finally sold the last of his Colonial Chain of Picture Houses, he sold the remaining furniture that was displayed in those houses to the John Wannamaker Stores of New York, were it went on display for a period of time. This catalog listed the items for sale and the asking prices.

Letters and Correspondence

Wallace Nutting was a relatively famous individual during the 1910 – 41 period and he wrote and received a large number of letters from customers, friends, and business associates. As is still typical today, most correspondence was discarded shortly after being read, so any remaining Wallace Nutting letters and correspondence have become increasingly collectible. Although there are probably hundreds of Wallace Nutting letters still in existence, a large percentage of them are in private collections or historical archives.

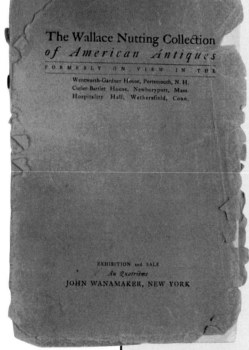

Wanamaker Catalog of Wallace Nutting's remaining early American antiques after the sale of his Colonial Chain of Homes, $125.00 – 175.00.

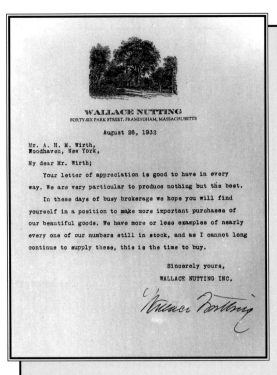

Wallace Nutting letter, typed & signed, with the most common letterhead.

The value of Wallace Nutting letters is generally determined by several factors, including:

a) the subject matter contained in the letter

b) whether the letter was entirely hand written, or simply typed and hand signed

c) the type of letterhead on the stationary

d) whether the letter includes the original envelope

e) and most obviously, condition.

One letter we have seen included Nutting's vital statistics (5'9", 175 lbs., hat size 7). Another indicated that he had visited my hometown of Doylestown, PA, in 1938. And still another discussed Nutting's disdain for income taxes and the poor state of his business in the late 1930s. In June 1996, we sold an interesting lot which included a series of letters between Nutting and his publisher where Nutting negotiated back the publishing rights to several of his books, "not because they had any financial value, but for sentimental reasons." And then, one year later, Nutting republished the books through a new publisher.

But perhaps the most interesting letter we have ever sold included a letter from Nutting to Gustov Stickley, with Nutting basically accusing Stickley of stealing his furniture designs, and Stickley's separate reply, telling Nutting where he could go. This letter sold for more than $600.

Wallace Nutting letter, typed & signed, with a rarer letterhead.

Calendars

Original calendars, with the calendar portion complete, are quite rare. (How many people actually keep a calendar at the

Calendar, with snow scene, $100.00 – 200.00.

end of the year?) Pages 901 – 917 of *The Wallace Nutting Expansible Catalog* show more than 50 different calendar styles that Nutting was selling in 1915. These were calendars which contained a hand-colored picture, a verse, and the actual calendar all mounted upon a thick paper backing, and were typically thrown away at the end of the year. Very few of these remain.

Two calendars, with exterior scenes, $75.00 – 150.00 each.

One calendar style introduced in later years included a calendar which hung on two colorful ribbons beneath a hand-colored picture, framed within a thin metal frame, approximately 4" x 5". This style enabled the owner to trim off the calendar ribbon at the end of the year and keep the hand-colored picture hanging on the wall. Complete calendars will generally be more valuable than incomplete calendars, and the rarity of the picture and condition of the calendar will determine its overall value.

Greeting Cards

Original greeting cards are also quite rare. Like calendars, how many people actually keep their greeting cards after an event has passed? Pages 951 – 954 of *The Wallace Nutting Expansible Catalog* reveal approximately 25 different greeting card styles. As a result, greeting cards are generally considered to be quite rare, and came in the form of Christmas, Easter, Mother's Day, friendship, bachelor, new birth, new home, and Valentine's Day cards. The rarity of the picture and the condition of the card will determine its overall value.

Blowing Bubbles greeting card, sold at auction for $960.00.

Silhouettes

Beginning around 1927, in an attempt to improve sagging picture sales, Nutting introduced a series of machine-produced silhouettes originally drawn by his assistant, Ernest John Donnelly. The majority of Donnelly-drawn silhouettes consisted of women either in the home or garden. Other silhouettes come in the form of famous couples (Abe and Mary Todd Lincoln; George and Martha Washington; John Alden and Priscilla, etc.), and silhouette note and greeting cards. There are more than 40 different Wallace Nutting silhouettes, which come in a variety of sizes including 4" x 4", 5" x 5", and 7" x 8". Most are identified with either a "WN" (obviously for Wallace Nutting), an "EJD" or "ED" (for Ernest John Donnelly, the artist), or with both a "WN" and "EJD."

Silhouettes, unusual oval shape, $35.00 – 75.00 each.

Nutting Collecting Tip: Original Wallace Nutting silhouette labels on the back of a silhouette can add 10% – 25% to the price a of silhouette.

Black & White Glossies

Uncolored black & white platinotype pictures were generally quite dull in color, and not bright enough to be used in the higher quality half-tone reproduction process needed to reproduce Nutting pictures in his *States Beautiful* books, advertising literature, other books that he produced, etc. As a result he found it necessary to reproduce slicker, shinier, and glossier pictures for such purposes. There are literally hundreds of black and white glossies still in existence. But what makes them more unique is that in most instances, only one black and white glossy was produced per picture. (When you consider that Nutting published ten *States Beautiful* books, each having approximately 300 photographs, that alone represents 3,000 original black and white glossies). As a result, this may be the only way for a collector to locate a specific rare and unusual scene that they want to add to their collection.

Silhouettes, Abe Lincoln and Mary Todd Lincoln, George and Martha Washington, $100.00 – 175.00 per pair.

Most Nutting black and white glossies will have several distinct markings on the back of the picture, including a purplish "Wallace Nutting" stamp, the title, size (usually a letter code, eg, "C"), and the Nutting studio number. The rarer the picture, the greater the value. Pictures which contain Nutting's personal hand-written notes on the back add even more value.

Process Prints

During the later years of the Great Depression of the 1930s, Nutting resorted to machine-producing eight of his favorite titles in an attempt to reduce the high costs associated with the hand-coloring process. In 1942, four new process prints titles were added, with the 12 process print titles including:

1) A Barre Brook
2) A Little River
3) A Sheltered Brook
4) All Sunshine
5) Primrose Cottage
6) Bonnie Dale
7) Decked As a Bride
8) A Garden of Larkspur
9) Nethercote
10) October Glories
11) Among October Birches
12) Red, White & Blue

Assorted black and white glossies.

Nutting printed literally thousands of these machine-produced process prints...at a fraction of the cost of hand coloring. However, process prints never succeeded in replacing the more popular hand-colored pictures. (Note that the term "process print" refers to the manner in which these pictures were reproduced!...i.e., in the four standard "process colors."..red, blue, yellow, and black). Sometimes process prints will have a Nutting Label on the back referring to the picture being an "Original Process Print."

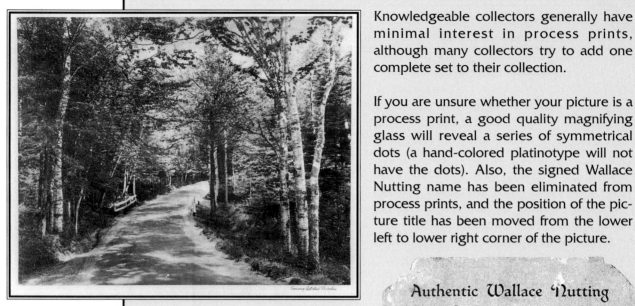

Machine-produced process print, 16"x 20" mat, 12"x 15" picture. Note that there is no signature and the title has been moved to the lower right position.

Knowledgeable collectors generally have minimal interest in process prints, although many collectors try to add one complete set to their collection.

If you are unsure whether your picture is a process print, a good quality magnifying glass will reveal a series of symmetrical dots (a hand-colored platinotype will not have the dots). Also, the signed Wallace Nutting name has been eliminated from process prints, and the position of the picture title has been moved from the lower left to lower right corner of the picture.

Authentic Wallace Nutting Process Pictures must bear this label. All others are unauthorized.

No. __2710__

Label identifying the pictures as a process print, meaning machine produced.

Pirate Prints

During the 1920s when Nutting's pictures were at the peak of their popularity, a competing company began machine reproducing a limited number of Nutting's pictures and commercially selling them at a price lower than Nutting's hand-colored pictures. Upon first seeing these reproductions, Nutting was quoted as saying "Why, those pirates!" Hence the name, pirate prints. Nutting won a lawsuit against the company, forcing them to cease production, but not until a limited number had been put into circulation.

Some pirate print titles include:
1) Blethen Gardens   6) Confidences
2) Joy Path   7) A Grandpa & Grandma Bed
3) Honeymoon Stroll   8) A Sheltered Brook
4) The Garden Gate   9) A Woodland Cathedral
5) A Checkered Road   10) The Turf Path

Pirate prints can be readily identified because while the picture title remains in the lower left position beneath the picture, the name "Wallace Nutting" usually positioned in the lower right corner has been eliminated. Pirate prints can also be detected by using a good quality magnifying glass. Knowledgeable collectors generally have a very limited interest in pirate prints.

Pirate print. Note that the title remains in the lower left position, and the signature has been eliminated.

Studio Memorabilia

Some of the most interesting items sought after by collectors include items that were originally used in the actual Wallace Nutting picture studio or furniture workshop. Some examples of these items would include: studio photographs, paint brushes, porcelain paint trays and palettes, original Winsor & Newton watercolors, shop tools, signs, and posters.

The biggest problem associated with collecting Wallace Nutting Studio memorabilia is provenance, that is...how do you authenticate it? In the past, we have sold items directly consigned by either former colorists from the Nutting Studios, or families of former colorists. This makes the studio memorabilia relatively easy to authenticate.

Certain pieces are clearly identifiable. Sometimes letters or old correspondence can be used to authenticate such items. However, keep in mind that without verifiable provenance or an ironclad guarantee, it may be very difficult to confirm that a specific item was actually from the Wallace Nutting Studio and should be priced accordingly.

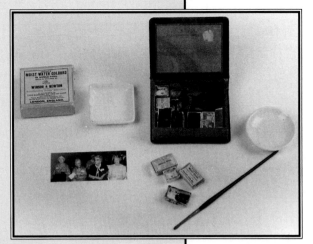

Miscellaneous studio memorabilia: porcelain paint palette, Winsor & Newton watercolors, colorist's brush, photograph of colorist.

Unmatted, Hand-Colored Pictures

When the Wallace Nutting Picture Studio was finally closed in the 1940s, there were literally thousands of loose, unmounted, hand-colored pictures remaining in inventory. Although Esther Svenson (the individual who inherited Nutting's business in 1944) continued selling a limited number of Wallace Nutting pictures into the 1960s, literally thousands of loose pictures were left after she passed away in 1972.

Miscellaneous unmounted hand-colored platinotypes are often close-framed.

Many long-time collectors remember Hilda Cushing (Esther Svenson's sister, who inherited most of the remaining items after Esther Svenson passed away in 1972) coming to many of the Wallace Nutting Collector's Club Annual Conventions in the early-mid 1970s with cardboard boxes loaded with literally hundreds of loose pictures each year. After several conventions, many of the rarer and more desirable pictures became picked over but some of the more common pictures were still being offered for sale at many future conventions.

What was done with the loose, unmounted pictures? They were either close-framed within smaller frames, they were placed on a newer matting and subsequently retitled and re-signed, or they were simply filed away for future use. Keep in mind that although these loose, unmounted pictures still may have considerable value, they will probably never be as valuable as an original matted, titled, signed, and framed picture of the same subject.

> **Nutting Collecting Tip:** Many unmounted pictures have been close-framed in new or older frames. Although not as valuable as matted pictures with an original signature, this is a good way to preserve and display unmatted pictures.

Uncolored Pictures and Proof Sheets

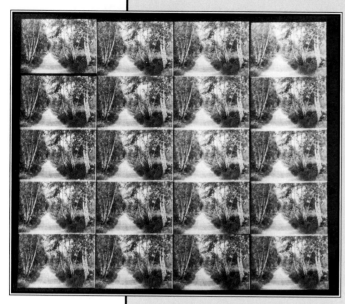

Proof sheet, exteriors with birches, 20 pictures per sheet, $50.00 – 100.00.

Similar to the unmatted, hand-colored pictures, loose uncolored black and white platinotype pictures also remained in inventory when the Nutting Studio was closed. Depending upon the actual size of the picture, larger pictures were developed as one single picture per sheet, while smaller pictures were grouped together onto one single sheet. Proof sheets were typically 11" x 14", and had anywhere from 4 to 20 of the same picture on the same sheet.

In the picture production process, these uncolored black and whites were sent to the colorists for hand coloring. Larger pictures (typically 7" x 9" or larger) would be colored individually while proof sheets with up to 20 pictures on the page would be colored all at the same time, then sent to be cut down to size and matted.

Because they were uncolored, they are generally not as attractive and appealing to collectors as hand-colored pictures. However, many collectors enjoy having a framed proof sheet in their collection which symbolizes a portion of the Wallace Nutting picture process.

Wooden Treenware

Treenware, small salt dish and plate. Note the clearly visible impressed Wallace Nutting marking on the bottom of each.

Although shown in the various furniture catalogs, and having furniture identification numbers, Treenware is generally regarded as memorabilia. Wallace Nutting produced a very limited amount of woodenware, including such items as candlesticks, picture frames, mirrors, salt & pepper shakers, ink wells, pen & pencil trays, handy boxes, cups, saucers, and assorted dishes. (For a more complete listing of Nutting's Treenware, see the section at the end of the Wallace Nutting General Catalog, Supreme Edition marked

"Small Articles.") More often than not, Nutting's Treenware was made from curly maple, and marked with either a small "Wallace Nutting" brand or incised punch. Occasionally a paper label was originally applied.

In over 20 years of collecting, we have seen probably fewer than 50 – 75 pieces of Nutting Treenware, which should give you an indication of its rarity.

Original Glass Negatives

Most of Wallace Nutting's original glass negatives were approximately 8" x 10". Whenever additional pictures were needed, the dark room man would use the glass negative to produce however many black and white platinotypes were needed. The black and whites would be sent to the coloring room, and the original glass negative would be refiled until needed again. Hence, some glass negatives were used many thousands of times prior to the final closing of the Wallace Nutting company.

Supposedly it was Esther Svenson who decided to have all of the original glass negatives destroyed, rather than take the risk of having them fall into the hands of someone who would use them to reproduce new and inferior Wallace Nutting pictures. As the story goes, all of the negatives were thrown onto the back of a pick-up truck, carted to the local dump, and literally shoveled off the back of the truck into the dump. Most shattered upon impact. However, after the truck left the dump, some enterprising individual went through the pile of broken glass, salvaged whatever few unbroken negatives remained, and resold them to a local antique dealer. Hence, there are still a very limited number of Wallace Nutting glass negatives still available. How many? No one really knows but, if I had to guess, I would put the number at fewer than 100.

Hand-Colored Glass Slides

By the mid 1920s, Nutting had turned most of the day-to-day operations of his picture studios over to two of his key employees, Esther Svenson and Ernest John Donnelly. This enabled Nutting to devote his attention to some of his other interests, one of which included public speaking.

Nutting had developed a series of lectures which he would offer to women's clubs, men's groups, church groups, and non-profit-type organizations around the country. (Nutting was frequently paid $100 – $200 plus travel

Hand-colored glass slides and magic lantern projector, sold at auction for $1100.00.

expenses per speaking engagement.) Some of his topics included Old American Homes and Their Furnishings…Old Homes and Their Settings…Maryland and the South: Landscapes and Dwellings…New York Beautiful…New England Beautiful: Landscapes, Gardens & Dwellings. Since this was long before the invention of 35mm slides, Nutting resorted to hand-colored glass slides of his various topics, which would be used with a magic lantern-type projector. These glass slides were hand colored by one of his colorists, and they enabled Nutting to visually illustrate his subject matter to his audiences.

Nutting's glass slides are quite rare and command strong prices.

Old Sales Literature, Advertising & Articles

One of the least expensive areas of Wallace Nutting memorabilia is in the ephemera area, ie, paper. Some examples include:

a) ***Magazine Advertisements***: Wallace Nutting frequently advertised his pictures, books, and furniture in various magazines, newspapers, and periodicals. For example, The Magazine Antiques regularly contained different ads for Nutting's bench-made furniture reproductions during the 1920s – 30s. Many collectors have been gathering as many different advertisements as they can locate.

b) ***Sales Literature***: Over the years, Nutting frequently put together flyers and sales pieces promoting his pictures, books, furniture…and of course, himself. Any advertising pieces promoting Nutting and his businesses are quite collectible.

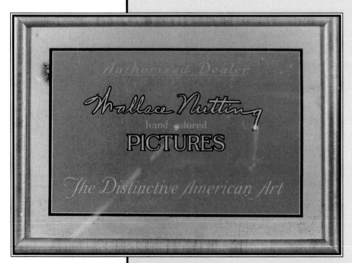

Glass advertising sign, $450.00 – 650.00.

c) ***Advertising Signs***: There are basically two types of signs. Glass advertising signs are quite rare because of their fragile nature. We have only sold a few of these over the years and they can command a very strong price if in good condition. Paper advertising signs typically either promoted his products, or announced Nutting's appearance at a specific time and location. Although not as expensive as glass signs, paper advertising signs can still command a very good price with collectors.

d) ***Articles about Wallace Nutting***: Articles were appearing about Wallace Nutting quite early in his career, and continue appearing in different newspapers, trade papers, magazines, and periodicals even as we speak. Many Nutting enthusiasts enjoy collecting as many different original articles as they can find. One Nutting collector has even published an extensive bibliography listing the date and source of every Nutting article he has been able to locate.

Paper advertising sign, $100.00 – 175.00.

WALLACE NUTTING

whose pictures are in all homes

AUTHOR

of Six Books on Early Furniture and

Fourteen Other Volumes on

OLD AMERICA - In and Out of Doors

WILL LECTURE HERE

Showing 180 Colored Lantern Slides

AT

Miscellaneous Memorabilia

As one final catch-all category, we will use this section to list some additional forms of Wallace Nutting memorabilia that you may run across in your travels:

a) ***Postcards***: We have occasionally seen actual postcards whose subject matter has included Nutting's homes *(Nutting-hame & Nuttingholme)*, his pictures, the Saugus Iron Works, and other items pertaining to Wallace Nutting.

b) ***Old Photographs***: We have sometimes run across old photographs pertaining to the Nutting Studios, the Nutting's themselves, their houses, colorists, and photos pertaining to the businesses.

c) ***Oil Paintings***: We have run across a few oil-on-canvas and oil-on-board paintings of original Nutting photographs. These copies of Nutting's pictures are usually exteriors, and the story we usually hear goes something like: "This is very rare because it was hand painted by Wallace Nutting himself." (Not true, because Nutting really had very little artistic talent himself.)

Oil-on-canvas painting, after The Swimming Pool, $150.00 – 250.00.

d) **Model Pictures**: Early in the picture process, Nutting would prepare a model picture which would include specific instructions regarding how a particular title should be colored by the colorists. Model pictures are quite collectible, and model pictures with the coloring instructions included are even more collectible.

6 6 8 4
A HARTFORD BROOK

SKY PRUSSIAN BLUE:CHINESE WHITE
DISTANCE MAUVE:GRAY GREEN:BURNT SIENNA:HOOKERS GREEN:INDIAN YELLOW:ALIZARIN SCARLET
TREES HOOKERS GREEN   BLOSSOMS ROSE MADDER
FOREGROUND HOOKERS:BURNT SIENNA:INDIAN YELLOW:SAP GREEN
TREE TRUNKS SEPIA
REFLECTIONS SAME AS ABOVE

e) ***Framed Book Cover Dust Jackets***: Sometimes we have seen the front of a book jacket cut down to size and framed. (This may be a new use for those dust jackets that may be in less-than-perfect condition.)

Model picture, with colorist's coloring instructions, $150.00 – 250.00.

f) ***Wooden Furniture Parts & Patterns***: On two occasions we have sold some of the original furniture patterns and designs that were used in making Wallace Nutting furniture. We have also even sold specific parts of Wallace Nutting furniture that may be subsequently displayed as part of a Wallace Nutting collection (eg, chair seats, rungs, spindles).

In my opinion, many memorabilia items are still undervalued. Many of the items sold are one-of-a-kind items that cannot be found anywhere else...letters, glass negatives, colorist's instructions, items actually used by colorists...yet they sometimes sell for prices lower than the very common Larkspur or The Swimming Pool-type pictures...of which there are literally hundreds or thousands of similar pieces.

You should realize that when compared to many other areas of antique collecting, Wallace Nutting collecting is still in its infancy. Whereas people were actively collecting Currier & Ives in the 1920s and 1930s, Wallace Nutting collecting didn't really actively begin on a widespread basis until the late 1970s – early 1980s. And even within the past 10 years, Wallace Nutting collecting is still evolving and being redefined as more is learned. This new Collector's Guide to Wallace Nutting Pictures is evidence of how quickly things have evolved only since 1991. A few advanced collectors have been tucking some of these items away for later years, but, as I have already said, I definitely believe this is still one of the most undervalued areas of Wallace Nutting today.

This chapter on Wallace Nutting Memorabilia covers a wide variety of Wallace Nutting items that are currently being collected by Wallace Nutting collectors from around the country. If I can leave you with this one thought, it would be this: "If it pertains to Wallace Nutting, it will be desirable to Wallace Nutting collectors."

Wallace Nutting Collecting Tips

* Wallace Nutting memorabilia has become increasingly collectible in recent years

* The most desirable and expensive Wallace Nutting items are his picture books & portfolios. Old New England Pictures, which sold at auction in 1993 for $10,175, is still the auction record for any single Wallace Nutting item.

* Many forms of Wallace Nutting memorabilia can be very inexpensive to collect, while others can become increasingly expensive

* If an item is not clearly identifiable and attributable to Wallace Nutting, the value will decrease.

* Nearly all forms of Wallace Nutting memorabilia are collectible.

Wallace Nutting Potpourri

Here are a few thoughts and topics that just don't seem to fit elsewhere, yet are still worth discussing.

Chapter 6

Untitled Pictures

As we have already seen, Wallace Nutting pictures were produced in many different sizes. The medium and large pictures generally contained both the title and the Wallace Nutting name on the mat.

It was very difficult, however, to tastefully put both the title and signature on smaller pictures. It would have looked too crowded. As a result, the title was omitted and only the signature was added to pictures smaller than 10" x 12". Some of these pictures contained the full Wallace Nutting signature; others used the abbreviated W.Nutting signature, and on small 5" x 7"s only a W.N. was added.

Wallace Nutting untitled exterior scenes generally consisted of smaller pastoral views. In most instances, untitled exteriors were smaller versions of Nutting's more popular and bestselling outdoor pictures. Typical scenes included apple blossoms, orchards, country lanes, birches, stone walls, ponds, lakes, and streams. Most untitled exterior scenes are fairly common.

An untitled picture having a signature but no title.

Wallace Nutting untitled interior scenes generally were smaller versions of Nutting's more popular and bestselling colonial indoor pictures. Typical scenes included women, usually near a large fireplace, performing some common household chore…sewing, cooking, polishing silver, reading, braiding a rug, etc.

Wallace Nutting untitled foreign scenes were smaller versions of Wallace Nutting's more popular and bestselling foreign scenes. These pictures usually included cottages, windmills, gardens, castles, cathedrals, and other stately houses.

As we have already discussed, large pictures are generally more desirable than smaller pictures and that definitely holds true regarding untitled pictures. Collectors generally prize titled pictures more than untitled pictures. Beginning collectors will frequently purchase untitled pictures because of their lower price. More serious collectors, on the other hand, will only purchase an untitled picture when they cannot obtain a larger version of the same picture.

Nutting Collecting Tip: Untitled exterior scenes are usually the least expensive form of Wallace Nutting pictures and are especially desirable to new collectors or to those individuals looking for a nice, modestly-priced gift.

Pictures Framed within Mirrors and Serving Trays

Wallace Nutting pictures framed within mirrors are highly sought-after items. Specifically, these were framed mirrors with a Wallace Nutting picture (or pictures) mounted above, or alongside, the mirror itself. Some mirrors I have seen contain a signed and mounted picture; others contain only a signed or copyrighted picture without the mat.

I have seen several mirrors with the name Wallace Nutting branded onto the back of the mirror. This would be a definite indication that the mirror was produced by Wallace Nutting. Most mirrors do not contain the branded signature, making it much more difficult to authenticate. These mirrors could have been produced by Wallace Nutting; they could have been framed and sold by a department store 60 years ago; or they could have been put together privately, either many years ago, or perhaps as recently as last week.

Since relatively few mirrors are readily available, prices are generally higher. Generally, the standard guidelines for pricing apply. Large mirrors of excellent quality, with the rarest pictures, command the highest prices. Smaller mirrors, with exterior scenes, in less than excellent condition, command proportionately lower prices. Unless the mirror is specifically signed, you should probably assume it was *not* manufactured by Wallace Nutting.

The same holds true for pictures framed within serving trays. Wallace Nutting as a rule did not produce serving trays. Like some mirrors, Wallace Nutting pictures framed within serving trays were most likely put together by department stores or privately. Unless the serving tray is specifically marked, you should probably assume that it was *not* manufactured by Wallace Nutting.

Value should be guided by three things:

* value of the picture itself
* value of the mirror or serving tray itself
* added value of the picture/mirror-serving tray combination.

Start with the Price Guide on page 30 and add whatever additional premium value you feel the mirror or serving tray adds to the picture. In any event, if you have a mirror or serving tray with a great Wallace Nutting picture, you have a very desirable piece. If you want to buy one, expect to pay top dollar for it.

Types of Collectors

As in any other field of collecting, serious collectors value rare and unusual items more than the beginning collector. Therefore, they are willing to pay more for a special item for their own collection.

You should be aware that there are many different types of Wallace Nutting collectors. Some try to collect as many different pictures as they can find and afford, including exteriors, interiors, foreign, and miscellaneous unusual topics. Some collect only interiors, while others collect strictly exterior scenes.

Others specialize in a specific area: birch trees, ladies with bonnets, Windsor chairs, clocks, foreign scenes: any country, foreign scenes: specific country only (e.g., only Italy), special states (eg.,Virginia, New Hampshire), sheep, and children.

And these are only some of the areas of specialization. Some people collect only their special area. Others make their specialty the center of their collection, but still collect other types of Wallace Nuttings as well.

In any event, you should be aware that a seascape is more valuable to a collector of seascapes than to a general collector, just as an Italian picture is more valuable to a collector specializing in Italian scenes.

Wallace Nutting's Earliest Signature

Although most people think of the script Wallace Nutting signature as the only marking Nutting used on his pictures, it appears that for a short time around 1905 he experimented with a very different and unique signature.

Based upon several early pictures we have seen dating from the time of the 1905 Cruise of the 800, it would appear that Nutting first experimented with a variation on the first letters of his first and last name. He took the "W" laid it over the "N" and obtained a "$\cancel{W}$" This marking made very little impression with us the first several times we saw it but, after seeing it on several different pictures, we finally concluded that this must have been Nutting's earliest attempt at a signature-trademark.

We have not seen this marking on any pictures other than early Cruise of the 800 pictures and it would appear that Wallace Nutting learned very quickly that his highly recognizable Wallace Nutting signature would become a much better business trademark than his coded "$\cancel{W}$."

Common State vs. Rarer State Pictures

I'm sometimes surprised at the number of collectors who don't seem to recognize that pictures from certain states are rarer than other states.

According to the Wallace Nutting Biography, Nutting began his first photographic work in New England during the summer of 1897, while he was a congregational minister in Providence, RI. Over the next few years Nutting took pictures in all six New England states. By 1905, he had resigned from the ministry and opened his first photography studio in Southbury, Conn., where his picture business greatly expanded. As his business continued to grow over the next seven years, Nutting continued to confine his work primarily to New England.

After moving to Framingham in 1912, his business had greatly expanded. Looking for new sources for pictures, Nutting turned primarily to expanding the variety of interior scenes in his inventory of pictures. Purchasing his Chain of Old Colonial Homes, Nutting continued to photograph primarily New England subjects.

However, as his business continued to increase into the 1920s, he felt an increasing demand for new pictures…from new areas. And after he hired a staff to assume many of his day-to-day duties, Nutting began to travel more in order to photograph scenes beyond the borders of New England.

Probably the best record of Wallace Nutting's travels outside of New England would correspond with the publication dates of his *States Beautiful* book series. His earliest five books were all New England States…*Vermont Beautiful* (1922)…*Massachusetts Beautiful* (1923)…*Connecticut Beautiful* (1923)…*New Hampshire Beautiful* (1923)…and *Maine Beautiful* (1924). This would seem to imply that Wallace Nutting was able to churn out five books within a two-year period by using pictures he had taken over the past 20 – 25 years.

With his New England series out of the way, Nutting was able to begin traveling more extensively to newer, yet-untapped areas. For example, Pennsylvania Beautiful, published in 1924, was probably photographed in 1922 – 23. England & Ireland Beautiful, published in 1925 and 1928 respectively, were photographed primarily during his third and final trip abroad early in 1925 (combined with some of his earlier photographs taken during his 1904 and 1915 European trips). New York Beautiful (1927) and Virginia Beautiful (1930) were also photographed significantly later than the New England states.

So, using 1941 (the year of Nutting's death) as the final year of pictures sales (although a very limited number were sold by Mrs. Nutting and Esther Svenson after Nutting's death), pictures from New England were sold over a 40-year period, while pictures from New York, Pennsylvania, and Virginia were sold over only a 10 – 20-year period. Hence, significantly fewer pictures were sold in these later states. Factoring in the extremely low sales during the Depression years, the degree of rarity becomes even greater.

> **Nutting Collecting Tip:** Pictures from New York, Pennsylvania, and Virginia will usually be rarer than pictures from the New England States and should be priced accordingly.

However, there are always exceptions to general rules of thumb. For example, The Natural Bridge, a Virginia picture, was very popular and sold many thousands of copies. Other less popular New England pictures sold relatively few copies, and are therefore rarer today. As a general rule, however, keep in mind that pictures from the later states will usually be rarer than those from the earlier New England states.

Wallace Nutting Collecting Tips

* Untitled exterior scenes are the most common type of Wallace Nutting pictures, are typically the least expensive, and are often purchased by beginning collectors.

* Pictures framed within mirrors and trays, although not always old, are highly collectible.

* There are many different kinds of Wallace Nutting collectors having many different areas of specialty.

* Although Wallace Nutting's distinctive script signature came to be recognized as his trademark, he did use another "W over N" trademark during his very early years.

* Pictures from several states are generally rarer and considered more valuable than most of the New England states.

Wallace Nutting Reproductions & Fakes
Process Prints

Chapter 7

In the face of declining picture sales due primarily to the effects of the Great Depression, Wallace Nutting resorted to machine producing eight of his favorite titles in the 1930s in an attempt to reduce the high costs associated with hand coloring his pictures. By machine producing these pictures, Nutting was able to run off tens-of-thousands of each title...at a fraction of the cost of hand coloring. For various reasons, process prints never reached the high level of popularity enjoyed by his hand-colored pictures. (Note: The term process print refers to the manner in which these pictures were reproduced...i.e., in the four standard process colors...red, blue, yellow, and black.)

A process print. Note the title under the lower right corner of the picture.

A total of twelve Nutting titles were reproduced as process prints...eight in the 1930s...and four more in 1942 (one year after his death in 1941)...including:

1) A Barre Brook	5) A Little River	9) A Sheltered Brook
2) All Sunshine	6) Among October Birches	10) Bonny Dale
3) Decked As A Bride	7) A Garden of Larkspur	11) Nethercote
4) October Glories	8) Primrose Cottage	12) Red, White & Blue

Because these were actually produced by Wallace Nutting, these are not technically reproductions or fakes. However, these are not hand colored and few collectors prefer process prints to hand-colored pictures. The biggest problem associated with process prints is that all too often people buy them thinking that they are hand-colored pictures when in fact they are not.

Process prints are of limited collectible value.

What To Look For?

* Because these were machine produced, a magnifying glass will reveal a series of tiny symmetrical dots.

* Process print pictures were always 12" x 15". If matted and signed, the mat measured 16" x 20".

* Beware that process print pictures could be less than 12" x 15" if someone has cut one down in size. They can never be larger than 12" x 15".

* There was never any Wallace Nutting signature on process prints, although some process prints do contain a block copyright on the print itself.

* The title was moved from the lower-left corner to the lower-right corner underneath the picture.

* Process prints frequently still have their labels on the back. Note that these labels state that the pictures were "Authentic Wallace Nutting Process Pictures," with the word process inferring the four-color printing process.

Pirate Prints

During the 1920s, with Wallace Nutting's hand-colored pictures enjoying the peak of their popularity, a competing company began machine reproducing a limited number of Nutting pictures and selling them at a price below Nutting's. Upon seeing some of the reproductions Nutting was quoted as saying, "Why, they are pirates." Hence the name "pirate" prints. Nutting won a lawsuit against the company, forcing them to cease production, but not until a limited number of pictures had been reproduced and sold.

Pirate prints are of limited collectible value.

A pirate print. Note the title under the lower left corner, and the absence of a signature under the lower right corner.

Some pirate print titles include:

* Blethen Gardens	* Honeymoon Stroll	* The Garden Gate
* A Grandpa & Grandma Bed	* A Sheltered Brook	* A Checkered Road
* Joy Path	* Confidences	* A Woodland Cathedral
* The Turf Path		

What To Look For?

* Because these were machine produced, a magnifying glass will reveal a series of tiny symmetrical dots.

* Pirate prints generally have a colored border around the picture itself.

* Pirate prints were reproduced in several different mat sizes including 11" x 14", 13" x 16", and 16" x 20".

* The titles always remained under the lower left corner of the picture as did Nutting's titles. The Wallace Nutting name was simply eliminated and left blank.

* Beware that some people have signed the Wallace Nutting name onto pirate prints giving them a more authentic look. The presence of a signature does not automatically mean the picture is authentic.

1970s Reproductions

These reproductions first appeared in the 1970s. Apparently, a nationally advertised reproduction wholesaler from Pennsylvania began selling a series of four different interior scenes. The titles included:

* An Elaborate Dinner   * A Chair for John
* Confidences   * One untitled interior

The reproduction wholesaler was legitimately selling those pictures as reproductions for approximately 50% what authentic Wallace Nutting pictures were selling for at that time. The problems arose when they began circulating through flea markets, auctions, and antique shows and were resold as authentic by both knowing and unsuspecting dealers.

1970s reproduction. Note the dark picture.

1970s reproductions have no collectible value except as a reference piece.

What To Look For?

* Because the pictures were actually photographs of photographs, a magnifying glass cannot by used to detect a 1970s reproduction.

* However, these are fairly easy to detect because:
    1) each picture has a darker color and glossy tint
    2) the mats are all paper thin
    3) the signatures have a purplish color.

* When originally sold, each was framed in a newer frame, although some may have been reframed with older frames over the years.

Wallace Nutting-Like Hand-Colored Pictures Signed with a Wallace Nutting Name

An added, fake Wallace Nutting signature. Note how the title and signature do not match.

If you have already read the book, *The Guide to Wallace Nutting-Like Photographers of the Early 20th Century,* you know that many different people were producing and selling hand-colored photography during the early twentieth century. Although some are collectible in their own right, many hand-colored pictures have limited collector interest and sell for very little. Some individuals have started purchasing those hand-colored pictures that are either unsigned by anyone, or signed in pencil with an easily erasable signature…and have been signing the Wallace Nutting name.

These are fakes and have no collectible value.

What To Look For?

* The best way to detect these is by closely looking at the quality and detail. Nutting pictures usually have good color and detail and if either are not very good…beware.

* Ask yourself whether both the mat and signature appear to be 60 – 90 years old.

* Closely check the signature area for possible erasures, inconsistencies, or evidence of a newer signature.

Wallace Nutting Calendar Pictures

1990 calendar. The other years (1991 – 1993) looked very similar to this.

Wallace Nutting calendars first appeared in 1990, appeared annually until 1993, and it didn't take long for thieves to begin cutting up the calendars, mounting and signing the pictures, and selling them as originals. Although this not a big problem, look closely before buying.

These have no collectible value.

What To Look For?

* Because calendars are machine produced, a magnifying glass will reveal a series of tiny symmetrical dots.

* Most of the pictures used in the calendars were of the more unusual nature.

* Your best defense is to obtain a copy of each year's calendar just to see what might be appearing in the next generation of fakes.

The Latest Round of Wallace Nutting Fakes

In approximately 1989, a new generation of fakes appeared in Massachusetts. Unlike some of the other types of reproductions and fakes previously mentioned, these fakes have been totally fabricated from scratch and made to appear old. What someone has done is:

1) Taken a photograph of a photograph...so the dots will not appear.

2) Mounted the picture upon a non-indented mat, signing the title and signature in fountain pen-type ink...to give an older appearance.

3) Framed them in old frames...to give an older appearance.

4) Put brown craft backing paper on the back, along with a pre-printed brown label which reads: "This picture is (WN Studio #) by Wallace Nutting in Process Color"...to provide a look of authenticity.

Shearing Time   *Wallace Nutting*

Typical Wallace Nutting-like sheep scene, with fake signature and title.

5) Stamped a fake date (e.g., Mar 21, 1925) on the backing paper with an ink stamp pad...to give an older appearance.

6) Used rare, but actual Wallace Nutting titles from *The Alphabetical & Numerical Index to Wallace Nutting Pictures*, with pictures of a corresponding subject matter (e.g., Tivoli was a picture that was obviously an Italian scene. Yet because Nutting's Tivoli was so rare and unusual, no one would have ever seen the original to know if the picture in question was a fraud or not).

Some of the titles include:

1) Moss
2) Tivoli
3) On the Waterway
4) The Lake in the Mountains

5) Washington Cherry Blossoms
6) A Mere on the Links
7) Evening Water
8) Three untitled pictures

Fortunately this generation of fakes seems to have been fairly limited, probably because of all the work that went into their creation. Although we have rarely seen these fakes in a flea market or antique show, several people have mailed us some of the fakes they had purchased.

What To Look For?

* In addition to the above-mentioned characteristics, the photographs were glossy and brightly colored.
* Generally these pictures seem to sell in the $35 – $55 range.

What Is Your Best Defense Against Fakes?

1) Be aware that there is a small group of Wallace Nutting reproductions and fakes just waiting to be purchased by some unsuspecting collectors. Too many people are now aware of the increasing value of Wallace Nutting pictures and are looking for a way to capitalize on it. Beware of any deal that looks too good. If the price appears ridiculously low, before reaching for your wallet…ask yourself why?

2) Become a knowledgeable collector. Read books, join the Wallace Nutting Collector's Club, read the club newsletter, attend the WNCC Annual Convention, or attend a Wallace Nutting auction where you can see several hundred Wallace Nutting pictures all in one place.

3) When possible, buy from a knowledgeable and reputable dealer who specializes in Wallace Nutting pictures. Five years ago you could count the number of dealers who specialized in Wallace Nutting pictures on one hand. Today, there are several dozen. And the number is growing. These people know Wallace Nutting, and they know the difference between average, good, and great Wallace Nutting pictures. They know them, they specialize in them, and they will guarantee what they sell.

This doesn't mean you shouldn't buy from other sources when the opportunity presents itself. Rather, it means that you should give any potential purchase special scrutiny before buying.

4) Regardless of who you buy your Wallace Nutting pictures from…get a guarantee. Most antique dealers I know are hard working, honest, and underpaid individuals. They are dealing in antiques because they love antiques, not to make big bucks. Most could make more money doing something else if that's what they really wanted to do.

But at the same time, most antique dealers specialize in their own one or two areas of specialty, and dabble throughout the rest of the general line field. No dealer is an expert in everything. I know a great deal about Wallace Nutting pictures, and I know furniture pretty well, but I would have a hard time telling the difference between an original iron doorstop from a reproduction, or a piece of brilliant cut glass from a piece made in the Orient last week.

Know what you are buying before you spend your money. Make certain that the dealer you are buying from is reputable and will guarantee what they sell.

You should understand that Wallace Nutting reproductions and fakes are not a major problem. Most are easily detectible if you do your homework and if you deal with reputable and knowledgeable dealers. This overview is simply intended to summarize some of the things you may see in your travels, and to create a better awareness of reproductions and fakes in Wallace Nutting collectors.

Wallace Nutting Collecting Tips

Questions to Ask Yourself if You Are Unsure if It Is an Authentic Wallace Nutting Picture

* Does the color, quality, and detail appear good enough to be a Wallace Nutting?

* Does the topic or theme of the picture seem to be consistent with what Nutting would have done?

* Does the signature appear to be authentic and 60 – 90 years old, or does it appear to be ball point pen?…new?…erased?

* Does the mat appear to be 60 – 90 years old?

* Does the frame appear to be 60 – 90 years old?

* Does the picture have a Wallace Nutting copyright on the picture?

* Does the picture have an original backing or does it appear to have been recently taken apart?

* Is the dealer reputable and knowledgeable in Wallace Nutting? (Remember, honesty and integrity will not guarantee that an unknowledgeable dealer is not unknowingly selling a bad picture.)

* Is it the only Wallace Nutting in the dealer's booth? If so, you might be getting a bargain or you might be buying their mistake. If you are a newer collector, you are generally safer purchasing from someone who specializes in Wallace Nutting.

* Will the dealer give you a full refund if you later find the picture to be a fake?

* If the title or subject matter appears extremely rare, your ears should perk up. Ask yourself these two questions: "Why has every professional dealer at this show passed on this rare picture before I got to it?" and "Am I just lucky today, being the first person to spot this particular title…or does everyone else know something that I don't know?"

A picture that fails any one of these questions does not necessarily mean that the picture is a fake. However, if a picture fails several of these questions, you should become somewhat suspicious and we would suggest that you take a good, hard look before buying.

Chapter 8

Best known among the general public for his hand-colored pictures, Wallace Nutting was also widely recognized as one of the leading authors of his time. He personally authored 19 books, contributed photographs to three other books, published many picture and furniture catalogs, and wrote numerous magazine articles about antiques and colonial living.

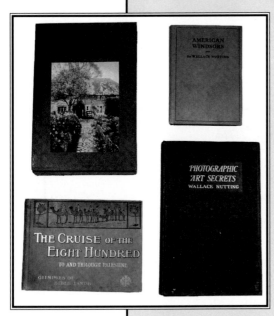

England Beautiful, in cardboard sleeve (1928); American Windsors (1918); The Cruise of the Eight Hundred (1905); Photographic Art Secrets (1927).

Some of Nutting's earliest photographs were first published in 1905. During the previous year he sailed on a cruise through the Bible lands along with a large group of ministers, missionaries, and other religious individuals. One result of this trip was the publication of the book *The Cruise of the Eight Hundred To and Through Palestine.* Although Wallace Nutting himself didn't write or publish this book, he did contribute many of the pictures included throughout its nearly 400 pages.

Over the years Nutting contributed photographs to several other books that he did not write, including *Social Life in Old New England* and *Pathway of the Puritans.*

In 1912, Wallace Nutting put together a leather-bound book entitled *Up at the Vilas Farm* for his friend, Charles Nathaniel Vilas. Apparently Mr. Vilas, a wealthy businessman from Alstead, NH, commissioned Nutting to photograph a series of pictures throughout his estate, have them hand colored, and included in a book which Mr. Vilas gave as gifts to several of his friends or clients.

Up at the Vilas Farm did not include actual copy, but it did have a leather cover, and more than 20 individual pages, each containing a hand-colored photograph, mounted and signed upon an indented, mat-like page. I am aware of only three existing copies of this book.

It was this book that apparently inspired Nutting to publish his first book the following year…*Old New England Pictures.* This book was similar to the *Up at the Vilas Farm* book in that it included 30+ pages of hand-colored pictures, each mounted upon a signed mat-like page. But taking this endeavor several steps further, Nutting added titles to each of the pictures, and more importantly, he included 64 pages of copy on old New England houses. This was his first copyrighted book (1913).

He was more widely known for his *States Beautiful* series. As Wallace Nutting traveled throughout America taking his photographs, he wrote eight books about states that he visited. Each book contained approximately 300 of his pictures which had been photographed throughout the state, and copy about the state's key regions and its houses, history, people, and charm.

These books had two primary markets. First, the residents of each particular state. Most people like reading about themselves, or at least about something near and dear to them…their home state. As a result, he would sell a considerable number of books to residents of each state that he wrote about.

Secondly, this was an era before travel became inexpensive and convenient. Commercial air travel had not yet arrived, transAtlantic ocean voyages were lengthy and expensive, and the automobile was still being perfected. Books were the easiest way to travel. Libraries were frequent purchasers of his States Beautiful books, as well as those individuals interested in learning about new and far-away places.

Overall, Nutting published 10 States Beautiful books:

Vermont Beautiful (1922, 1936)
Massachusetts Beautiful (1923, 1935)
Connecticut Beautiful (1923, 1937)
New Hampshire Beautiful (1923, 1935)
Maine Beautiful (1924, 1935)
Pennsylvania Beautiful (1924, 1935)
Ireland Beautiful (1925, 1935)
New York Beautiful (1927, 1936)
England Beautiful (1928, 1936)
Virginia Beautiful (1930, 1935)

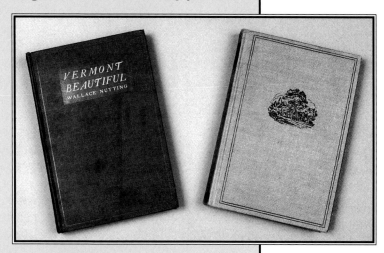

First edition States Beautiful books had a green cover; second edition States Beautiful books had a tan cover.

This States Beautiful series also included two books on European countries, England and Ireland, using pictures taken on several of his trips overseas.

Five other States Beautiful books were under consideration: Ohio, Colorado, California, New Jersey, and Florida, but none of these were ever published. The dust jacket of the first edition Connecticut Beautiful book went so far as to state that Florida Beautiful was released in 1924 but that apparently never occurred. Twenty-five pages of the unpublished manuscript were found, but no such book was ever published.

England Beautiful (first edition), had a cardboard sleeve rather than a dust jacket. Cardboard sleeves are rare and can add 50% or more to the price of the book.

Nutting sold many States Beautiful books. Based upon comments in *Wallace Nutting's Biography* (Wallace Nutting wrote and published his own biography in 1936), approximately 10,000 copies of most first editions were sold. Second editions were released in the mid 1930s.

The success of the States Beautiful books led Nutting to publish several other books on subjects where he possessed significant knowledge: clocks and pho-

New York Beautiful (first edition), had a cardboard sleeve rather than a dust jacket. Cardboard sleeves are rare and can add 50% or more to the price of the book.

tography. In 1924, he published one of the most definitive books ever written on the subject of clocks...*The Clock Book*. This book pictured nearly 250 clocks, described in detail many forms and variations of different types of clocks, and compiled the most extensive listing of American clock makers known at that time.

Photographic Art Secrets was published in 1927, and included Nutting's philosophy and knowledge of successful photography. Chapters included such diverse topics as The Tripod, The Shutter, Exposure, Composition, Latitude From The Equator, Animal Pictures, and much more. For serious picture collectors, this book is a must because it contains many pictures that were never published in any of his States Beautiful books or picture catalogs.

With all of his numerous publications over the years, Nutting published many of his books through his own publishing company, the Old America Company. Other books were published by Dodd, Mead & Company, and Marshall, Jones and Company. Later editions were published by Garden City Publishing Company, and MacMillan Publishing Company. You should also recognize that Bonanza Books republished many of these books in the 1970s. Bonanza reprints are typically used as working copies and have minimal value to collectors.

If Wallace Nutting became well-known for his States Beautiful series, he became even more famous for the books he published on his true passion: early American antiques.

Nutting claimed that the search for attractive backgrounds for his interior pictures was responsible for his fascination with antiques. Through the accumulation of antiques for his interior scenes and for several of his homes, Wallace Nutting had the opportunity to see such a diverse assortment and large quantity of antiques that he began to record what he saw...through his camera.

It was in 1917 that he published his first book on antique furniture...*American Windsors*. Although many antique collectors are aware of Charles Santore's publication of two excellent volumes on Windsor chairs, relatively few are aware that Wallace Nutting

Although the dust jacket called this book Windsor Chairs, the title printed on the book was American Windsors. (See photo on page 76.)

wrote the first comprehensive book on Windsor chairs more than 70 years ago...*American Windsors* (the dust jacket called the book *Windsor Chairs*). Nearly 200 pages long, this book was the first serious study of the Windsor form with chairs dating from 1725 to 1825. Picturing nearly 100 different Windsors, this book included an in-depth discussion of Windsor variations, and each chair's merit, dating, and frequency of occurrence.

Nutting's passion for antiques then led to his publication in 1921 of *Furniture of the Pilgrim Century*. This work went beyond the Windsor form to include American chests, desks, tables, non-Windsor chairs, mirrors, clocks, utensils, and hardware.

Nutting felt that World War I stirred a great deal of patriotism and stimulated interest in the work of our forefathers. Some credit him with playing a significant role in the Colonial Revival Movement. More than 500 pages long, and including more than 1,000 photos of items dating between 1620 – 1720, Wallace Nutting tried to include only things made in America...of native American woods.

In 1924, *Furniture of the Pilgrim Century* was revised, eliminating some pieces which had been later determined to be of non-American origin, adding a few new sections, and eliminating a few controversial pages on ironwork.

Wallace Nutting took most of the photos used in this book, and wrote all copy. Except for the more serious collectors, this extensive publication was all but forgotten because it was eclipsed by his most important work...*The Furniture Treasury*.

Furniture of the Pilgrim Century (1921).

The Furniture Treasury, still available in bookstores today, is really not one book, but three separate volumes. Volumes I & II, published in 1928, contained more than 5,000 photos of American furniture and utensils. Somewhat overlapping the *Furniture of the Pilgrim Century*, this work covers 1650 to the end of the Empire Period which, according to Nutting, "brings us to the beginning of the degraded styles."

In 1933, Nutting published a third volume of *The Furniture Treasury*. Intended as a

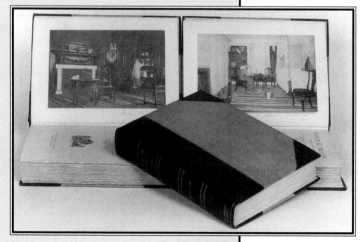

Rare version of the three-volume Furniture Treasury. This rare deluxe edition included a hand-colored interior scene at the front of Volumes I & II, with a special blue binding (vs. the standard rust-brown binding).

supplement to Volumes I & II, this book supplied additional details concerning styles, dates, construction, and origins of the previous volumes. It also provided a listing of early American clock makers which supplemented the listing in his 1924 publication of *The Clock Book*. Unlike the first two volumes of *The Furniture Treasury*, Volume III had no photographs. Rather, it was illustrated with hundreds of sketches, mostly drawn by his assistant, Ernest John Donnelly.

After more than 60 years in print, *The Furniture Treasury* still has not been superseded as the finest and most complete visual reference book of early American antiques ever published.

Wallace Nutting Collecting Tips

* First edition States Beautiful books have a green cover; second edition States Beautiful books have a tan cover; Bonanza reprints usually have a dark blue, dark green or white cover.

* First edition States Beautiful books are usually more desirable and priced approximately 25% – 50% higher than second edition books.

* If a book has a dust jacket in good condition, add $5 – 15 to the price.

* Wallace Nutting attended many book signings and as a result, signed copies of his books are uncommon, but not rare. If a book is signed by Wallace Nutting, add $10 – $20 to the price.

* *England Beautiful* is usually the hardest first edition book to find.

* *New Hampshire Beautiful* is usually the hardest second edition book to find.

* *England Beautiful* and *New York Beautiful* first editions had cardboard sleeves instead of dust jackets. A cardboard sleeve can increase the value by 50% or more.

* First edition dust jackets were white with black printing; second edition dust jackets were more colorful. It is not uncommon to find a second edition dust jacket on a first edition book.

Wallace Nutting Book Prices

Title	Type	Rate	Amount	Date
American Windsors	Book	4	$72.00	4/95
American Windsors	Book	4	$77.00	6/95
American Windsors	Book	3	$77.00	3/96
American Windsors	Book	3.5	$61.00	4/95
American Windsors	Book	3.75	$52.00	6/96
American Windsors	Book	4	$110.00	12/98
Clock Book, The (1st Ed)	Book	4	$110.00	1/96
Clock Book, The (1st Ed)	Book	3	$83.00	3/96
Clock Book, The (1st Ed)	Book	4	$75.00	12/98

Title	Type	Rate	Amount	Date
Clock Book, The (2nd Ed)	Book	3	$55.00	12/95
Clock Book, The (2nd Ed)	Book	4	$75.00	5/96
Clock Book, The (2nd Ed)	Book	4	$41.00	11/94
Clock Book, The (2nd Ed)	Book	4	$65.00	2/96
Clock Book, The (2nd Ed)	Book	4	$50.00	12/98
Connecticut Beautiful (1st Ed)	Book	3	$17.00	6/96
Connecticut Beautiful (1st Ed)	Book	4	$50.00	6/95
Connecticut Beautiful (1st Ed)	Book	4	$50.00	12/98
Connecticut Beautiful (2nd Ed)	Book	4	$44.00	6/95
Connecticut Beautiful (2nd Ed)	Book	3	$22.00	4/95
Connecticut Beautiful (2nd Ed)	Book	4	$35.00	12/98
Cruise of the 800, The	Book	3	$95.00	7/95
Cruise of the 800, The	Book	3.5	$83.00	6/96
Cruise of the 800, The	Book	3	$165.00	4/95
Cruise of the 800, The	Book	4	$132.00	11/95
Cruise of the 800, The	Book	4	$125.00	12/98
England Beautiful (1st Ed)	Book	4	$41.00	6/96
England Beautiful (1st Ed)	Book	4	$72.00	3/96
England Beautiful (1st Ed, cardboard jacket)	Book	4	$150.00	4/96
England Beautiful (1st Ed)	Book	4	$85.00	12/98
England Beautiful (2nd Ed)	Book	4	$44.00	6/95
England Beautiful (2nd Ed)	Book	4	$45.00	12/98
Furniture of the Pilgrim Century	Book	3	$50.00	6/95
Furniture of the Pilgrim Century	Book	4	$44.00	11/95
Furniture of the Pilgrim Century	Book	4	$165.00	7/95
Furniture of the Pilgrim Century	Book	4	$125.00	12/98
Furniture of the Pilgrim Century (Rev 1924 Ed)	Book	3.5	$44.00	6/95
Furniture Treasury, DeLuxe Edition (Vol I – II – III)	Book	4	$231.00	6/95
Furniture Treasury, Vol I – II – III (1st Ed)	Book	4	$250.00	12/98
Furniture Treasury, Vol I – II – III (1st Ed)	Book	3.75	$77.00	6/96
Furniture Treasury, Vol I – II – III (1st Ed)	Book	4	$154.00	6/95
Furniture Treasury, Vol I – II – III (1st Ed)	Book	4	$385.00	3/96
Furniture Treasury, Vol I – II – III (1st Ed)	Book	4	$175.00	5/95
Furniture Treasury, Vol III (1st Ed)	Book	4	$39.00	6/95
Furniture Treasury, Vol I – II (1954 Ed)	Book	4	$25.00	6/95

Title	Type	Rate	Amount	Date
Furniture Treasury, Vol I – II				
(1948 Ed)	Book	4	$83.00	3/96
Ireland Beautiful (1st Ed)	Book	4	$50.00	6/96
Ireland Beautiful (1st Ed)	Book	4	$55.00	12/98
Ireland Beautiful (1st Ed,				
with dust jacket)	Book	4	$83.00	4/94
Ireland Beautiful (2nd Ed)	Book	4	$50.00	11/95
Ireland Beautiful (2nd Ed)	Book	4	$41.00	4/95
Ireland Beautiful (2nd Ed)	Book	4	$45.00	12/98
Maine Beautiful (1st Ed)	Book	4	$39.00	6/96
Maine Beautiful (1st Ed)	Book	4	$60.00	3/95
Maine Beautiful (1st Ed)	Book	4	$45.00	12/98
Maine Beautiful (2nd Ed)	Book	4	$33.00	6/96
Maine Beautiful (2nd Ed)	Book	3.75	$39.00	6/95
Maine Beautiful (2nd Ed)	Book	4	$30.00	12/98
Maine Beautiful (2nd Ed,				
with dust jacket)	Book	4	$45.00	3/95
Massachusetts Beautiful (1st Ed)	Book	3.5	$33.00	6/96
Massachusetts Beautiful (1st Ed)	Book	4	$39.00	6/96
Massachusetts Beautiful (1st Ed)	Book	4	$30.00	5/95
Massachusetts Beautiful (1st Ed)	Book	4	$35.00	12/98
Massachusetts Beautiful (1st Ed,				
with dust jacket)	Book	4	$61.00	11/95
Massachusetts Beautiful (2nd Ed)	Book	4	$61.00	6/94
Massachusetts Beautiful (2nd Ed)	Book	4	$14.00	6/96
Massachusetts Beautiful (2nd Ed)	Book	3	$22.00	6/96
Massachusetts Beautiful (2nd Ed)	Book	4	$50.00	12/98
New Hampshire Beautiful (1st Ed)	Book	4	$33.00	6/96
New Hampshire Beautiful (1st Ed)	Book	4	$44.00	11/95
New Hampshire Beautiful (1st Ed)	Book	4	$55.00	12/98
New Hampshire Beautiful (2nd Ed)	Book	4	$44.00	4/95
New Hampshire Beautiful (2nd Ed)	Book	4	$39.00	10/95
New Hampshire Beautiful (2nd Ed)	Book	4	$40.00	12/98
New York Beautiful (1st Ed)	Book	3.5	$121.00	6/96
New York Beautiful (1st Ed)	Book	4	$94.00	6/95
New York Beautiful (1st Ed)	Book	4	$75.00	12/98
New York Beautiful (1st Ed,				
with cardboard jacket)	Book	4	$125.00	7/95
New York Beautiful (2nd Ed)	Book	4	$41.00	6/96
New York Beautiful (2nd Ed)	Book	4	$44.00	3/96
New York Beautiful (2nd Ed)	Book	4	$50.00	12/98
Pathways of the Puritans	Book	4	$33.00	11/95
Pathways of the Puritans	Book	4	$85.00	12/98
Pathways of the Puritans	Book	3	$39.00	6/95
Pathways of the Puritans	Book	4	$50.00	6/96

Title	Type	Rate	Amount	Date
Pathways of the Puritans	Book	4	$55.00	12/98
Pathways of the Puritans	Book	4	$33.00	11/95
Pennsylvania Beautiful (1st Ed)	Book	4	$44.00	3/96
Pennsylvania Beautiful (1st Ed)	Book	4	$45.00	12/98
Pennsylvania Beautiful (1st Ed, with dust jacket)	Book	4	$55.00	4/96
Pennsylvania Beautiful (2nd Ed)	Book	4	$35.00	12/98
Pennsylvania Beautiful (2nd Ed)	Book	4	$33.00	4/95
Pennsylvania Beautiful (2nd Ed, with dust jacket)	Book	4	$36.00	6/96
Photographic Art Secrets	Book	3	$242.00	6/95
Photographic Art Secrets	Book	3.5	$187.00	6/95
Photographic Art Secrets	Book	3	$204.00	3/96
Photographic Art Secrets	Book	4	$242.00	11/95
Photographic Art Secrets	Book	4	$150.00	12/98
Set of 10 States Beautiful Books (1st Ed)	Book	3	$308.00	6/94
Set of 10 States Beautiful Books (1st Ed)	Book	3	$374.00	11/94
Set of 10 States Beautiful Books (2nd Ed)	Book	3	$220.00	11/94
Set of 10 States Beautiful Books (2nd Ed)	Book	3 – 4	$248.00	6/95
Set of 10 States Beautiful Books (2nd Ed)	Book	3	$165.00	4/95
American Chair, The (Illus. by Ernest Donnelly)	Book	4	$39.00	6/96
Vermont Beautiful (1st Ed)	Book	4	$50.00	11/95
Vermont Beautiful (1st Ed)	Book	4	$50.00	12/98
Vermont Beautiful (1st Ed, with dust jacket)	Book	3	$88.00	11/95
Vermont Beautiful (2nd Ed)	Book	4	$44.00	3/96
Vermont Beautiful (2nd Ed)	Book	4	$40.00	12/98
Virginia Beautiful (1st Ed)	Book	3.75	$55.00	4/95
Virginia Beautiful (1st Ed)	Book	4	$50.00	3/96
Virginia Beautiful (1st Ed)	Book	4	$65.00	12/98
Virginia Beautiful (2nd Ed, with dust jacket)	Book	4	$50.00	6/95
Virginia Beautiful (2nd Ed)	Book	4	$45.00	12/98
Wallace Nutting Biography	Book	4	$55.00	11/95
Wallace Nutting Biography	Book	4	$149.00	6/95
Wallace Nutting Biography	Book	4	$61.00	3/96
Wallace Nutting Biography	Book	4	$85.00	12/98

Chapter 9

What's in the Future for Wallace Nutting Pictures?

In the past I have sometimes heard the comment that all Wallace Nutting pictures look alike. To the serious collector, nothing could be further from the truth.

Wallace Nutting pictures offer such a wide variety of topics, sizes, and areas of specialty that no two look alike. Since each was hand colored, even the same picture with the same title and size can look different. You can literally spend years searching for these pictures and still find something you have never seen before.

Where will prices go as we approach the year 2000?

My personal feeling has always been that the price of Wallace Nutting pictures will follow the same pattern as Currier and Ives. Initially, Currier and Ives pictures were mass-produced, inexpensive, and readily available to everyone (Phase I).

As they fell from style, few people wanted them. Since they were so inexpensive when originally purchased, many were damaged, destroyed or thrown away, and no one really cared (Phase II).

Slowly, they came back into favor. Large numbers were still available and people started collecting them. Books were written about them, research was conducted, a collectors club was formed, and people became much more knowledgeable in the area (Phase III).

Today, most Currier and Ives pictures are in private homes and collections. Common pictures bring top dollar, with medium folio pictures, in average condition, usually bringing hundreds of dollars. Rarer large folio pictures in excellent condition bring thousands of dollars, with the best selling for over $20,000. And whenever a rare or special picture becomes available, it doesn't stay on the market long (Phase IV).

Wallace Nutting pictures have just entered Phase IV. They have already achieved their initial widespread popularity where they were mass-produced, inexpensive, and available to everyone (Phase I, 1900 – 1930s). They then went out of style (Phase II, 1930s – 1960s).

Phase III has occurred over the past 30 years, as they were slowly assembled into personal collections.

We are now in the early stages of Phase IV. Good quality, rare pictures are no longer easily available. Collectors continually complain that they can't find good pictures anymore, and when they do, the quality is bad or the prices are too high.

Well, you had probably better get used to higher prices, because the days of easy-to-find Wallace Nutting rarities seems to be over. 1988 saw the $1,000 barrier broken on several pictures and 1989 saw the $5,000 mark nearly broken. Wallace Nutting pictures are no longer cheap. But bargains are still around…if you look hard enough. Undoubtedly there will be ups and downs in the Wallace Nutting market in the coming years, just as there are in nearly every other market.

Traditionally antiques have been defined as things over 100 years old. The earliest copyright date I have seen on a Wallace Nutting picture is 1898. That means they are on the verge of becoming technically termed as legitimate antiques. Things that are classified as collectibles are valuable; things that are classified as antiques are even more valuable.

Wallace Nutting pictures have reached the threshold of antiquity.

A Collection of Some Rare and Unusual Wallace Nutting Pictures

Chapter 10

No. 1: **The Coming Out of Rosa**. . . *Wallace Nutting's most popular picture.*

No. 2: **Nuttinghame Blossoms**. . . *taken near Nutting's house in Southbury, CT.*

No. 3

No. 4

No. 6

No. 5

No. 7

No. 8

No. 3: **The Marvin Door**. . .*an architectural scene from Portsmouth, N.H.*

No. 4: **A Sip of Tea**. . .*a popular Nuttinghame interior scene.*

No. 5: **The Natural Bridge**. . .*a very popular scene from Virginia.*

No. 6: **An Airing at the Haven**. . .*a Holland scene with a foreign-man-child triple rarity.*

No. 7: **A Studious Maid**. . .*a more unusual interior scene.*

No. 8: **Sea Ledges**. . .*Nutting's bestselling seascape.*

No. 9

No. 11

No. 10

No. 12

No. 13

No. 14

No. 9: **Summer Clouds**...a basic exterior scene.
No. 10: **The Way It Begins**...with a man in a red jacket.
No. 11: **The Mills at the Turn**...a very popular Dutch scene.
No. 12: **Hawthorne Cottage**...thatch-roofed cottage scenes sold very well for Nutting.
No. 13: **Dutch Maids**...a rare and beautiful Dutch scene.
No. 14: **The Meeting Place**...one of the most popular, and expensive Nutting pictures today.

No. 15

No. 16

No. 17

No. 18

No. 20

No. 19

No. 15: **Embroidering**...taken at the Hazen-Garrison House in Haverhill, MA.
No. 16: **The Village Vale**...New England countrysides were Nutting's favorite scenes.
No. 17: **A Como Crest**...sold at auction form $935 in March 1996.
No. 18: **Hepatica**...a rare floral still-life scene.
No. 19: **Rheinstein**...a very rare German scene. Nutting sold very few German scenes, probably resulting from the World War I era anti-German sentiment.
No. 20: **Affectionately Yours**...a very popular Massachusetts interior scene.

88

No. 21

No. 22

No. 24

No. 23

No. 25

No. 26

No. 27

No. 21: **A Dutch Bridge**...a rare scene from Holland.

No. 22: **Flume Falls**...a New Hampshire exterior scene.

No. 23: **Capri Bay**...a rare foreign scene with ocean liners at anchor.

No. 24: **Summer Wind**...was taken outside of Nuttinghame, Southbury, CT.

No. 25: **At the Well, Sorrento**...an unusual Italian child pictured with several people meeting around the town well.

No. 26: **Larkspur**...Nutting's most popular European scene and one of his bestselling pictures.

No. 27: Untitled farmhouse...smaller pictures were usually untitled.

No. 28

No. 29

No. 30

No. 31

No. 32

No. 33

No. 28: **An Old Time Gallant**...*rare man in blue jacket.*

No. 29: **The Guardian Mother**...*still holds the Wallace Nutting auction record price for a single picture, $4,950.*

No. 30: **A Canal in Sunshine**...*rare Italian scene.*

No. 31: **Vico Equense**...*rare Italian scene.*

No. 32: *Pair of miniature florals...very popular with collectors.*

No. 33: *Pair of silhouettes...first produced in 1927.*

No. 34

No. 35

No. 36

No. 37

No. 38

No. 39

No. 40

No. 34: **Fireroom Accessories**…a fireplace built at Nutting's Framingham studio to display his ironwork utensils.

No. 35: **The Age of Romance**…Bryce House, Annapolis, MD. Daisy Ryder was the model.

No. 36: **Jonquils**…Harwood House, Annapolis, MD.

No. 37: **Watching for Papa**…a much rarer version featuring little Rosa and her mother.

No. 38: **The Goose Chase Pattern**…taken at the Quincy Homestead, Quincy, MA.

No. 39: **The Torn Hem**…Hazen-Garrison House, Haverhill, MA.

No. 40: **A Virginia Reel**…taken in Framingham, MA., not Virginia. The "Virginia" refers to the type of yarn winder rather than the location where the picture was taken.

No. 41

No. 42

No. 43

No. 44

No. 45

No. 46

No. 47

No. 41: **A Little Orchard Home**...rare Wytheville, VA, picture.

No. 42: **Arches and Domes**...an unusual stone Italian bridge.

No. 43: **Indecision**...a rare South Carolina interior scene.

No. 44: **Dr. Wallace Nutting**...in his fireside easy chair.

No. 45: **Mrs. Marietta Nutting**...relaxing beside the fire.

No. 46: **Benn's Church**...despite being a minister, Nutting shot relatively few churches.

No. 47: **Colonial Grace**...rare Bryce House interior scene, Annapolis, MD.

No. 48

No. 49

No. 50

No. 51

No. 52

No. 53

No. 48: **Wayside Inn Dining Room**...*at the Historic Wayside Inn, Sudbury, MA.*

No. 49: **The Eighteenth Century**...*a popular Nuttinghame scene.*

No. 50: **Where Grandma Was Wed**...*a very popular Woodbury, CT, scene.*

No. 51: **A Little Helper**...*a rare child scene taken at the Hazen-Garrison House.*

No. 52: **Ballinabad Castle**...*a very rare Irish cow and castle scene.*

No. 53: **An Ancestral Chamber**...*Broadhearth, Saugus, MA.*

No. 54: **An Affectionate Greeting**...*Woodstock, Vermont.*

No. 54

No. 55

No. 56

No. 57

No. 58

No. 59

No. 60

No. 61

No. 55: **Flower Laden**...*Chase House, Annapolis, MD.*

No. 56: **Saben Hall from Garden**...*rare Virginia architectural scene.*

No. 57: **Coming from Confession**...*rare California scene with two young children.*

No. 58: **At a Welsh Cottage**...*very rare scene with Mrs. Nutting in the backseat of their Steven's-Duryea car, driven by their chauffeur Maurice Young.*

No. 59: **The Expected Letter**...*This is the same lady who appeared in* **Larkspur**.

No. 60: **The Halo of a Bride**...*very rare interior scene with large wooden staircase, Lee Mansion, Marblehead, MA.*

No. 61: **Saturday Baking**...*Wentworth-Gardner House kitchen, Portsmouth, NH.*

No. 63

No. 64

No. 62

No. 65

No. 67

No. 66

No. 62: **A Snow Road**...*a very rare and desirable snow scene featuring a horse-drawn sleigh.*

No. 63: **Spinning, 1831**...*black and white scene with lady and large porch spinning wheel.*

No. 64: **A Basket Running Over**...*very rare and large basket of gourds scene.*

No. 65: **A Warm Spring Day**...*Nutting's most popular sheep scene, taken while he was a minister in Rhode Island.*

No. 66: **Luncheon Time**...*rare Hazen-Garrison House interior scene.*

No. 67: **An Amused Recollection**...*Hospitality Hall-Webb House, Wethersfield, CT.*

No. 68: **A Comforting Cup**...*rare New York State interior scene, Scotia, NY.*

No. 68

No. 69

No. 70

No. 71

No. 72

No. 73

No. 74

No. 75

No. 69: **Blossoms by the Lake**...New York State exterior scene. Nutting sold relatively few New York pictures.

No. 70: **A Cupboard Conference**...Hazen-Garrison House, Haverhill, MA.

No. 71: **Tea in Yorktown Parlor**...Webb House, Wethersfield, CT.

No. 72: **A Leisurely Afternoon**...a very rare European scene with two ladies in a courtyard.

No. 73: **On the Heights**...this is a very rare Italian scene. Note that Nutting also had another "On the Heights" picture as well.

No. 74: **The Charms of Home**...a cat and child near Framingham fire with mother.

No. 75: **Awaiting a Visitor**...a rare interior scene with some extremely decorative wallpaper.

Summary of Top Prices Listed in this Book

This chapter is intended to provide you with a summary of some of the top prices that are reported in Chapter 12. I have a feeling that many people will be surprised at what they see. Note that prices include the 10% buyer's premium, where applicable.

Top 25 Exterior Scenes

A Pennsylvania Stream	14x17	Ext	5	$770.00	6/96
Squirrel Bridge	13x16	Ext	5	$451.00	4/95
Champlain Shores	13x15	Ext	4.5	$440.00	3/96
Palmetto Grace	14x17	Ext	4	$440.00	3/96
A Perkiomen October	13x16	Ext	4	$429.00	4/95
A Wilkes Barre Brook	13x16	Ext	4.5	$429.00	6/96
Flume Falls	13x17	Ext	4	$385.00	4/95
A Delaware Canal Turn	11x14	Ext	3	$363.00	6/96
A Mohonk Drive	14x18	Ext	3	$363.00	11/95
An October Array	13x16	Ext	5	$352.00	4/95
Mossy Logs	18x22	Ext	5	$330.00	11/95
The Great Wayside Oak	22x26	Ext	4.5	$330.00	4/95
A Pasture Stream	11x17	Ext	4	$319.00	6/96
A Gambrel-Roofed Road (b&w)	16x20	Ext	4	$297.00	6/96
Yosemite Water	10x12	Ext	3	$281.00	6/94
River Grasses	13x16	Ext	4	$275.00	11/95
Vilas Gorge	13x16	Ext	4	$275.00	4/94
Purity and Grace	20x24	Ext	5	$264.00	6/96
A Wilderness Camp	13x22	Ext	3	$259.00	6/94
The Curve of the Hill Road	13x22	Ext	4	$253.00	4/95
Watersmeet	13x17	Ext	4	$253.00	4/95
Homestead Blossoms	13x15	Ext	4	$248.00	6/95
A Berkshire Brook	10x16	Ext	4	$242.00	3/96
The Seven Bridge Road	12x15	Ext	4	$242.00	6/94
A Berkshire Crossroad	14x17	Ext	4	$237.00	3/96

Top 25 Interior Scenes

An Absorbing Tale	13x16	Int	4.5	$660.00	6/95
At the Spinnet	14x17	Int	4	$550.00	3/96
The Weaver	13x16	Int	4	$495.00	6/94
Triple Interior Grouping	16x33	Int	3	$468.00	6/96
Untitled Interior ("The Maple Sugar Cupboard")	5x7	Int	4	$462.00	4/95
A Call at the Manor	13x16	Int	4	$451.00	4/95
A Knickerbocker Fireplace	14x17	Int	4.5	$440.00	11/95
An Old Drawing Room	16x20	Int	4	$429.00	4/94
A Chair for John	16x20	Int	4	$425.00	11/94
A Call at the Manor	13x17	Int	4	$413.00	6/95
Fireside Contentment	14x17	Int	3.5	$413.00	6/95
Colonial Dames at Tea	14x17	Int	5	$407.00	4/94

Fire Room Accessories	8x10	Int	5	$396.00	6/94
Proud as Peacocks	16x20	Int	4	$395.00	10/95
A Nuttinghame Nook	14x17	Int	4.5	$375.00	9/94
In the Midst of Her China	14x17	Int	4.5	$375.00	4/96
Old Wentworth Days	16x20	Int	4	$375.00	5/95
A Fine Effect	12x20	Int	4	$369.00	3/96
Feminine Finery	13x16	Int	4	$358.00	6/95
Morning Duties	14x17	Int	5	$358.00	4/95
A Chair for John	14x17	Int	4	$352.00	6/94
Afternoon Tea	18x22	Int	4	$352.00	6/95
What Shall I Answer?	15x22	Int	4	$352.00	6/96
A Knickerbocker Fireplace	11x14	Int	4	$350.00	2/96
Wayside Inn, Old Dining Room	10x12	Int	4	$336.00	4/94

Top 25 Foreign Scenes

Wine Carrier, Ravello	11x17	Foreign	3.75	$1,705.00	6/94
View from Casino, Funchal	12x16	Foregin	4.5	$1,540.00	3/96
A Como Crest	13x16	Foreign	5	$935.00	3/96
Caherlough	20x28	Foregin	5	$743.00	3/96
The Cheese Market, Alkmaar	13x17	Foregin	3.5	$743.00	6/96
The Donjon, Chenanceau	13x16	Foregin	3	$660.00	6/96
The Foot Bridge by the Ford	16x20	Foregin	4.5	$660.00	6/95
Children of Sorrento	12x20	Foregin	4	$633.00	4/94
Stepping Stones Bolton Abbey	13x16	Foreign	4	$633.00	3/96
A Water Garden in Venice	14x17	Foreign	4	$605.00	11/94
D'Este Garden	13x15	Foreign	3	$605.00	3/96
The Donjon, Chenanceau	14x17	Foreign	4	$575.00	8/95
A Vine Gabled Mill	13x15	Foreign	2	$523.00	3/96
Patti's Favorite Walk	13x16	Foreign	3	$468.00	6/95
Water Paths of Venice	10x14	Foreign	4	$468.00	6/94
Vico Esquene	11x13	Foreign	3.5	$440.00	6/94
Dutch Sails	9x15	Foreign	4	$413.00	6/95
Old Italian Arches	12x20	Foreign	4	$413.00	4/96
On the Heights	10x16	Foreign	3.5	$413.00	6/95
Warwick Castle	11x17	Foreign	4	$413.00	3/96
A Listless Day	14x17	Foreign	4	$385.00	4/95
The Bay at Capri	14x17	Foreign	3	$385.00	11/95
The Mills at the Turn	18x22	Foreign	4	$385.00	6/95
Bridge of Sighs	14x17	Foreign	4	$375.00	10/95
A Nova Scotia Idyl	16x20	Foreign	4	$374.00	4/95

Top 25 Miscellaneous Unusual Scenes

The Meeting Place	18x22	Horse/Cows	4.5	$2,420.00	6/96
The Meeting Place	13x16	Horse/Cows	4	$2,035.00	6/94
Mammy's Darling	13x16	Child	3.5	$1,925.00	11/95
The Guardian Mother	11x17	Child	4	$1,625.00	10/95
The Winter Welcome Home	8x12	Snow	4	$1,430.00	6/94
A Basket of Gourds	9x13	Floral	4	$1,320.00	6/95
Four O'Clock	14x17	Cows	4	$1,293.00	6/96

Arlington Hills	12x18	Cow	4	$1,265.00	6/95
Snow Scene with House	9x11	Snow	4	$1,265.00	4/94
Hollyhocks	16x20	Floral	5	$1,238.00	11/95
Roses and Larkspur	13x16	Floral	4	$1,210.00	6/96
The Meeting Place	17x20	Misc Un	3.5	$1,155.00	6/95
Colonial Days	14x17	Misc Un	4.5	$1,128.00	6/96
A Basket Running Over	16x20	Floral	3	$1,100.00	6/95
A Patchwork Siesta	13x16	Child	4	$1,100.00	9/94
Christmas at the Farm	11x14	Snow	3.75	$1,100.00	4/95
Going for the Doctor	12x16	Children	3	$1,100.00	6/96
Naptime Stories	14x17	Child	4	$1,050.00	11/94
The Guardian Mother	9x14	Child	3.5	$990.00	4/95
Reading from Arabian Nights	13x16	Misc Un	4	$975.00	7/95
Spring Basket	8x10	Floral	5	$963.00	4/94
Children of the Sea	11x14	Child	4	$908.00	6/95
Arlington Hills	10x20	Cow	3	$880.00	4/94
At the Foot of the Hill	14x17	Cow	4	$880.00	4/95
Four O'Clock	13x16	Cow	4	$850.00	2/96

Top 25 Memorabilia Items

Pilgrimage Prints		Misc	3.5	$6,325.00	6/95
Original Nutting Picture Studio Catalog		Misc	4	$1,012.00	6/96
B&W Glossies (10 misc.)		Misc	4	$715.00	11/94
Letter (Wallace Nutting)		Misc	4	$660.00	3/96
Birthday Book		Misc	3	$605.00	11/95
Glass Negative	8x10	Misc	4	$605.00	4/94
Letter (Two Letters, Wallace Nutting)		Misc	4	$605.00	11/95
Letter (Wallace Nutting, 2 page)		Misc	4	$605.00	6/94
Memorabilia Lot (Misc. items)		Misc	4	$451.00	11/95
Hand-Colored Glass Slide	3x4	Misc	4	$440.00	4/95
Letter (Two Letters, Wallace Nutting)		Misc	4	$440.00	11/94
Letter (Wallace Nutting)		Misc	4	$440.00	4/94
Greeting Card (large)	11x14	Misc	3.5	$396.00	11/95
Hand-Colored Glass Slide	3x4	Misc	4	$385.00	3/96
Letter (Wallace Nutting)		Misc	4	$385.00	4/95
Letter (Wallace Nutting)		Misc	4	$358.00	6/95
WN/Dodd Mead Contract Lot		Misc	4	$358.00	6/96
Easter Card		Misc	5	$352.00	4/95
Letter (Wallace Nutting)		Misc	4	$352.00	6/94
Oil Painting ("Slack Water")	19x28	Misc	4	$352.00	6/94
Birthday Card	5x9	Misc	5	$330.00	6/96
Glass Negative, Rare Double	8x10	Misc	4	$330.00	6/96
Hand-Colored Glass Slide	3x4	Misc	4	$330.00	3/96
Mother's Day Card		Misc	4	$330.00	11/94
Bachelor Card	5x9	Misc	5	$319.00	6/96

Top 50 Wallace Nutting Pictures Overall

Pilgrimage Prints		Misc	3.5	$6,325.00	6/95
The Meeting Place	18x22	Horse/Cows	4.5	$2,420.00	6/96

The Meeting Place	13x16	Horse/ Cows	4	$2,035.00	6/94
Mammy's Darling	13x16	Child	3.5	$1,925.00	11/95
Wine Carrier, Ravello	11x17	Foreign	3.75	$1,705.00	6/94
The Guardian Mother	11x17	Child	4	$1,625.00	10/95
View from Casino, Funchal	12x16	Foreign	4.5	$1,540.00	3/96
The Winter Welcome Home	8x12	Snow	4	$1,430.00	6/94
A Basket of Gourds	9x13	Floral	4	$1,320.00	6/95
Four O'Clock	14x17	Cows	4	$1,293.00	6/96
Arlington Hills	12x18	Cow	4	$1,265.00	6/95
Snow Scene with House	9x11	Snow	4	$1,265.00	4/94
Hollyhocks	16x20	Floral	5	$1,238.00	11/95
Roses and Larkspur	13x16	Floral	4	$1,210.00	6/96
The Meeting Place	17x20	Misc Un	3.5	$1,155.00	6/95
Colonial Days	14x17	Misc Un	4.5	$1,128.00	6/96
A Basket Running Over	16x20	Floral	3	$1,100.00	6/95
A Patchwork Siesta	13x16	Child	4	$1,100.00	9/94
Christmas at the Farm	11x14	Snow	3.75	$1,100.00	4/95
Going for the Doctor	12x16	Children	3	$1,100.00	6/96
Naptime Stories	14x17	Child	4	$1,050.00	11/94
Original Nutting Picture Studio Catalog		Misc	4	$1,012.00	6/96
The Guardian Mother	9x14	Child	3.5	$990.00	4/95
Reading from Arabian Nights	13x16	Misc Un	4	$975.00	7/95
Spring Basket	8x10	Floral	5	$963.00	4/94
A Como Crest	13x16	Foreign	5	$935.00	3/96
Children of the Sea	11x14	Child	4	$908.00	6/95
Arlington Hills	10x20	Cow	3	$880.00	4/94
At the Foot of the Hill	14x17	Cow	4	$880.00	4/95
Four O'Clock	13x16	Cow	4	$850.00	2/96
A Cliff Corner	11x14	Misc Un	3	$825.00	3/96
Christmas Welcome Home	10x16	Snow	3.5	$825.00	11/95
A Jar of Posies (close-framed)	8x10	Floral	4	$798.00	11/95
The Herd in the Stream	13x22	Cow	4	$798.00	11/95
The Pool at Sandwich	13x16	Misc Un	4.5	$798.00	11/95
Toward Slumberland	13x16	Child	5	$798.00	11/94
Fording the Connecticut	13x16	Man	4	$775.00	11/95
Pasture Dell	13x16	Cow	4	$775.00	1/96
Above the Mahogany	16x20	Floral	5	$770.00	11/95
An Eventful Journey	14x17	Misc Un	4	$770.00	9/95
Upper Brandon with Roses	13x16	Misc Un	5	$770.00	11/95
A Dahlia Jar (close-framed)	8x10	Floral	5	$743.00	6/94
Caherlough	20x28	Foreign	5	$743.00	3/96
Hepatica	13x15	Floral	5	$743.00	6/94
The Cheese Market, Alkmaar	13x17	Foreign	3.5	$743.00	6/96
A Chat at the Window	16x20	Misc Un	3.75	$715.00	11/95
A Little Helper	14x17	Child	5	$715.00	11/94
Black and White Glossies (10 misc.)		Misc	4	$715.00	11/94
The Old Time Gallant	11x14	Man	3.5	$715.00	4/95
Vanity & Constancy (close-framed)	8x10	Floral	5	$715.00	4/94

Numerical Grading System and Listing of Recent Prices

As mentioned in the Introduction, the prices in this section are derived from many different sources, including:

* Michael Ivankovich Antiques & Auction Co. auctions (1994 – 96)

* Other auction houses

* Retail and mail order sales

* Prices observed at antique shows and flea markets such as Brimfield, Farmington, and dozens of other such events

* Prices observed at the Wallace Nutting Collector's Club Annual Convention

* Various private collectors and dealers who regularly report prices they have observed in their travels

Most prices here represent prices actually paid. In some instances where we were unable to ascertain the final sale price, we have included the dealer asking price if we felt that it was appropriately priced and fell within the acceptable ranges. The sample of items listed here includes titles sold by us, seen by us, or reported to us. However, many Wallace Nutting pictures are sold throughout the country which are not reported to us, and therefore cannot be included in this listing.

Obviously not all titles are included here. I can't tell you how many people have called to tell me that since their picture title was not included in an earlier editions of the price guide, theirs must be quite rare. If you are simply looking to confirm the existence of a title, the first place to check is *The Alphabetical & Numerical Index of Wallace Nutting Pictures* which contains more than 10,000 Wallace Nutting picture titles.

We have tried to include as many titles and prices as possible in this listing to provide the broadest representative range of prices possible. Between all the sources listed above, I think that most titles will be found here.

However, if a title you are looking for is not found in this listing:

1) Look for a comparable title. Since all titles were individually hand written, there were occasional deviances from the actual title. For example, "An Afternoon Tea" became "Afternoon Tea," "A Canopied Road" became "Canopied Road," "The Natural Bridge" became "Natural Bridge," or "A Sip of Tea" became "The Sip of Tea." If yours isn't listed exactly, try looking under a comparable title.

2) If all else fails...refer to the Price Guide on page 30 and derive an approximate price using the pricing guidelines given in Chapter 3.

I should also clarify that there is no consistent or ironclad correlation between the Price Guide in Chapter 3 and the Listing of Recent Prices that follows. The Price Guide is intended to show *how to* set an approximate value on a Wallace Nutting picture, while the Listing of Recent Prices reports values that have already been set by the market place by virtue of an actual selling price. You will notice that some prices do not follow the Price Guide. Some pictures were sold too cheaply; others sold much higher than their current value. Overall, however, you will find that most prices included in this section do correspond to the Pricing Guide.

One major improvement we have tried to address in this all new *Collector's Guide to Wallace Nutting Pictures* is to provide some indication of the condition of the picture that was sold. As we have stressed earlier, *condition is the primary determinant of value*. In order to help you better relate the selling price to the actual condition of the picture, we have expanded the *Numerical Grading System* which we first introduced in 1991.

This special Numerical Grading System is something that we developed when cataloging pictures for our Wallace Nutting auctions. Every picture that is consigned to one of our sales is now assigned a Numerical Grading Code to help us estimate the approximate price that each picture might achieve at auction.

This code is especially helpful when calculating insurance values and when describing the picture over the telephone to our numerous absentee bidders. However, we do not include this code in our auction catalog so as not to unduly influence bidding.

One problem we encountered after introducing the Numerical Grading System in 1991 was that often times there was a major difference between pictures containing the same code. For example, a picture would be graded a "3" whether the water stain was huge and very visible, or tiny and nearly invisible, whether the mat was cropped down only ½" or right up to the signature, whether there was major or minimal foxing, or whether the mat blemish was minor or quite obvious. The way the initial grading system worked, there was no distinction between major or minor differences within the same grading.

Therefore, in this expanded Numerical Grading System we have introduced midpoints between the major grades to help differentiate levels with a specific grade.

Each picture listed in the section has been assigned a grading of 1 – 5, with 5 being the best, 1 being the worst. In order to arrive at the appropriate numerical grading, we have developed the following guidelines:

> ***5...Excellent Condition***...Recognizing that they are nearly 100 years old, these are pictures with absolutely no visible flaws. The picture has great color and detail, the mat is in excellent condition with proper size and aging, and the frame should be in near perfect condition and appropriate for the period. Very few pictures will ever achieve this grading.
>
> Only titled pictures can receive a "5." Smaller untitled pictures will generally not be graded a "5" because they are so typical and common.

4.5...Near-Excellent Condition...These are pictures with practically no visible flaws whatsoever. To reach this grading, the picture must have great color and detail, and the mat must be in excellent condition with proper aging. The frame must be attractive, appropriate for the period, but may not be quite perfect. Perhaps there may be a little dirt that needs to be cleaned from the mat or inside glass.

At this grading it might be possible to upgrade it to a "5" with a better frame, but it can never be upgraded to a "5" if the picture and mat are not nearly perfect.

4...Above-Average Condition...These are pictures that, although they may not have any visible flaws, just don't rate a "4.5" or "5." The picture has very good color and detail (but not great color and detail), the mat is nice and clean (but showing a certain amount of aging), and the frame is totally acceptable.

Occasionally, a "4" can be upgraded to a "4.5" with a better frame, or with a good cleaning on the inside of the glass.

The highest grading an untitled picture can receive is a "4."

In a very few instances, an especially rare or unusual picture with a minor blemish (e.g., a small, faint water stain on the mat) might be rated a "4" if that picture is rare enough that it would be quite difficult to find another picture in better condition.

3.5 Slightly Above-Average Condition...These are pictures that have minor damage, but not as extensive as a picture graded "3." Minor blemishes might include a small and barely visible stain, very minor foxing or dirt, a very minor mat reduction (no more than ⅓" – ¾"), or any other minor blemish.

Minor picture blemishes could also cause a picture to be graded a "3.5." An example of a minor picture blemish would be a few small, white spots on the picture. Or, a slightly damaged frame could cause a picture to be graded a "3.5."

A "3.5" picture whose only blemish is a slightly damaged frame or cleanable dirt or film on the glass can be upgraded to a "4" with a new frame or a good cleaning.

However, once the mat has a water stain, foxxing, or has been reduced, it can never be upgraded to a "4."

3...Average Condition...Although the picture must be in good condition, there will usually be some major visible mat damage. This damage could include water stains that are large and clearly visible, overmats, foxing, major dirt under the glass, mat creases or tears, or other significant blemishes. Re-mounted or re-signed pictures would also fall into this category.

A "3" picture that is very dirty or that has an unsightly frame can easily be upgraded to a "3.5" or "4" with a good cleaning or a new frame.

Any mat blemish that can be completely covered with an overmat would be considered a "3."

A nicely overmatted picture can never be rated higher than "3."

Pictures that have been either re-mounted or re-signed can never be rated higher than a "3."

2.5...Less Than Average Condition...These pictures have some major picture and/or mat blemishes. For example, a water stain that extends through the title or signature, some fairly major white spots on the picture, or an overmat that is in very poor condition.

2...Poor Condition...Pictures falling within this category generally have some very significant flaws or blemishes. Damage to the picture would include faded picture coloring, noticeable tears or corner chips, or highly visible white spots.

Mat damage would include things like large tears or creases, a very dark mat, water stains that cover all or a portion of the title or signature, or other major damage that cannot be entirely covered with an overmat.

Other examples of flaws that could cause a picture to be graded a "2" would be broken glass or a frame that is so damaged or unsightly that someone would probably not be interested in hanging a picture with such a frame.

Pictures that have broken glass or a horrible frame can be upgraded with the appropriate corrective action. Even an attractive picture with major mat damage might be upgraded to a "3" by re-mounting the picture. However, there is little that can be done to upgrade pictures with major picture damage.

1 – 1.5...Very Poor Condition...Quite frankly you very rarely see pictures with this grading because by the time they have reached this level, most have been trashed or thrown away. However occasionally they do turn up. Specifically, pictures that are rated "1" or "1.5" have irreparable damage to the picture itself. Specific examples would include pictures with major tears, pictures with unsightly spotting, pictures with ink spots, or other major damage making the picture unrepairable.

I can't think of any instance where a picture graded a "1" could be upgraded to a "2." In order to be graded a "1," the picture must be so bad that it is basically beyond repair.

I should remind you once again that this Numerical Grading System is nothing more than my personal system for evaluating Wallace Nutting pictures. It is not perfect, and it is very subjective. However, I feel comfortable using it and believe that other Wallace Nutting experts would agree with my ratings in a majority of cases. In the absence of a better system, you are welcome to use it. And, if you find that you are able to make any improvements to it, I would appreciate hearing from you.

Wallace Nutting Collecting Tips

* Very few pictures will ever be rated a "4.5" or "5."

* Most pictures will fall within the "3.0" – "4.0" category.

* There will be relatively few pictures in the "1.0" – "1.5" categories because by the time they reach this condition, they have either been discarded or thrown away.

* An overmatted picture can never be rated higher than a "3."

* A picture with a water stain can never be rated a "4" or higher, regardless of how large or small the stain or blemish actually is.

* A picture that has either been re-mounted or re-signed can never be graded higher than a "3."

Listing of Recent Prices

Title	Size	Type	Rate	Amount	Date
Above the Mahogany	13x16	Floral	3.5	$413.00	4/94
Above the Mahogany	16x20	Floral	5	$770.00	11/95
Above the Mahogany					
(close-framed)	8x10	Floral	5	$660.00	10/95
Above the Orchard	11x17	Ext	4	$155.00	1/95
Absorbing Tale, An	**13x16**	**Int**	**4.5**	**$660.00**	**6/95**
Absorbing Tale, An	11x14	Int	3	$44.00	11/94
Across the Charles	10x16	Ext	4	$72.00	4/95
Across the Farm	11x20	Ext	4	$45.00	12/98
Advertising Piece (b&w chair)	7x9	Misc	4	$28.00	3/96
Advertising Piece (b&w furniture)		Misc	4	$83.00	11/95
Advertising Piece (thermometer)		Misc	4	$66.00	4/95
Advertising Piece (thermometer)		Misc	4	$41.00	6/95
Advertising Piece ("University Press")		Misc	3	$22.00	11/94
Affectionately Yours	18x22	Int	4	$198.00	3/96
Affectionately Yours	11x14	Int	4	$77.00	6/95
Affectionately Yours	14x17	Int	5	$325.00	5/95
Affectionately Yours	13x16	Int	4	$145.00	12/98
Affectionately Yours	10x12	Int	4	$127.00	3/96
Afterglow	8x13	Ext	4	$75.00	12/98
Afternoon in Nantucket	13x16	Misc Un	4.5	$303.00	6/95
Afternoon Stroll, An	13x16	Misc Un	5	$319.00	4/94
Afternoon Tea, An	10x13	Int	4	$150.00	12/98

An Absorbing Tale

An Airing at the Haven

All the Comforts of Home

Among Saffron Sails

Title	Size	Type	Rate	Amount	Date
Afternoon Tea, An	14x17	Int	4	$100.00	12/98
Afternoon Tea, An	11x14	Int	4	$195.00	10/94
Afternoon Tea, An	14x17	Int	4	$185.00	7/95
Afternoon Tea	13x20	Int	3.5	$121.00	4/94
Afternoon Tea	13x15	Int	3	$66.00	6/96
Afternoon Tea	11x14	Int	3	$105.00	4/95
Afternoon Tea	18x22	Int	4	$352.00	6/95
Afternoon Tea	12x14	Int	3	$50.00	6/96
Afternoon Tea	12x14	Int	4	$225.00	7/94
Afternoon Tea	13x14	Int	3	$105.00	3/96
Airing at the Haven, An	**14x17**	**Foreign**	**4.5**	**$1,100.00**	**2/96**
All in a Garden Fair	14x17	Misc Un	4	$275.00	4/95
All in a Garden Fair	11x17	Misc Un	4	$175.00	6/95
All in a Garden Fair	13x16	Misc Un	4	$210.00	5/94
All in a Garden Fair	10x12	Misc Un	3	$77.00	6/94
All in a Garden Fair	14x17	Misc Un	4	$120.00	12/98
All in the Garden Fair	14x17	Misc Un	4	$176.00	6/96
All Smiles	13x16	Int	4	$210.00	11/95
All Smiles	14x17	Int	4	$100.00	12/98
All the Comforts of Home	**14x17**	**Cat**	**4**	**$303.00**	**6/96**
All the News and More	18x22	Int	5	$275.00	6/94
All the News and More	14x17	Int	4	$245.00	12/98
Almost Ready	11x14	Int	4	$155.00	12/98
Along Rock Creek	11x14	Ext	3	$90.00	2/95
Along the River	10x16	Ext	4	$66.00	11/94
American Colors	10x12	Ext	3	$44.00	4/94
Among October Birches	13x16	Ext	3.5	$77.00	6/94
Among October Birches	13x16	Ext	4.5	$105.00	3/96
Among Saffron Sails	**13x16**	**Foreign**	**4**	**$425.00**	**3/95**
Among the Rocks	11x20	Sheep	4	$275.00	4/95
Ancestral Chamber, An	16x20	Int	4	$182.00	6/94
Ancestral Cradle, The	15x22	Cat	2	$138.00	4/95
Ancestral Cradle, The	13x17	Cat	4	$523.00	4/95
Ancestral Hall, The	14x17	Int	4	$340.00	12/98
Ancestral Hall, The	11x14	Int	3	$44.00	6/96
Ancient Cemetery, Salem, The	11x17	Misc Un	3	$413.00	3/96
Anne Hathaway's Cottage	**13x16**	**Foreign**	**3.5**	**$308.00**	**6/96**
Announcement of Engagement	14x17	Int	4	$470.00	12/98
Anxious to Please	14x17	Int	4	$240.00	2/96
Apple Over the Brook, The	9x16	Ext	4	$85.00	12/98
Apple Pie	14x17	Int	4	$230.00	12/98
Apple Pie	10x12	Int	4	$209.00	6/96
Apple Pie	13x15	Int	3	$143.00	11/95
Apple Pool	16x20	Ext	4	$198.00	6/94
Apple Row	10x12	Ext	4	$44.00	4/95
Apple Tree Bend	13x15	Ext	4	$95.00	12/98
Apple Tree Bend	11x14	Ext	4	$140.00	5/95
Approach, The	10x15	Misc Un	3.75	$468.00	4/95
Arlington Hills	12x18	Cow	4	$1,265.00	6/95
Arlington Hills	13x22	Cow	3	$358.00	6/94

Title	Size	Type	Rate	Amount	Date
Arlington Hills	10x20	Cow	3	$880.00	4/94
Artist's River, An	18x22	Foreign	4	$187.00	4/95
As it Was in 1700	11x14	Misc Un	4	$305.00	12/98
At Broadhearth	10x16	Man	4	$385.00	6/96
At Broadhearth	10x13	Man	4	$175.00	12/98
At Grandmother's Highboy	8x10	Int	3	$25.00	3/96
At the Fender	11x14	Int	4	$193.00	3/96
At the Fender	17x20	Int	4	$355.00	12/98
At the Foot of the Hill	14x17	Cow	4	$880.00	4/95
At the Highboy	13x15	Int	3	$50.00	6/96
At the Landing	13x17	Int	4	$77.00	11/95
At the Side Door	13x16	Misc Un	4.5	$325.00	10/95
At the Spinnet	**14x17**	**Int**	**4**	**$550.00**	**3/96**
At the Spinnet, The Way It Begins	14x17	Man	3.5	$413.00	4/94
At the Village Finger Post	12x14	Foreign	3	$264.00	6/94
At the Well, Sorrento	10x17	Child	3	$176.00	11/95
At the Well, Sorrento	9x15	Child	3.75	$330.00	3/96
At the Well, Sorrento	11x17	Foreign	4.5	$625.00	4/96
At the Well, Sorrento	13x16	Foreign	4	$340.00	12/98
Auspicious Entrance, An	13x16	Ext	4	$88.00	6/96
Auspicious Entrance, An	14x17	Ext	4	$150.00	3/95
Autumn Canopy, The	11x14	Ext	4	$99.00	4/94
Autumn Glow	11x14	Ext	3	$83.00	11/94
Autumn Grotto	14x17	Ext	3	$70.00	8/95
Autumn Grotto	13x16	Ext	4	$160.00	3/96
Autumn Grotto	16x20	Ext	4	$195.00	12/98
Autumn Grotto	13x16	Ext	4	$135.00	7/95
Autumn Nook	14x17	Ext	4	$138.00	3/96
Autumn Waters	13x16	Ext	4	$60.00	12/98
Autumnal Peace	19x25	Ext	3.75	$176.00	3/96
Autumnal Peace	11x14	Ext	4	$105.00	6/96
Awaiting an Opening	12x16	Misc Un	3.5	$121.00	6/96
Awaiting an Opening	**10x15**	**Misc Un**	**3**	**$176.00**	**3/96**
Bachelor Card	5x9	Misc	5	$319.00	6/96
Bag and Baggage	**12x16**	**Misc Un**	**3**	**$358.00**	**3/96**
Baking Day	13x15	Int	3.75	$286.00	6/96
Banks of the Swift	13x16	Ext	4	$94.00	6/94
Baptistry at Canterbury, The	11x14	Foreign	3.5	$99.00	6/96
Barre Brook, A	10x16	Ext	4	$75.00	12/98
Barre Brook, A	12x20	Ext	4	$160.00	3/96
Barre Brook, A	13x19	Ext	4	$175.00	12/98
Barre Brook, A	14x17	Ext	4	$60.00	12/98
Barre Brook, A	14x17	Ext	4	$88.00	6/96
Bars Down to Beauty	22x25	Ext	4	$140.00	12/98
Basket of Gourds, A	9x13	Floral	4	$1,320.00	6/95
Basket Running Over, A	16x20	Floral	3	$1,100.00	6/95
Bay at Capri, The	14x17	Foreign	3	$385.00	11/95
Bay Farm	12x16	Foreign	4	$154.00	6/96
Bay Road	16x20	Foreign	5	$209.00	11/95

Anne Hathaway's Cottage

At the Spinet

Awaiting an Opening

Bag and Baggage

Birthday Book

Title	Size	Type	Rate	Amount	Date
Beckoning Road, The	10x16	Ext	4	$150.00	10/95
Beckoning Road, The	13x16	Ext	4	$72.00	11/94
Beech Borders	10x12	Foreign	4	$66.00	11/95
Beech Borders	16x20	Foreign	4	$120.00	12/98
Belle of the Herd, The	13x16	Cow	4	$385.00	6/95
Belle of the Olden Days, A	14x17	Ext	4	$66.00	6/95
Belle of the Olden Days, A	11x14	Ext	4	$61.00	11/95
Bells of San Gabriel	11x14	Misc Un	4	$175.00	12/98
Below the Arches	18x22	Foreign	3.75	$160.00	6/95
Below the Arches	10x12	Foreign	4	$165.00	7/94
Below the Arches	10x12	Foreign	3	$105.00	3/96
Below the Arches	16x20	Foreign	3	$154.00	6/96
Benedict Door	9x11	Misc Un	5	$204.00	3/96
Benedict Door, A	9x11	Misc Un	4	$170.00	1/96
Bennington Road, A	9x15	Ext	4	$265.00	12/98
Berkshire Brook, A	10x16	Ext	4	$242.00	3/96
Berkshire Brook, A	12x15	Ext	4	$145.00	12/98
Berkshire Brook, A	14x17	Ext	4	$85.00	12/98
Berkshire Brook, A	10x16	Ext	3	$61.00	11/94
Berkshire Crossroad, A	14x17	Ext	4	$237.00	3/96
Berkshire Crossroad, A	14x17	Ext	3.5	$50.00	4/95
Bethel Birches	9x11	Ext	3	$72.00	11/94
Between Cloud Crested Hills	13x22	Ext	3	$72.00	6/96
Between Hill and Tree	13x15	Foreign	4	$94.00	3/96
Between the Spruces	11x15	Ext	3	$127.00	3/96
Billows of Bloom	16x19	Ext	3	$72.00	6/96
Billows of Blossoms	13x16	Ext	3	$75.00	10/95
Billows of Blossoms	13x16	Ext	4	$72.00	11/94
Birch Bend	13x16	Ext	3	$36.00	6/96
Birch Bend	13x16	Ext	4	$120.00	12/98
Birch Brook	14x17	Ext	3	$80.00	12/95
Birch Drapery	13x16	Ext	4	$130.00	2/95
Birch Grove, A	11x14	Ext	4	$80.00	12/98
Birch Grove, A	13x15	Ext	4	$115.00	1/95
Birch Grove, A	11x14	Ext	4	$50.00	6/96
Birch Grove, A	18x22	Ext	3	$55.00	11/94
Birch Hilltop	10x16	Ext	4	$90.00	12/98
Birch Hilltop	14x17	Ext	3.5	$88.00	11/95
Birch Hilltop	11x14	Ext	4	$150.00	1/96
Birch Hilltop	13x16	Ext	3	$85.00	2/96
Birch Mountain Road, A	18x22	Ext	4	$185.00	2/95
Birch Paradise, A	10x13	Ext	3	$39.00	6/94
Birch Paradise, A	12x15	Ext	4	$66.00	4/95
Birch Strand, A	9x15	Ext	4	$65.00	12/98
Birches on Bomaseen	13x16	Ext	4	$88.00	6/95
Birthday Book		Misc	5	$286.00	3/96
Birthday Book		**Misc**	**3**	**$605.00**	**11/95**
Birthday Card	5x8	Misc	5	$198.00	4/95
Birthday Card	5x9	Misc	5	$330.00	6/96
Birthday Card	4x9	Misc	5	$220.00	6/95

Title	Size	Type	Rate	Amount	Date
Birthday Card	4x9	Misc	5	$105.00	6/95
Birthday Card	5x8	Misc	5	$297.00	4/95
Birthday Flowers	**10x14**	**Int**	**4**	**$210.00**	**12/98**
Bit of Gossip, A	12x15	Int	3	$231.00	6/95
Bit of Paradise, A	10x12	Foreign	4	$165.00	3/96
Bit of Sewing, A	11x14	Int	3	$85.00	1/96
Bit of Sewing, A	14x17	Int	3	$65.00	2/96
Bit of Sewing, A	13x16	Int	4	$185.00	2/95
Bit of Sewing, A	16x20	Int	3	$47.00	6/96
Bit of Sewing, A	13x15	Int	4	$100.00	12/98
Black Head, The	12x14	Ext	3	$88.00	6/96
Blooms at the Bend	11x17	Ext	3.75	$149.00	3/96
Blossom Bordered	16x20	Ext	4	$99.00	6/96
Blossom Bordered	14x16	Ext	3	$77.00	3/96
Blossom Bordered	16x20	Ext	4	$66.00	11/94
Blossom Cottage	11x14	Ext	3	$120.00	2/96
Blossom Cove	11x19	Ext	4	$77.00	6/96
Blossom Cove	10x16	Ext	4	$35.00	12/98
Blossom Cove	12x16	Ext	4	$110.00	11/95
Blossom Cove	12x16	Ext	4	$83.00	6/95
Blossom Cove	16x20	Ext	4	$135.00	12/98
Blossom Dale	12x16	Ext	3	$90.00	4/96
Blossom Drive	11x14	Ext	4	$160.00	5/96
Blossom Landing	13x16	Ext	4	$145.00	12/98
Blossom Pasture	13x22	Cow	4	$275.00	4/95
Blossom Pasture	12x18	Cow	3	$143.00	6/96
Blossom Point	12x15	Ext	4	$100.00	12/98
Blossoms at the Bend	11x17	Ext	4	$90.00	12/98
Blossoms at the Bend	**11x17**	**Cows**	**3.5**	**$185.00**	**10/95**
Blossoms at the Bend	14x17	Ext	4	$94.00	4/95
Blossoms by the Lake	13x16	Ext	4	$176.00	11/95
Blossoms by the Lake	12x16	Ext	4	$198.00	11/95
Blossoms on the Housatonic	10x16	Ext	3	$75.00	2/96
Blossoms on the Houstanoic	11x14	Ext	4	$140.00	1/96
Blossoms that Meet	14x17	Ext	3	$72.00	6/95
Blue Lustre Pitcher, A	8x10	Floral	5	$468.00	11/94
Bonnet Curve, A	11x14	Ext	4	$55.00	11/94
Bonnie May	11x14	Ext	3	$50.00	11/95
Bonny Dale	16x20	Ext	4	$190.00	12/98
Book by the Window, A	13x17	Int	3	$231.00	4/94
Book Settle, The	10x16	Int	4	$120.00	12/98
Book Settle, The	10x16	Int	2	$83.00	11/94
Book Settle, The	11x17	Int	4	$275.00	12/94
Bordering the Stream	10x12	Ext	4	$165.00	4/96
Bossington Street	11x14	Foreign	3	$110.00	4/94
Bowered	14x17	Ext	4	$99.00	3/96
Boy's Delight	13x16	Ext	4	$80.00	12/98
Boy's Joy, A	13x16	Ext	4	$132.00	11/95
Braiding a Rug	10x12	Int	3.5	$132.00	3/96
Braiding a Rug	10x12	Int	3.75	$66.00	6/95

Birthday Flowers

Blossoms at the Bend

Braiding a Straw Hat

Bridge End

Bridge of Sighs

Title	Size	Type	Rate	Amount	Date
Braiding a Straw Hat	10x12	Int	4	$175.00	5/95
Braiding a Straw Hat	**13x16**	**Int**	**4**	**$320.00**	**12/98**
Breakfast Hour, The	9x14	Sheep	3	$132.00	11/95
Bridal of the Beech, The	13x16	Foreign	3.5	$121.00	4/95
Bride's Maids of the Wood	18x22	Ext	5	$165.00	4/95
Bridesmaid's Procession, The	20x40	Ext	4	$198.00	11/95
Bridesmaid's Procession, The	12x20	Ext	4	$80.00	12/98
Bridesmaid's Procession, The	10x12	Ext	4	$61.00	11/95
Bridge Bows	13x16	Ext	4	$187.00	6/96
Bridge End	**14x16**	**Foreign**	**3**	**$209.00**	**11/95**
Bridge of Sighs, The	11x17	Foreign	3	$198.00	6/94
Bridge of Sighs	14x20	Foreign	3	$165.00	11/95
Bridge of Sighs	**14x17**	**Foreign**	**4**	**$375.00**	**10/95**
Bridge of Three Arches	11x14	Foreign	3	$198.00	4/94
Bridgewater Road, A	13x16	Ext	3	$28.00	6/94
Broken Waters	10x12	Ext	4	$66.00	11/94
Brook and Blossom	11x14	Ext	4	$145.00	3/96
Brook Blossoms	14x16	Ext	3	$55.00	6/95
Brook Borders	10x12	Ext	4	$72.00	4/94
Brook in Doubt, A	13x16	Ext	4	$198.00	11/95
Brookside Blooms	10x12	Ext	3	$80.00	4/96
Brookside Blossoms	14x17	Ext	3.5	$61.00	11/94
Burlington Glimpse, A	12x16	Ext	4	$165.00	3/95
By the Meadow Gate	14x17	Ext	4	$150.00	5/96
By the Stone Wall	13x16	Ext	4	$77.00	6/95
By the Streams of Peace	13x18	Sheep	4	$468.00	6/94
By the Wayside	9x12	Sheep	3	$121.00	4/95
B&W Glossies (10 misc.)		Misc	4	$66.00	6/95
B&W Glossies (10 misc.)		Misc	4	$88.00	6/94
B&W Glossies (10 misc.)		Misc	4	$110.00	6/94
B&W Glossies (10 misc.)		Misc	4	$143.00	6/95
B&W Glossies (10 misc.)		Misc	4	$55.00	4/94
B&W Glossies (10 misc.)		Misc	4	$715.00	11/94
B&W Glossies (10 misc.)		Misc	4	$55.00	4/94
B&W Glossies (10 misc.)		Misc	4	$193.00	4/95
B&W Glossies (10 misc.)		Misc	4	$121.00	6/95
B&W Glossy (Bear Mt. Bridge, framed)	5x7	Misc	4	$50.00	6/95
B&W Glossy (car picture, framed)	6x8	Misc	4	$55.00	11/94
B&W Glossy (church pew, framed)	6x8	Misc	4	$72.00	4/94
B&W Glossy (cottage, framed)	7x9	Misc	4	$61.00	4/95
B&W Glossy (Isaac Walton Brook, framed)	8x10	Misc	4	$77.00	4/94
B&W Glossy (prison, framed)	7x9	Misc	4	$66.00	4/95
B&W Glossy (Virginia house, framed)	6x8	Misc	4	$55.00	6/94
B&W Glossy (VA house, framed)	6x8	Misc	4	$33.00	6/94
B&W Glossy ("Very Dutch," framed)	8x10	Misc	4	$39.00	11/94
B&W Man in Red Coat	8x10	Man	4	$110.00	11/95

Title	Size	Type	Rate	Amount	Date
B&W Picture with Uncle Sam	12x15	Man	3	$132.00	11/95
B&W Picture (from Cruise of the 800)	10x12	Misc	4	$127.00	3/96
B&W Picture (Mrs. Nutting)	9x12	Misc	4	$61.00	6/95
B&W Sepia (WN's logo house)	3x4	Misc	4	$39.00	6/95
B&W Sheep Scene	13x15	Sheep	3	$105.00	4/95
B&W Snow (close-framed)	3x4	Snow	4	$88.00	11/94
Caherlough	10x16	Foreign	3	$115.00	4/95
Caherlough	**20x28**	**Foreign**	**5**	**$743.00**	**3/96**
Calendar, 1914	5x12	Misc	4	$176.00	6/96
Calendar, 1917		Misc	2	$125.00	4/95
Calendar, 1918		Misc	4	$110.00	4/96
Calendar, 1925		Misc	3	$125.00	7/95
Calendar, 1927	8x14	Misc	4	$165.00	6/96
Calendar, 1930		Misc	4	$209.00	6/95
Calendar, 1934		Misc	4	$209.00	6/95
Calendar, 1936		Misc	4	$175.00	7/95
California Hill Top	14x16	Misc Un	3.5	$105.00	11/94
California Hilltops	11x14	Ext	3	$85.00	1/96
California Oak, A	14x17	Ext	4	$230.00	12/98
Call at the Manor, A	13x17	Int	3	$61.00	11/95
Call at the Manor, A	13x17	Int	4	$413.00	6/95
Call at the Manor, A	13x16	Misc Un	4	$180.00	2/96
Call at the Manor, A	**13x16**	**Int**	**4**	**$451.00**	**4/95**
Call at the Manor, The	13x17	Int	3	$83.00	4/94
Call for More, A	10x13	Child	4	$375.00	12/98
Call for More, A	16x20	Child	4	$275.00	4/95
Call for More, A	11x14	Child	3.5	$193.00	3/96
Call for More, A	14x17	Child	5	$440.00	6/94
Call in State, A	13x16	Misc Un	4	$190.00	3/96
Call of the Road, The	16x20	Ext	4	$45.00	12/98
Call of the Road, The	11x14	Ext	3.5	$55.00	4/95
Call on Priscilla, A	14x17	Int	4	$143.00	4/95
Call to Liberty, A	8x10	Int	3	$88.00	6/96
Call to Liberty, A	12x14	Int	3.5	$187.00	4/95
Caller's at the Squire's	14x17	Misc Un	3	$132.00	4/95
Caller's at the Squire's	11x14	Misc Un	3	$187.00	4/95
Caller's at the Squire's	13x15	Misc Un	4	$225.00	10/95
Camden Harbor	13x16	Misc Un	4	$165.00	12/95
Camden Mountains	10x16	Ext	4	$132.00	4/95
Canal in Sunshine, A	**12x15**	**Foreign**	**3**	**$231.00**	**11/95**
Canal Road, The	9x12	Foreign	3	$39.00	4/94
Canal Row, The	10x16	Foreign	3.5	$121.00	11/95
Canopied Road, A	14x17	Ext	4	$83.00	11/95
Canopied Road, A	13x16	Ext	4	$145.00	12/98
Canopied Road, A	11x17	Ext	3	$83.00	6/95
Canterbury Close	13x16	Foreign	4	$193.00	3/96
Canterbury Gate, A	14x18	Foreign	3	$39.00	4/94
Capri Bay (close-framed)	7x9	Foreign	4	$72.00	6/95

Caherlough

A Call at the Manor

A Canal in Sunshine

The Capture of a Redcoat

Title	Size	Type	Rate	Amount	Date
Capri Bay	13x16	Foreign	4.5	$615.00	10/95
Capture of a Redcoat, The	**11x14**	**Man**	**4**	**$390.00**	**12/98**
Caputian Convent, Amalfi, The	8x10	Foreign	3	$187.00	6/94
Caroline's Garden	10x12	Child	4	$578.00	6/95
Cathedral Brook	9x11	Ext	4	$55.00	3/96
Cathedral Brook	9x11	Ext	3.5	$72.00	4/94
Catskill Bank, A	14x17	Ext	4	$140.00	5/95
Catskill Blooms	13x15	Ext	4	$99.00	6/96
Catskill Summit Blooms	14x17	Ext	3.5	$149.00	4/94
Catskill Summit Blooms	14x17	Ext	4	$155.00	2/96
Century of Age, A	10x13	Ext	3.75	$66.00	6/94
Chair for John, A	12x14	Int	4	$145.00	12/98
Chair for John, A	10x12	Int	3	$77.00	11/95
Chair for John, A	13x16	Int	4	$275.00	6/96
Chair for John, A	11x14	Int	3	$44.00	6/96
Chair for John, A	16x20	Int	4	$425.00	11/94
Chambord from the Casson	13x16	Foreign	4	$205.00	9/95
Champlain Shores	13x15	Ext	3	$135.00	1/95
Champlain Shores	13x15	Ext	4	$440.00	3/96
Charles River Elm	10x12	Ext	3	$90.00	3/96
Charles River Elm	13x16	Ext	4	$125.00	12/98
Charm of the Birch, The	9x11	Ext	4	$83.00	3/96
Chat at the Window, A	16x20	Misc Un	3.75	$715.00	11/95
Check (Old America Co., framed)	8x10	Misc	4	$55.00	3/96
Checkers	11x14	Man	4	$374.00	12/98
Cheese Market, Alkmaar, The	13x17	Foreign	3.5	$743.00	6/96
Children of Sorrento	12x20	Foreign	4	$633.00	4/94
Children of the Sea	11x14	Child	4	$908.00	6/95
Chimney Corner, The	13x15	Int	3	$50.00	3/96
Choosing a Bonnet	11x14	Int	3	$61.00	6/95
Christmas at the Farm	11x14	Snow	3.75	$1,100.00	4/95
Christmas Card (with silhouette)	6x8	Misc	4	$35.00	12/98
Christmas Card (with snow scene)		Misc	4	$143.00	11/95
Christmas Gifts	14x17	Int	4	$187.00	6/95
Christmas Jelly	10x14	Int	3	$110.00	6/96
Christmas Jelly	13x16	Int	4	$135.00	12/94
Christmas Jelly	14x17	Int	4	$175.00	9/94
Christmas Jelly	11x14	Int	3	$88.00	11/94
Christmas Jelly	12x16	Int	3.5	$143.00	6/96
Christmas Welcome Home	10x16	Snow	3.5	$825.00	11/95
Church by the Stream, The	**11x14**	**Foreign**	**4**	**$100.00**	**12/98**
Cliff Corner, A	13x16	Misc Un	4	$375.00	12/98
Cluster of Zinnias, A	16x20	Floral	4	$523.00	6/94
Cluster of Zinnias, A	16x20	Floral	4.5	$605.00	6/95
Cluster of Zinnias (close-framed), A	8x10	Floral	4	$220.00	4/95
Cluster of Zinnias (close-framed), A	8x10	Floral	4	$187.00	6/95
Clustered Roses	10x12	Foreign	4	$154.00	4/95
Clustered Roses	13x16	Foreign	4	$200.00	12/98
Clyffe Pypard	13x16	Foreign	4	$105.00	6/95
Cobb's Creek Banks	10x12	Ext	4	$160.00	4/96

Title	Size	Type	Rate	Amount	Date
Cold Day, A	13x17	Int	4	$265.00	9/94
Cold Day, A	14x17	Int	3	$154.00	6/96
Cold Day, A	11x14	Int	3.5	$110.00	4/94
Cold Day, A	13x16	Int	4	$185.00	4/95
Colonial China	11x14	Int	4	$180.00	4/96
Colonial Corner, A	13x17	Int	4	$80.00	12/98
Colonial Dames at Tea	**14x17**	**Int**	**5**	**$407.00**	**4/94**
Colonial Dames at Tea	13x15	Int	4	$165.00	4/94
Colonial Days	14x17	Misc Un	4.5	$1,128.00	6/96
Colonial Days	14x17	Misc Un	4	$285.00	4/96
Colonial Kitchen, A	14x17	Int	3	$132.00	11/94
Colonial Stair, A	9x15	Int	3.75	$231.00	6/95
Come Into the Garden	13x16	Misc Un	5	$341.00	4/94
Come Into the Garden	16x20	Misc Un	3	$132.00	11/94
Comfort and a Cat	14x17	Cat	3	$132.00	6/96
Comfort and a Cat	14x17	Cat	3.75	$242.00	6/94
Comfort and the Cat	13x15	Cat	3.5	$248.00	6/95
Coming Out of Rosa, The	13x15	Child	4	$407.00	6/96
Coming Out of Rosa, The	11x14	Child	4	$193.00	3/96
Coming Out of Rosa, The	16x20	Child	4	$302.00	6/96
Coming Out of Rosa, The	11x14	Child	4	$135.00	12/98
Coming Out of Rosa, The	18x22	Child	4	$231.00	6/95
Coming Out of Rosa, The	14x17	Child	4	$275.00	12/98
Coming Out of Rosa, The	14x17	Child	4	$138.00	3/96
Coming Out of Rosa, The	14x17	Child	3	$132.00	6/96
Coming Out of Rosa, The	12x16	Child	3	$154.00	6/96
Commencement	10x12	Ext	3	$39.00	11/94
Como Crescent, A	13x16	Foreign	4	$77.00	11/94
Como Crest, A	**13x16**	**Foreign**	**5**	**$935.00**	**3/96**
Concord Birches	13x16	Ext	3	$95.00	5/96
Confidences	11x17	Int	3.5	$105.00	6/96
Confidences	9x15	Int	3.5	$154.00	4/96
Confidences	11x17	Int	4	$175.00	12/95
Confidences	13x17	Int	4	$110.00	4/95
Connecticut Arches	11x14	Ext	3.5	$110.00	11/95
Connecticut Blossoms	11x14	Ext	4	$90.00	12/98
Connecticut Blossoms	10x16	Ext	4	$83.00	6/95
Connecticut Blossoms	11x14	Ext	4	$155.00	1/95
Copper Engraving Plate		Misc	4	$39.00	6/96
Copper Engraving Plate	3x4	Misc	4	$35.00	12/98
Copper Engraving Plate of Wallace Nutting		Misc	4	$72.00	6/95
Corner Cupboard, The	9x16	Int	3	$39.00	11/94
Corner Cupboard, The	10x16	Int	4	$150.00	2/96
Corner in China, A	13x16	Int	4	$275.00	4/96
Corner in China, A	13x16	Int	4	$85.00	12/98
Corner in China, A	11x14	Int	3	$95.00	4/95
Corner in China, A	13x16	Int	3	$121.00	7/95
Corner of Capistrano, A	13x15	Misc Un	3	$303.00	4/95
Corner of the Field, A	13x16	Ext	4	$125.00	6/95

The Church by the Stream

Colonial Dames at Tea

A Como Crest

113

Cosmos and Larkspur

A Cranford Tea Pouring

Title	Size	Type	Rate	Amount	Date
Cosmos and Larkspur	**16x20**	**Floral**	**4.5**	**$605.00**	**6/95**
Cosmos & Larkspur	8x10	Floral	4	$635.00	12/98
Cottage Garden, The	12x16	Foreign	4	$245.00	12/98
Cottage Path, The	11x14	Ext	3	$83.00	11/95
Cozy Corner	11x14	Int	3.5	$110.00	6/96
Cranford Tea Pouring, A	**13x16**	**Int**	**4**	**$175.00**	**1/96**
Creature Comforts	13x15	Int	3	$99.00	4/94
Critical Examination, A	12x16	Misc Un	4	$200.00	4/96
Crossing of the Creek, The	14x16	Ext	4	$193.00	6/94
Crossing of the Creek, The	14x16	Ext	4	$160.00	4/94
Cup that Cheers, The	10x12	Int	3	$88.00	11/95
Cup that Cheers, The	11x14	Int	3	$127.00	6/94
Cup that Cheers, The	11x14	Int	3	$72.00	11/94
Cup that Cheers, The	11x13	Int	5	$215.00	7/94
Cup that Cheers, The	14x17	Int	3	$143.00	4/94
Curtsy, In Grandma's Days, The	11x14	Man	3	$468.00	6/96
Curve of the Hill Road, The	13x22	Ext	4	$253.00	4/95
Daguerreotype, The	13x16	Int	3.5	$105.00	6/95
Dahlia Jar, A	16x20	Floral	4	$355.00	12/98
Dahlia Jar (close-framed), A	10x13	Floral	4	$358.00	6/95
Dahlia Jar (close-framed), A	8x10	Floral	5	$743.00	6/94
Dahlia Jar (close-framed), A	16x20	Floral	5	$550.00	3/96
Dainty China	9x15	Int	3.5	$149.00	4/94
Dainty China	11x14	Int	4	$275.00	5/94
Dainty China	18x22	Int	3.5	$143.00	11/95
Dainty China	10x17	Int	4	$75.00	12/98
Daisy Shore, A	13x16	Ext	4	$165.00	11/94
Daughter of the Revolution, A	14x17	Int	4	$180.00	2/96
Day in June, The	11x14	Misc Un	4	$230.00	12/98
Decked as a Bride	13x16	Ext	4	$135.00	2/96
Decked as a Bride	16x20	Ext	4	$225.00	11/94
Decked as a Bride	14x17	Ext	3.5	$61.00	3/96
Decked as a Bride	16x20	Ext	4	$150.00	12/98
Decked as a Bride	18x22	Ext	4	$75.00	12/98
Decorated Bank, A	13x16	Ext	3	$85.00	7/95
Delaware Canal Turn, A	11x14	Ext	3	$363.00	6/96
Delicate Stitch, A	11x14	Int	3	$286.00	6/95
Delicate Stitch, A	16x20	Int	3	$44.00	6/96
Delicate Stitch, A	13x15	Int	4	$132.00	4/95
Delicate Stitch, A	10x12	Int	3	$77.00	6/94
Dell Dale Road	13x16	Ext	3	$90.00	2/95
Dell Dale Road	14x17	Ext	4	$150.00	3/95
Dell Dale Road	14x17	Ext	3.5	$99.00	6/96
Derby Village, A	13x16	Foreign	4	$61.00	11/94
Derwentwater	11x14	Foreign	4	$165.00	12/94
Designing Maid, A	18x22	Int	4	$100.00	12/98
D'Este Garden	**11x14**	**Foreign**	**3**	**$125.00**	**2/96**
D'Este Garden	13x15	Foreign	3	$605.00	3/96
Disappearing Curve, A	14x17	Ext	4	$135.00	8/95

Title	Size	Type	Rate	Amount	Date
Disappearing Path, A	13x16	Misc Un	3.95	$121.00	11/95
Discovered Under Mistletoe	**18x22**	**Man**	**4**	**$375.00**	**12/98**
Discovery, A	14x17	Int	3	$145.00	6/94
Discovery, A	13x17	Int	4	$175.00	9/95
Discovery, A	11x14	Int	4	$72.00	6/95
Discovery, A	10x12	Int	3.5	$72.00	6/96
Discovery, The	10x12	Int	4	$99.00	11/95
Distinction	11x14	Floral	3.5	$375.00	8/95
Divining Cup, A	13x16	Int	4	$95.00	12/98
Dixie Creek, A	14x17	Misc Un	2	$160.00	3/96
Dixville Shadows	11x14	Ext	4	$105.00	4/94
Dixville Shadows	13x16	Ext	4	$135.00	5/95
Dixville Shadows	14x17	Ext	4	$175.00	2/96
Donjon, Chenanceau, The	13x16	Foreign	3	$660.00	6/96
Donjon, Chenanceau, The	14x17	Foreign	4	$575.00	8/95
Dorothy Q	**13x16**	**Misc Un**	**4**	**$165.00**	**11/95**
Double Border, A	12x16	Ext	4	$77.00	4/94
Double Drawing Room, A	10x16	Int	3	$154.00	4/95
Double Drawing Room, A	11x17	Int	4	$195.00	5/95
Double Drawing Room, A	13x16	Int	4	$225.00	5/95
Doughnut Day	16x20	Int	4	$220.00	6/95
Doune Banks	10x12	Foreign	3	$154.00	6/94
Dream and Reality	15x22	Ext	4	$88.00	11/95
Dream and Reality	10x12	Ext	3	$50.00	4/95
Dream and Reality	11x17	Ext	4	$90.00	12/98
Dream and Reality	11x17	Ext	4	$72.00	4/95
Dream Birches	11x14	Ext	3.5	$55.00	4/95
Dreaming Stream, A	13x16	Ext	3	$127.00	3/96
Drying Apples	13x16	Man	4	$495.00	12/98
Drying Apples	13x15	Man	3.75	$303.00	6/95
Drying Apples	14x17	Man	4	$575.00	10/95
Drying Apples	13x15	Man	3	$198.00	6/96
Durham	14x17	Foreign	4	$310.00	12/98
Durham	14x17	Foreign	4	$198.00	6/96
Durham	14x17	Foreign	3	$155.00	10/95
Durham	13x16	Foreign	4	$275.00	9/95
Durham	14x17	Foreign	4	$195.00	10/95
Durham (Untitled)	7x9	Foreign	3.75	$55.00	11/95
Durham Cove, A	13x16	Ext	4	$187.00	4/94
Dutch Maid & a Dutch Door, A	11x14	Misc Un	3	$253.00	11/95
Dutch Maids (untitled)	10x12	Foreign	3.5	$330.00	6/95
Dutch Sails	9x15	Foreign	4	$413.00	6/95
Dutch Sails	10x16	Foreign	4	$265.00	6/94
Dutch Sails	11x17	Foreign	3.5	$195.00	7/95
Dutch Twins	12x15	Foreign	5	$336.00	6/94
Dykeside Blossoms	8x13	Foreign	4	$150.00	12/98
Dykeside Blossoms	13x16	Foreign	4	$215.00	4/96
Early Candle Lighting	14x17	Int	4	$193.00	6/95
Early Foliage	12x16	Ext	4	$35.00	12/98

D'Este Garden

Discovered Under the Mistletoe

Dorothy Q

El Capitan

Entering the Old Bridge

Title	Size	Type	Rate	Amount	Date
Early June Brides	11x17	Ext	4	$115.00	12/98
Easter Card		Misc	4	$83.00	11/94
Easter Card		Misc	5	$149.00	6/95
Easter Card		Misc	5	$352.00	4/95
Easter Card		Misc	5	$198.00	11/95
Easy Mark at Home, The	6x8	Man	3	$330.00	6/95
Echo Lake Borders	9x11	Ext	5	$94.00	11/94
El Capitan	**10x12**	**Misc Un**	**4**	**$355.00**	**12/98**
Elaborate Christmas Dinner	16x20	Int	4	$121.00	6/95
Elaborate Dinner, An	9x15	Int	3	$143.00	3/96
Elaborate Dinner, An	13x15	Int	4	$200.00	12/98
Elaborate Dinner, An	14x17	Int	5	$265.00	7/95
Elaborate Dinner, An	12x15	Int	4	$85.00	12/98
Elaborate Dinner, An	13x16	Int	4	$195.00	12/98
Elizabeth and Her Pets	14x17	Child	4	$2,200.00	6/91
Elm Birch Arch, An	14x20	Ext	4	$105.00	3/96
Elm Birch Arch	15x22	Ext	3	$61.00	4/95
Elm Curves	10x12	Ext	3	$60.00	4/95
Elm Drapery	13x16	Ext	4	$140.00	5/95
Embroidering	13x16	Int	4	$250.00	2/96
Embroidering	11x14	Int	4	$190.00	5/96
Embroidering for Christmas	14x17	Int	2	$77.00	11/95
Embroidering for Christmas	12x15	Int	3	$242.00	11/94
Enchantment	13x16	Ext	3	$65.00	6/95
Enchantment	10x12	Ext	3	$66.00	6/94
Endless Battle, The	13x16	Seascape	3	$154.00	6/96
English Door, An	11x14	Foreign	3	$55.00	11/94
English May, An	10x16	Foreign	3	$83.00	4/94
Entering the Old Bridge	14x17	Misc Un	3.5	$220.00	11/94
Entering the Old Bridge	**13x16**	**Misc Un**	**4**	**$605.00**	**6/94**
Enticing Waters	13x16	Ext	4	$88.00	3/96
Enticing Waters	6x20	Ext	4	$99.00	3/96
Enticing Waters	16x20	Ext	4	$83.00	6/96
Enticing Waters	18x22	Ext	4.5	$121.00	11/95
Enticing Waters	13x16	Ext	3	$61.00	11/95
Enticing Waters	10x12	Ext	4	$85.00	12/98
Equinox Pond, The	9x17	Ext	3	$99.00	4/94
Esther Svenson Contract		Misc	4	$22.00	6/96
Esther Svenson Contract		Misc	4	$61.00	6/96
Esther Svenson Contract		Misc	4	$61.00	6/96
Evangeline Bough	**9x11**	**Foreign**	**4**	**$135.00**	**12/98**
Evangeline Lane	16x20	Foreign	4	$187.00	11/95
Evangeline Lane	9x11	Foreign	4	$190.00	12/98
Evening at Killarney	14x20	Foreign	3	$253.00	3/96
Eventful Journey, An	13x15	Misc Un	4	$635.00	12/98
Eventful Journey, An	13x16	Misc Un	4	$468.00	3/96
Eventful Journey, An	**14x17**	**Misc Un**	**4**	**$770.00**	**9/95**
Eventful Journey (close-framed)	6x8	Misc Un	4	$143.00	6/95
Evergreen Shadows	13x16	Ext	3	$55.00	6/96
Expected Letter, The	**11x14**	**Foreign**	**4**	**$200.00**	**11/95**

Title	Size	Type	Rate	Amount	Date
Fair Autumn	13x17	Ext	4	$110.00	6/95
Fair Banks	13x16	Ext	3	$66.00	11/94
Fair Banks	12x20	Ext	3.75	$61.00	11/94
Fair Woodstock	13x16	Ext	4	$110.00	6/95
Fairhaven Blossoms	12x15	Ext	4	$143.00	11/95
Fairway	13x17	Ext	3.75	$77.00	6/96
Fairway	11x14	Ext	4	$60.00	12/98
Far Dixie	11x14	Misc Un	4	$175.00	2/96
Farm Borders	10x16	Ext	4	$77.00	3/96
Farm Cart Track, A	9x11	Ext	4	$121.00	3/96
Farm Causeway, The	8x12	Ext	3	$50.00	6/94
Farm Road, The	14x17	Ext	4	$110.00	11/94
Farm Road, The	14x17	Ext	3.5	$66.00	11/95
Favorite Corner, A	14x17	Sheep	4	$385.00	11/94
Favorite Corner, A	16x20	Sheep	4	$248.00	11/95
Favorite Corner, A	14x17	Sheep	5	$550.00	11/94
Favorite Corner, A	14x17	Sheep	4	$305.00	12/98
Favorite Corner, A	11x14	Sheep	4	$253.00	4/95
Favorite Waterside, A	12x15	Ext	3	$90.00	9/95
Feathered Elms	10x12	Ext	4	$50.00	6/96
Feminine Finery	13x16	Int	4	$358.00	6/95
Fern Path	13x16	Ext	4	$132.00	6/94
Fine Effect, A	12x20	Int	4	$369.00	3/96
Fine Effect, A	8x10	Int	4	$85.00	12/98
Fine Effect, A	11x14	Int	4	$132.00	11/95
Fine Effect, A	10x12	Int	4	$55.00	6/96
Fine Effect, A	11x14	Int	4	$270.00	3/96
Fine Orchard, A	14x17	Ext	4	$140.00	10/95
Finger Lake Stream, A	14x17	Ext	3	$95.00	11/95
Fire Room Accessories	8x10	Int	5	$396.00	6/94
Fireside Contentment	14x17	Int	4	$170.00	12/98
Fireside Fancies	13x16	Cat	4	$250.00	9/95
Five O'Clock	12x20	Foreign	4	$185.00	11/95
Five O'Clock	13x22	Foreign	4	$175.00	12/95
5 O'Clock	12x20	Foreign	4	$165.00	11/94
Fleck of Sunshine, A	14x17	Int	3.5	$275.00	3/96
Fleck of Sunshine, A	13x17	Int	4	$165.00	4/94
Fleck of Sunshine, A	**11x17**	**Int**	**4**	**$195.00**	**7/95**
Fleck of Sunshine, A	10x14	Int	3	$105.00	6/96
Flock, The	16x20	Sheep	4	$209.00	4/95
Flock, The	18x22	Sheep	3.5	$248.00	4/94
Florida Grace	13x16	Misc Un	3	$116.00	3/96
Florida Grace	13x16	Misc Un	4	$425.00	4/96
Florida Sunrise, A	13x16	Misc Un	4	$210.00	5/96
Flower Laden	13x16	Misc Un	4	$180.00	3/96
Flower Maiden, The	**8x15**	**Misc Un**	**3.75**	**$143.00**	**11/95**
Flower Missionary, The	8x13	Misc Un	3	$121.00	4/94
Flower Missionary, The	10x16	Misc Un	4	$235.00	9/95
Flower Missionary, The	11x17	Misc Un	4	$195.00	4/95
Flowered Approach, A	9x11	Misc Un	4	$143.00	11/95

Evangeline Bough

An Eventful Journey

The Expected Letter

A Fleck of Sunshine

Flower Maiden

Title	Size	Type	Rate	Amount	Date
Flowering Time	13x16	Ext	4	$77.00	6/95
Flowering Time	14x20	Ext	4	$85.00	12/98
Flowery Path, A	13x16	Foreign	4	$143.00	6/96
Flowery Path, A	13x16	Foreign	4	$105.00	11/94
Flowery Path, A	13x16	Foreign	4	$116.00	4/94
Flowery Path, A	14x20	Foreign	3	$143.00	6/96
Flowery Path, A	8x10	Foreign	3.5	$94.00	11/95
Flume Falls	13x17	Ext	4	$385.00	4/95
Flush Banks	11x14	Ext	4	$75.00	12/98
Flush Banks	8x10	Ext	3	$165.00	11/95
Flush Banks	10x12	Ext	3	$61.00	3/96
Foot Bridge and the Ford	16x20	Foreign	4	$165.00	1/96
Foot Bridge by the Ford, The	16x20	Foreign	4.5	$660.00	6/95
For a Little Guest	14x17	Int	3	$39.00	11/94
For Easter Sunday	13x16	Misc Un	3	$209.00	6/94
Fording the Connecticut	20x27	Man	3	$165.00	11/94
Fording the Connecticut	13x16	Man	4	$775.00	11/95
Forest Window, A	11x14	Ext	4	$145.00	12/95
Formal Call, A	16x20	Int	4.5	$275.00	6/96
Four O'Clock	14x17	Cows	4	$1,293.00	6/96
Four O'Clock	14x17	Cow	4	$1,100.00	12/98
Four O'Clock	13x16	Cow	4	$850.00	2/96
Fox Glove	10x16	Floral	3	$550.00	6/94
Fragrant Highway, A	11x14	Ext	3	$44.00	3/96
Fragrant Highway, A	11x14	Ext	3	$85.00	3/96
Framed River, A	12x15	Ext	3	$90.00	1/96
Franconia Brook, A	10x12	Ext	4	$150.00	2/96
Friendly Bough, The	13x16	Ext	4	$99.00	6/96
Friendly Reception, A	11x14	Misc Un	3	$143.00	3/96
From Berkshire Crests	10x12	Ext	3	$61.00	6/96
From Pocono Heights	10x14	Ext	3	$94.00	6/94
From the Mountain	10x16	Ext	4	$135.00	7/95
From the Mountain	11x17	Ext	3	$70.00	8/95
Fruit Luncheon, A	14x17	Int	4	$175.00	12/98
Fruit Luncheon, A	13x15	Int	4	$220.00	7/95
Fruit Luncheon, A	13x16	Int	3.75	$154.00	11/95
Fruit Luncheon, A	14x16	Int	3	$72.00	11/94
Fruit Luncheon, A	11x14	Int	3.5	$275.00	6/96
Fruit Luncheon, A	14x16	Int	3	$110.00	11/95
Full Summer	13x16	Floral	4	$578.00	6/95
Furniture Catalog, 1918 Windsor Catalog		Misc	4	$143.00	11/95
Furniture Catalog, 1926		Misc	4	$155.00	11/95
Furniture Catalog, 1926		Misc	4.5	$77.00	11/94
Furniture Catalog, 1926		Misc	3	$45.00	5/95
Furniture Catalog, 1927 – 28 (hardcover)		Misc	4	$85.00	12/98
Furniture Catalog, 1927		Misc	4	$72.00	11/94
Furniture Catalog, 1930 Supreme Edition		Misc	2	$33.00	4/95
Furniture Catalog, 1930 Supreme Edition		Misc	4	$50.00	6/94
Furniture Catalog, 1930 Supreme Edition		Misc	4	$110.00	11/94
Furniture Catalog, 1927 –28		Misc	4	$40.00	12/98

Title	Size	Type	Rate	Amount	Date
Furniture Catalog, 1937 Final Edition		Misc	3	$50.00	6/95
Furniture Catalog, 1937 Final Edition		Misc	3.5	$50.00	6/95
Furniture Catalog, 1937 Final Edition		Misc	4	$44.00	6/96
Furniture Catalog, 1937 Final Edition		Misc	4	$121.00	11/94
Furniture Catalog, 1937 Final Edition		Misc	2	$44.00	4/95
Furniture Catalog, 1937 Final Edition		Misc	4	$85.00	12/98
Furniture Patterns (Wood, Misc Lot)		Misc	3	$28.00	4/94
Furniture Patterns (Wood, Misc Lot)		Misc	3	$28.00	4/94
Furniture Receipt (framed)	6x9	Misc	4	$25.00	6/96
Furniture Receipt (framed)		Misc	4	$41.00	3/96
Furniture Receipts (two, framed)		Misc	5	$66.00	6/95
Gambrel-Roofed Road, A	11x17	Ext	3	$72.00	4/95
Gambrel-Roofed Road, A	**18x22**	**Ext**	**4**	**$231.00**	**4/95**
Gambrel-Roofed Road, A (b&w)	16x20	Ext	4	$297.00	6/96
Garden Exit, A	9x11	Ext	3	$22.00	11/94
Garden Gossip	**9x11**	**Misc Un**	**3.5**	**$121.00**	**11/95**
Garden of Larkspur, A	13x16	Foreign	4	$66.00	6/96
Garden of Larkspur, A	10x12	Foreign	3.5	$66.00	6/96
Garden of Larkspur, A	14x17	Foreign	4	$85.00	12/98
Garden of Larkspur, A	11x14	Foreign	3	$132.00	11/95
Garden of Larkspur, A	9x11	Foreign	4	$150.00	12/98
Garden of Larkspur, A	13x16	Foreign	4	$132.00	6/95
Garden of Larkspur, A	10x12	Foreign	4	$77.00	11/95
Garden of Larkspur, The	9x11	Foreign	4	$154.00	4/95
Garden Scene (Untitled)	8x10	Misc Un	4	$143.00	6/96
Gardner Parlor, A	10x13	Int	4	$132.00	11/95
Gardner Parlor Corner, A	14x17	Int	4	$242.00	4/94
Genealogy Books (Nutting Family)		**Misc**	**4**	**$187.00**	**11/95**
Genial Stream, The	11x20	Cow	3.75	$468.00	6/94
Gettysburg Crossing, A	10x13	Ext	3	$132.00	6/96
Gettysburg Crossing, A	14x17	Ext	4	$275.00	12/98
Gift of the Hills, A	13x16	Foreign	2	$28.00	6/96
Girl by Large Home	13x16	Misc Un	3	$143.00	4/94
Glance in Passing, A	**13x16**	**Int**	**3**	**$165.00**	**3/96**
Glass Negative	8x10	Misc	4	$116.00	3/96
Glass Negative	8x10	Misc	4	$110.00	6/95
Glass Negative	8x10	Misc	4	$120.00	12/98
Glass Negative	8x10	Misc	4	$182.00	6/94
Glass Negative, Rare "Double"	8x10	Misc	4	$330.00	6/96
Gloucester Peter, A	**14x17**	**Man**	**4**	**$2,200.00**	**10/93**
Going Back to Nature	10x16	Ext	3.75	$88.00	3/96
Going Back to Nature	11x17	Ext	4	$50.00	11/94
Going for the Doctor	12x14	Child	4	$1,200.00	12/98
Going Forth of Betty, The	13x17	Misc Un	3	$135.00	5/94
Going Forth of Betty, The	18x22	Misc Un	4	$286.00	11/95
Going Forth of Betty, The	10x12	Misc Un	4	$121.00	6/94
Golden Birches	11x14	Ext	4	$83.00	6/96
Golden Birches	13x17	Ext	4	$121.00	11/95
Golden River, A	12x15	Ext	3	$39.00	6/96

A Grambel Roofed Road

Garden Gossip

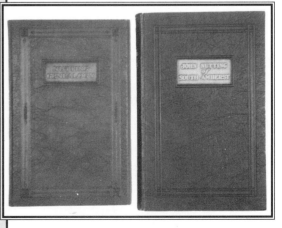

Genealogy Books

A Glance in Passing

A Gloucester Peter

Good Night!

Title	Size	Type	Rate	Amount	Date
Golden River, A	13x16	Foreign	4	$121.00	11/95
Golden River, A	11x14	Ext	4	$165.00	5/96
Golden Twilight	10x16	Ext	4	$94.00	6/95
Golden West, The	11x14	Ext	4	$145.00	11/95
Gondolier's Dock, A	7x9	Foreign	3	$110.00	6/95
Good Night	11x14	Int	4	$99.00	6/96
Good Night!	**11x14**	**Int**	**4**	**$235.00**	**6/95**
Good Night!	13x16	Int	4	$175.00	6/96
Good Night!	11x14	Int	4	$225.00	5/95
Good Night!	13x16	Int	4	$94.00	11/94
Good Night!	13x16	Int	3	$94.00	3/96
Good Story, A	14x17	Int	4	$275.00	6/94
Goodman is Coming, The	13x16	Foreign	4	$275.00	6/94
Goodman is Coming, The	11x14	Foreign	4	$176.00	6/95
Goose Chase Pattern, A	11x14	Int	3	$105.00	4/94
Goose Chase Pattern, The	12x14	Int	4	$90.00	12/98
Goose Chase Quilt, The	11x15	Int	3	$160.00	6/95
Goose Chase Quilt, The	13x22	Int	4	$175.00	12/98
Gorgeous May	14x17	Ext	4	$145.00	11/95
Gorgeous May	13x16	Ext	3	$75.00	10/95
Gorgeous May	12x16	Ext	4	$140.00	9/95
Grace	10x12	Ext	4	$145.00	12/98
Grace	10x12	Ext	3	$28.00	6/96
Grace	10x12	Ext	3	$80.00	12/95
Grace	10x12	Ext	3.5	$83.00	4/95
Grace	10x12	Ext	4	$204.00	3/96
Grace	13x16	Ext	4	$135.00	7/95
Grace	11x14	Ext	4	$150.00	1/96
Grace before Meat	13x15	Man	4	$413.00	6/95
Graces, The	14x17	Ext	4	$72.00	4/95
Grafton Windings	13x16	Ext	4	$155.00	3/96
Grafton Windings	12x20	Ext	3	$85.00	2/96
Grafton Windings	12x20	Ext	4	$88.00	11/95
Grafton Windings	13x22	Ext	4	$85.00	12/98
Grafton Windings	13x16	Ext	4	$155.00	6/95
Grandfather's Clock	13x16	Int	4	$240.00	3/96
Grandmother's China	11x17	Int	4	$132.00	11/95
Grandmother's China	14x17	Int	4	$265.00	10/95
Grandmother's Garden	11x14	Foreign	4	$150.00	12/98
Grandmother's Guests	11x14	Int	4	$143.00	11/95
Grand'pa and Grand'ma Bed, A	9x15	Int	3	$121.00	6/94
Grand'pa & Grand'ma Bed, A	12x16	Int	4	$105.00	11/94
Great American Idea Catalog		Misc	3.5	$83.00	6/96
Great Wayside Oak, A	14x17	Ext	3	$96.00	11/95
Great Wayside Oak, The	22x26	Ext	4.5	$330.00	4/95
Great Wayside Oak, The	**11x14**	**Ext**	**4**	**$198.00**	**11/95**
Great Wayside Oak, The	14x17	Ext	4	$165.00	2/95
Great Wayside Oak, The	13x16	Ext	3	$110.00	10/95
Green Mountain Range, The	11x17	Ext	4	$145.00	4/94
Green Mountain Range, The	13x22	Ext	3.5	$61.00	3/96

Title	Size	Type	Rate	Amount	Date
Green Mountain Range, The	10x18	Ext	4	$90.00	12/98
Green Mountain Range, The	14x17	Ext	4	$165.00	11/95
Greeting, A	11x14	Foreign	3.5	$72.00	11/95
Greeting, A	10x12	Foreign	4	$110.00	10/95
Greeting, A	**10x12**	**Foreign**	**4**	**$115.00**	**9/94**
Greeting, The	10x12	Misc Un	3	$28.00	4/95
Greeting Card	4x5	Misc	4	$121.00	6/95
Greeting Card	5x9	Misc	5	$105.00	3/96
Greeting Card	4x5	Misc	5	$270.00	3/96
Greeting Card	4x5	Misc	4	$83.00	3/96
Greeting Card, Folding	5x6	Misc	4	$33.00	6/96
Greeting Card, Folding		Misc	3	$30.00	6/96
Greeting Card (Framed)	5x10	Misc	5	$176.00	11/95
Greeting Card (Framed)	5x10	Misc	5	$198.00	11/95
Greeting Card (Large)	11x14	Misc	3.5	$396.00	11/95
Greeting Card					
(two framed silhouette cards)	8x10	Misc	4	$61.00	6/95
Greeting Card (with ext scene)	4x6	Misc	4	$33.00	6/94
Greeting Card (with silhouette)	4x5	Misc	4	$83.00	4/95
Greeting Card (with silhouette)	4x5	Misc	4	$19.00	3/96
Greeting Card (with silhouette)	4x6	Misc	4	$8.00	11/94
Greeting Card (with silhouette)	4x5	Misc	4	$19.00	6/95
Greeting Card (with silver white)	5x8	Misc	3	$55.00	4/95
Greeting Card					
(with "A Memory of Childhood")	6x7	Misc	3	$72.00	4/94
Greeting Card					
(with "Charles River Elm")	4x6	Misc	4	$72.00	6/94
Guardian Mother, The	9x14	Child	3.5	$990.00	4/95
Guardian Mother, The	13x17	Child	4	$660.00	6/94
Guardian Mother, The	11x17	Child	4	$1,625.00	10/95
Half Tide in October	13x16	Ext	3	$121.00	11/95
Half-Tide in October	10x12	Ext	4	$99.00	11/95
Hand-Colored Glass Slide	3x4	Misc	4	$275.00	6/95
Hand-Colored Glass Slide	3x4	Misc	4	$198.00	6/96
Hand-Colored Glass Slide	3x4	Misc	3.75	$303.00	6/95
Hand-Colored Glass Slide	3x4	Misc	4	$385.00	3/96
Hand-Colored Glass Slide	3x4	Misc	4	$121.00	6/96
Hand-Colored Glass Slide	3x4	Misc	4	$94.00	6/94
Hand-Colored Glass Slide	8x10	Misc	4	$94.00	6/94
Hand-Colored Glass Slide	3x4	Misc	4	$330.00	3/96
Hand-Colored Glass Slide	3x4	Misc	4	$165.00	6/95
Hand-Colored Glass Slide	3x4	Misc	4	$440.00	4/95
Hanging Winter Herbs	13x16	Int	4	$308.00	3/96
Happy Valley Road	14x17	Ext	4	$95.00	12/98
Happy Valley Road	13x16	Ext	5	$72.00	6/94
Happy Valley Road	10x16	Ext	3	$44.00	6/95
Harbingers of Spring	13x16	Floral	4	$325.00	12/98
Harbingers of Spring	**13x16**	**Floral**	**3**	**$286.00**	**6/95**
Harmony	**13x19**	**Int**	**4**	**$165.00**	**12/98**

The Great Wayside Oak

A Greeting

Harbingers of Spring

Harmony

Hesitation

Title	Size	Type	Rate	Amount	Date
Harmony	14x17	Int	3	$66.00	6/96
Harmony	14x17	Int	4	$160.00	3/96
Harpsichord, The	11x17	Int	4	$210.00	3/96
Hawthorn Cottage	14x20	Foreign	3	$176.00	6/96
Hawthorn Cottage	14x20	Foreign	4	$150.00	12/98
Hawthornden	14x17	Foreign	4	$155.00	12/98
Heifers by the Stream	11x17	Cow	4	$407.00	11/95
Heifers by the Stream	11x17	Cow	4	$495.00	6/94
Heifers by the Stream	11x17	Cow	3.5	$193.00	4/95
Helping Mother	13x16	Child	3	$121.00	11/95
Hepatica	13x15	Floral	5	$743.00	6/94
Her First "At Home"	13x16	Int	3.5	$175.00	7/95
Her First Hand Mirror	13x16	Int	3	$66.00	6/96
Her Old Trundle Bed	14x17	Int	3	$165.00	6/95
Her Old Trundle Bed	14x17	Int	4	$204.00	11/94
Herd in the Stream, The	13x22	Cow	4	$798.00	11/95
Hesitancy	11x14	Man	4	$550.00	12/98
Hesitation	**13x16**	**Man**	**4.5**	**$700.00**	**2/96**
Hidden Cove, A	16x20	Ext	3	$39.00	4/95
High Rollers	13x16	Seascape	4	$248.00	4/95
High Rollers	10x16	Seascape	4	$165.00	3/96
High Rollers	13x16	Seascape	3	$83.00	3/96
Highland Blossoms	12x15	Ext	4	$110.00	6/96
Highland Blossoms	13x17	Ext	4	$83.00	6/96
Highland Brae, A	11x14	Ext	4	$61.00	11/94
Hingham Road, A	11x14	Ext	3	$22.00	11/95
Hingham's Lane	14x17	Misc Un	4	$185.00	4/96
Hint of September, A	14x17	Ext	4	$155.00	4/96
His First Letter	11x17	Int	3	$121.00	6/96
His First Letter	11x17	Int	4	$220.00	4/94
His Move	14x17	Man	3	$358.00	11/95
His Move	**13x16**	**Man**	**4**	**$600.00**	**7/95**
His Move	13x16	Man	3.5	$330.00	6/95
His Rose	11x17	Int	4	$275.00	7/95
His Rose	11x17	Int	3.5	$127.00	6/94
His Rose	11x17	Int	3	$132.00	3/96
Hiway or Byway	16x20	Misc Un	4	$303.00	4/94
Holland Express	10x16	Foreign	5	$330.00	6/94
Hollyhock Cottage	13x16	Foreign	4	$187.00	4/94
Hollyhock Cottage	18x22	Foreign	4	$209.00	3/96
Hollyhock Cottage	13x16	Foreign	4	$140.00	12/98
Hollyhock Cottage	14x17	Foreign	4	$195.00	8/96
Hollyhock Cottage	16x20	Foreign	4	$285.00	4/95
Hollyhock Cottage (untitled)	7x9	Foreign	3	$61.00	6/94
Hollyhock Cottage (untitled)	7x9	Foreign	4	$44.00	11/94
Hollyhock Cottage (untitled)	6x8	Foreign	4	$77.00	6/96
Hollyhock Cottage (untitled)	7x9	Foreign	3	$61.00	11/94
Hollyhock Row	14x17	Misc Un	4	$190.00	12/98
Hollyhocks	16x20	Floral	5	$1,238.00	11/95
Hollyhocks	8x10	Floral	4	$360.00	12/98

Title	Size	Type	Rate	Amount	Date
Home Charm	14x17	Misc Un	3	$121.00	11/95
Home Garden, The	13x16	Misc Un	4	$187.00	11/94
Home Hearth, The	13x22	Int	3	$88.00	11/94
Home Hearth, The	13x22	Int	4	$264.00	6/96
Home Lane	12x20	Ext	3.5	$61.00	11/95
Home Room, The	13x17	Int	3	$72.00	11/95
Home Room, The	14x17	Int	4	$182.00	3/96
Home Room, The	14x17	Int	4	$115.00	12/98
Home Sweet Home	**11x14**	**Misc Un**	**4**	**$396.00**	**11/95**
Homestead Blossoms	13x15	Ext	4	$248.00	6/95
Homestead Decorations	9x12	Misc Un	3	$39.00	11/94
Homeward Bound	13x16	Ext	3.5	$30.00	11/94
Honeymoon Blossoms	11x14	Ext	4	$95.00	12/98
Honeymoon Blossoms	14x17	Ext	4	$145.00	7/95
Honeymoon Blossoms	10x12	Ext	4	$55.00	11/95
Honeymoon Cottage	12x16	Ext	4	$125.00	12/98
Honeymoon Cottage	10x16	Ext	4	$83.00	4/95
Honeymoon Cottage	13x16	Ext	4	$55.00	11/95
Honeymoon Cottage	10x16	Ext	4	$77.00	11/94
Honeymoon Cottage	11x14	Ext	4	$83.00	6/96
Honeymoon Drive	11x14	Ext	4	$80.00	12/98
Honeymoon Drive	14x17	Ext	4	$150.00	12/98
Honeymoon Drive	14x16	Ext	3	$55.00	11/95
Honeymoon Shore	9x11	Ext	4.5	$121.00	11/94
Honeymoon Stroll	11x14	Ext	3	$39.00	6/96
Honeymoon Stroll	10x12	Ext	4	$83.00	3/96
Honeymoon Stroll	9x11	Ext	4	$155.00	12/98
Honeymoon Stroll	13x15	Ext	3.5	$72.00	11/95
Honeymoon Stroll	11x14	Ext	3	$55.00	3/96
Honeymoon Stroll	13x16	Ext	4	$75.00	12/98
Honeymoon Windings	15x22	Ext	4	$83.00	11/95
Honeymoon Windings	8x10	Ext	3	$72.00	11/95
Honeymoon Windings	10x16	Ext	3	$66.00	6/96
Honeymoon Windings	10x12	Ext	4	$135.00	12/98
Honeymoon Windings	11x14	Ext	4	$75.00	12/98
Hope	16x20	Ext	4	$187.00	6/96
Hope	16x20	Ext	4	$165.00	12/98
Hope	13x16	Ext	4	$154.00	11/95
Hope	13x16	Ext	4	$125.00	2/96
Hope	9x11	Ext	4	$154.00	11/95
Hope of the Year, The	9x11	Ext	4	$72.00	3/96
Hope of the Year, The	11x14	Ext	4	$65.00	12/98
Housatonic Blossoms	11x17	Ext	3.75	$55.00	11/94
House Lane, The	10x12	Misc Un	3.5	$176.00	4/95
Hurrying Brook, A	11x14	Ext	3	$80.00	5/96
Idle Mill, The	**13x16**	**Foreign**	**4**	**$275.00**	**6/96**
Ilfracombe	11x14	Seascape	3	$176.00	6/95
In Garden of Gods, Colorado	13x16	Misc Un	4	$303.00	4/95
In Grandma's Days	8x10	Misc Un	3	$132.00	6/95

His Move

Home Sweet Home

The Idle Mill

In the Old Parlor

Indian Maidens

Title	Size	Type	Rate	Amount	Date
In John Hancock's Chair	13x16	Int	2.5	$176.00	4/94
In Tenderleaf	12x20	Ext	4.5	$132.00	6/95
In Tenderleaf	10x16	Ext	3	$83.00	11/95
In Tenderleaf	9x11	Ext	4	$75.00	12/98
In Tenderleaf	16x20	Ext	5	$165.00	3/96
In Tenderleaf	16x20	Ext	3.75	$99.00	6/96
In the Brave Days of Old	13x16	Int	4	$176.00	11/95
In the Brave Days of Old	16x20	Int	3	$132.00	11/95
In the Brave Days of Old	10x12	Int	4	$175.00	12/98
In the Garden of the Gods, Colorado	13x16	Misc Un	3	$358.00	6/96
In the Midst of Her China	14x17	Int	4	$220.00	6/96
In the Midst of Her China	13x16	Int	4	$185.00	6/95
In the Midst of Her China	14x17	Int	4.5	$375.00	4/96
In the Midst of Her China	12x15	Int	3.75	$275.00	4/95
In the Old Parlor	**14x17**	**Int**	**3.5**	**$99.00**	**6/96**
Indian Maidens	14x17	Misc Un	4	$1,500.00	7/95
Indian Maidens	**13x16**	**Misc Un**	**5**	**$3,410.00**	**11/96**
Indian Summer Haze	13x16	Ext	3	$39.00	4/94
Informal Call, An	10x12	Int	3	$116.00	3/96
Informal Call, An	11x14	Int	3	$75.00	4/94
Informal Call, An	11x14	Int	3.75	$110.00	6/96
Informal Call, An	11x14	Int	4	$225.00	2/96
Interrupted Letter, An	14x17	Int	4	$110.00	11/94
Interrupted Letter, An	11x17	Int	3	$275.00	8/94
Interrupted Letter, An	14x17	Int	4	$225.00	10/94
Interrupted Letter, An	13x16	Int	3	$99.00	6/96
Interrupted Letter, An	13x16	Int	3	$155.00	9/95
Interrupted Letter, The	14x17	Int	4	$215.00	4/96
Into the Birchwood	11x14	Ext	4	$110.00	11/95
Into the Birchwood	9x11	Ext	4	$65.00	12/98
Into the Birchwood	13x16	Ext	4	$155.00	8/95
Into the Birchwood	14x17	Ext	3	$39.00	11/95
Investigating an Heirloom	13x15	Int	3	$121.00	11/95
Iris & Lilies	8x10	Floral	4	$578.00	6/95
Isaac Walton Brook, The	14x17	Foreign	4	$210.00	12/98
Isle in the Tiber, The	12x20	Foreign	3	$80.00	3/96
Is the Fire Ready?	**14x17**	**Int**	**4**	**$165.00**	**12/98**
Italian Spring, An	11x14	Foreign	4	$225.00	4/96
Italian Spring, The	18x22	Foreign	3	$187.00	4/95
Italian Spring, The	14x17	Foreign	3	$116.00	6/95
Italian Spring, The	11x14	Foreign	4	$297.00	6/95
Italian Spring, The	10x13	Foreign	2	$72.00	3/96
Ivy and Rose Cloister	14x17	Misc Un	3	$143.00	11/95
Ivy and Rose Cloister	9x11	Misc Un	4	$325.00	8/94
Ivy and Rose Cloister	18x22	Misc Un	3	$105.00	4/94
Ivy and Rose Cloister	14x17	Misc Un	4	$340.00	12/98
Jacob's Ladder Brook	10x12	Ext	4	$66.00	6/94
Jane	**10x16**	**Misc Un**	**4**	**$190.00**	**5/96**

Title	Size	Type	Rate	Amount	Date
Jane (untitled)	8x12	Misc Un	4	$99.00	6/96
Jar of Posies (close-framed), A	8x10	Floral	4	$798.00	11/95
Jersey Blossoms	10x12	Ext	4	$90.00	12/98
Jersey Blossoms	11x14	Ext	4	$135.00	4/96
Jersey Blossoms	13x15	Ext	4	$110.00	3/96
John Hancock's Chair	12x16	Int	4	$99.00	4/94
Joy Path	13x16	Foreign	4	$185.00	6/95
Joy Path	13x16	Foreign	4	$95.00	8/94
Joy Path	13x15	Foreign	4	$155.00	12/98
Joy Path	11x14	Foreign	4	$160.00	11/94
Joy Path (untitled)	6x8	Foreign	4	$44.00	11/94
Joyous Anniversary, A	13x16	Foreign	4	$160.00	1/96
Judge's Daughter, The	12x16	Misc Un	3	$413.00	6/95
June Flowers	13x16	Int	4	$121.00	11/94
Just a Line	12x16	Int	3	$39.00	6/96
Justifiable Vanity	13x16	Int	5	$248.00	6/94
Keene Road, A	12x20	Ext	4	$100.00	12/98
Killarney Castle & Cove, A	12x16	Foreign	4	$410.00	12/98
Killarney Castle & Cove, A	10x16	Foreign	4	$242.00	11/94
Knickerbocker Fireplace, A	11x14	Int	4	$350.00	2/96
Knickerbocker Fireplace, A	14x17	Int	4.5	$440.00	11/95
Knickerbocker Fireplace, A	14x17	Int	4	$190.00	12/98
Knitting for Uncle Sam	13x16	Man	4	$675.00	7/95
Knitting for Uncle Sam	14x17	Man	4	$415.00	12/98
Knitting for Uncle Sam	14x17	Man	6	$385.00	4/95
Knoll by the Brook, The	11x13	Foreign	2	$83.00	11/95
LaJolla	13x16	Seascape	3	$380.00	6/94
LaJolla	17x24	Seascape	4	$275.00	5/95
LaJolla	14x17	Seascape	4	$209.00	6/96
LaJolla	9x15	Seascape	4	$138.00	3/96
LaJolla	12x16	Seascape	4	$231.00	11/95
LaJolla	13x22	Seascape	4	$195.00	12/98
LaJolla (close-framed)	12x20	Seascape	4	$165.00	3/96
Labor of Love, A	12x15	Int	3	$94.00	4/95
Lake Bank Birches	14x17	Ext	4	$150.00	12/98
Lake Brandt Birches	13x16	Ext	4	$149.00	3/96
Lambs at Rest	11x14	Sheep	3.75	$187.00	3/96
Lambs at Rest	**13x16**	**Sheep**	**4**	**$325.00**	**8/95**
Lambs at Rest	11x14	Sheep	3	$150.00	3/95
Lane in April, The	13x16	Ext	5	$83.00	6/94
Lane in Sorrento, A	11x17	Foreign	4	$170.00	2/96
Lane or Highway	13x16	Foreign	4.5	$176.00	6/95
Lane to Uncle Jonathan's	11x17	Ext	3	$90.00	4/96
Lane to Uncle Jonathan's, The	10x16	Ext	4	$127.00	3/96
Laneside	13x16	Ext	4	$135.00	12/95
Laneside	10x13	Ext	3	$61.00	6/95
Laneside	13x15	Ext	3	$99.00	6/96
Lane's End	10x14	Ext	3	$50.00	3/96

Is the Fire Ready?

Jane

Lambs at Rest

Langdon Door

A Lavender Canopy

Title	Size	Type	Rate	Amount	Date
Lane's End	14x17	Ext	4	$226.00	6/94
Langdon Door	9x11	Misc Un	3	$149.00	3/96
Langdon Door	**9x11**	**Misc Un**	**5**	**$149.00**	**3/96**
Langdon Door, The	14x17	Misc Un	3.5	$165.00	4/95
Langdon Door, The	14x17	Misc Un	3.75	$132.00	11/95
Larkspur	7x9	Foreign	4	$65.00	12/98
Larkspur	9x13	Foreign	4	$150.00	12/98
Larkspur	14x17	Foreign	4	$110.00	3/96
Larkspur	18x22	Foreign	5	$165.00	6/94
Larkspur	14x17	Foreign	4	$143.00	4/95
Larkspur (untitled)	7x9	Foreign	4	$66.00	4/95
Larkspur (untitled)	6x8	Foreign	4	$72.00	4/94
Larkspur (untitled)	8x10	Foreign	4	$149.00	3/96
Larkspur (untitled)	6x8	Foreign	4	$61.00	4/94
Larkspur (untitled)	7x9	Foreign	4	$182.00	3/96
Last Furrow, The	13x16	Man	4.5	$429.00	6/95
Last Furrow, The	13x16	Misc. Un	4	$395.00	6/96
Last Furrow, The	13x16	Man	3.75	$330.00	3/96
Last Touches, The	7x13	Int	3	$55.00	6/96
Last Touches, The	13x16	Int	4	$225.00	5/96
Last Word in Bonnets, The	13x22	Int	3.5	$231.00	11/94
Last Word in Bonnets, The	13x16	Int	3	$143.00	4/95
Laune at Dunloe, The	12x16	Foreign	4	$242.00	11/95
Laune at Dunloe, The	12x16	Foreign	4	$205.00	12/95
Lavender Canopy, A	**12x15**	**Misc Un**	**3**	**$154.00**	**11/95**
Leaf Stream Brook, A	10x12	Ext	4	$105.00	3/96
Leaf Strewn Brook , A	16x20	Ext	4	$165.00	12/98
Leaf Strewn Brook, A	11x17	Ext	4	$140.00	12/98
Leaf Strewn Brook, A	14x17	Ext	4	$204.00	3/96
Lecture Advertising Sign	11x14	Misc	4	$132.00	6/96
Letter, Mariet Nutting, 2 pg.		Misc	4	$209.00	6/96
Letter, Wallace Nutting, 2 pg-handwritten		Misc	4	$275.00	6/96
Letter (Esther Svenson)		Misc	4	$72.00	6/95
Letter (Henry Wood Irving)		Misc	5	$88.00	6/95
Letter (two letters, Wallace Nutting)		Misc	4	$605.00	11/95
Letter (two letters, Wallace Nutting)		Misc	4	$440.00	11/94
Letter (Wallace Nutting, 2 page)		Misc	4	$605.00	6/94
Letter (Wallace Nutting, and price list)		Misc	4	$83.00	11/95
Letter (W. Nutting, with bio & church item)		Misc	4	$121.00	4/94
Letter (Wallace Nutting)		Misc	4	$220.00	3/96
Letter (Wallace Nutting)		Misc	4	$660.00	3/96
Letter (Wallace Nutting)		Misc	4	$385.00	4/95
Letter (Wallace Nutting)		Misc	4	$303.00	4/95
Letter (Wallace Nutting)		Misc	4	$145.00	12/98
Letter (Wallace Nutting)		Misc	4	$358.00	6/95
Letter (Wallace Nutting)		Misc	5	$95.00	12/98
Letter (Wallace Nutting)		Misc	4	$165.00	6/95
Letter (Wallace Nutting)		Misc	4	$135.00	12/98
Life of the Golden Age, The	13x17	Sheep	3	$193.00	3/96
Life of the Golden Age, The	**15x22**	**Sheep**	**4**	**$425.00**	**1/96**

Title	Size	Type	Rate	Amount	Date
Life of the Golden Age, The	13x22	Sheep	4	$198.00	6/96
Life of the Golden Age, The	12x18	Sheep	4	$290.00	12/98
Life of the Golden Age, The	11x17	Sheep	4	$265.00	9/95
Life of the Golden Age, The	11x19	Sheep	3	$132.00	6/96
Liffey Crags	12x16	Foreign	2	$143.00	6/96
Light Side of the Road, The	11x15	Ext	3	$110.00	4/95
Lilac Cottage	10x16	Ext	4	$160.00	3/96
Lilac Cottage	10x16	Ext	3	$77.00	4/95
Lined with Petals	14x17	Ext	3.75	$160.00	3/96
Lined with Petals	13x15	Ext	3	$61.00	6/94
Lingering Water	10x12	Ext	4	$110.00	11/95
Lingering Water	10x12	Ext	4	$72.00	3/96
Lingering Water	12x20	Ext	3.5	$50.00	11/95
Lingering Waters	11x17	Ext	3	$61.00	11/95
Listless Day, A	11x14	Foreign	3.5	$154.00	11/95
Listless Day, A	11x14	Foreign	3.5	$176.00	4/95
Listless Day, A	14x17	Foreign	3	$187.00	6/96
Listless Day, A	10x12	Foreign	4	$275.00	6/95
Listless Day, A	**12x15**	**Foreign**	**4**	**$170.00**	**12/98**
Litchfield Minster	14x17	Foreign	4	$220.00	11/95
Litchfield Minster	10x12	Foreign	4	$90.00	12/98
Litchfield Minster	9x11	Foreign	3.5	$88.00	11/95
Litchfield Minster	13x16	Foreign	4	$187.00	3/96
Litchfield Minster (close-framed)	8x10	Foreign	4	$28.00	11/95
Litchfield Minster (untitled)	5x7	Foreign	4	$44.00	3/96
Litchfield Minster (untitled)	6x8	Foreign	4	$77.00	4/94
Litchfield Minster (untitled)	5x7	Foreign	3.5	$83.00	11/95
Little Corner House, The	11x14	Foreign	4	$171.00	6/94
Little Corner House, The	10x12	Foreign	3	$121.00	4/94
Little Corner House, The	10x12	Foreign	4	$187.00	4/95
Little Dutch Cove, A	11x14	Foreign	4	$180.00	3/96
Little Helper, A	**14x17**	**Child**	**4**	**$475.00**	**12/98**
Little Killarney Lake, A	16x20	Foreign	3	$231.00	4/95
Little Killarney Lake, A	13x16	Foreign	4	$193.00	3/96
Little Maine Cover, A	10x12	Ext	4	$61.00	6/96
Little Maine Village, A	13x16	Ext	4	$187.00	11/95
Little River, A	12x18	Ext	3	$99.00	3/96
Little River, A	14x20	Ext	4	$77.00	6/96
Little River, A	13x16	Ext	4.5	$121.00	4/95
Little River, A	20x26	Ext	4	$125.00	12/98
Little River, A	11x17	Ext	3	$61.00	6/96
Little River, A	12x20	Ext	4	$99.00	3/96
Little River with Mt. Washington, A	11x14	Ext	4	$100.00	12/98
Little River with Mt. Washington, A	10x16	Ext	4	$83.00	3/96
Little River with Mt. Washington, A	12x16	Ext	4	$116.00	3/96
Little River with Mt. Washington, A	13x19	Ext	4	$105.00	3/96

The Life of the Golden Age

A Listless Day

127

A Little Helper

A Lough Gill Cottage

Mammy's Darling

Title	Size	Type	Rate	Amount	Date
Lorna Doone	14x17	Foreign	4	$690.00	12/98
Lough Gill Cottage, A	**10x12**	**Foreign**	**4**	**$187.00**	**6/96**
Luscious May	13x16	Ext	4	$160.00	9/95
Luscious May	10x16	Ext	4	$150.00	4/96
Luscious May	14x17	Ext	3	$83.00	4/95
Luscious May	11x14	Ext	4	$160.00	5/96
Madonna Lilies	9x11	Misc Un	4	$255.00	12/98
Maid and a Mirror, A	11x17	Int	4	$94.00	11/94
Maid and the Mirror, The	10x16	Int	4	$121.00	6/95
Maiden Reveries	14x17	Int	4	$143.00	3/96
Maiden Reveries	13x15	Int	3.5	$127.00	3/96
Maiden Reveries	14x17	Int	5	$285.00	7/94
Maiden Reveries	14x17	Int	4	$176.00	11/95
Maiden Reveries	16x18	Int	4	$145.00	12/98
Maidenly Pleasures	11x13	Misc Un	4	$187.00	4/94
Maidenly Pleasures	8x10	Misc Un	3	$110.00	6/96
Maidenly Pleasures	11x14	Misc Un	4	$195.00	9/95
Maine Brook, A	11x14	Ext	3.5	$88.00	6/95
Maine Coast Sky, A	13x16	Seascape	4	$375.00	12/98
Maine Coast Sky, A	11x14	Seascape	3.5	$138.00	3/96
Maine Coast Sky, A	10x12	Seascape	4	$210.00	12/98
Maine Coast Sky	14x17	Seascape	4	$175.00	12/98
Maine Farm Entrance, A	14x17	Ext	4	$160.00	1/95
Mammy's Darling	**13x16**	**Child**	**3.5**	**$1,925.00**	**11/95**
Manchester Battenkill, The	16x20	Misc Un	4	$210.00	12/98
Manchester Battenkill, The	14x17	Ext	3	$80.00	12/95
Many Happy Returns	16x20	Ext	3.5	$150.00	1/96
Many Happy Returns	11x14	Ext	4	$95.00	10/95
Many Happy Returns	14x17	Ext	4	$145.00	8/95
Maple by the Stream, A	10x12	Ext	4	$39.00	4/95
Maple Drive	10x12	Ext	3	$72.00	11/94
Maple in May, A	13x16	Ext	3	$75.00	2/95
Maple Sugar Closet, The	13x17	Int	4	$185.00	6/95
Maple Sugar Cupboard	14x17	Int	4	$143.00	11/95
Maple Sugar Cupboard, The	13x15	Int	4	$187.00	4/95
Maple Sugar Cupboard, The	15x22	Int	4	$132.00	6/95
Maple Sugar Cupboard, The	14x16	Int	4	$145.00	12/98
Maple Sugar Cupboard, The	13x15	Int	4	$193.00	6/94
Maple Sugar Cupboard, The	16x20	Int	4	$165.00	3/96
Marlboro Roadside, A	13x16	Ext	4	$165.00	11/95
Marlboro Roadside, A	14x17	Ext	4.5	$187.00	11/95
Marlboro Shore, A	13x15	Ext	3.5	$83.00	6/96
Marsh Grass & Palm	14x17	Misc Un	3	$165.00	6/96
Mary Ball Washington's Parlor	**13x16**	**Misc Un**	**3**	**$303.00**	**3/96**
Mary's Little Lamb	14x17	Sheep	4	$341.00	11/95
Mary's Little Lamb	11x14	Sheep	4	$250.00	12/95
Mary's Little Lamb	11x14	Sheep	4	$190.00	12/98
Mary's Little Lamb	13x15	Sheep	3.75	$171.00	3/96
Mary's Little Lamb	11x14	Sheep	4	$155.00	12/98

Title	Size	Type	Rate	Amount	Date
May Beautiful	14x17	Ext	3.5	$55.00	11/94
May Countryside, A	13x16	Ext	4	$155.00	3/95
May Drive, A	13x16	Ext	4	$150.00	5/95
May Drive, A	11x14	Ext	3	$70.00	4/95
May Grasses	11x14	Ext	4	$125.00	9/95
Meadow Arches	10x12	Ext	4	$72.00	6/94
Meadow Beauty	12x15	Foreign	4	$94.00	11/94
Meadow Beauty	11x14	Foreign	3.5	$50.00	11/94
Meadow Beauty	14x17	Foreign	3.5	$99.00	11/94
Meadow Blossoms	11x14	Ext	4	$72.00	11/95
Meadow Gate, The	10x12	Foreign	4	$308.00	11/94
Meadow Gate, The	13x15	Foreign	3.5	$88.00	6/96
Meadow Lilies	13x16	Floral	3	$363.00	4/95
Meditative Pause, A	13x15	Int	4	$231.00	6/96
Meeting of the Ways, The	10x16	Ext	4	$138.00	3/96
Meeting of the Ways, The	13x16	Ext	4	$90.00	12/98
Meeting Place, The	13x16	Horse/Cows	4	$2,035.00	6/94
Meeting Place, The	18x22	Horse/Cows	4.5	$2,420.00	6/96
Meeting Place, The	17x20	Misc Un	3.5	$1,155.00	6/95
Mellow Birches	13x16	Ext	3.75	$83.00	6/95
Mellow May	13x17	Foreign	4	$209.00	6/96
Memory of Childhood, A	13x16	Misc Un	4	$170.00	4/95
Memory of Childhood, A	14x17	Misc Un	4	$150.00	8/95
Memory of Childhood, A	11x14	Misc Un	3.5	$77.00	6/95
Memory of Childhood, A	11x14	Misc Un	5	$286.00	4/94
Mending	13x15	Int	3	$165.00	6/96
Mending	11x14	Int	4	$170.00	5/96
Mending Day	12x16	Int	3	$66.00	4/94
Merchant's Daughter, The	11x16	Misc Un	3.75	$165.00	6/96
Met Half Way	**14x17**	**Misc Un**	**3.5**	**$165.00**	**3/96**
Metal Frame, Thin (w/ext scene)	4x5	Misc	4	$28.00	11/95
Metal Frames, Thin (Two, with ext scenes)	3x4	Misc	4	$154.00	6/95
Metal Frames, Thin (Two, with ext scenes)	4x5	Misc	4	$88.00	11/95
Mexican Zinnias	13x16	Floral	4	$675.00	12/98
Middlesex Glen & Camel's Hump	13x15	Ext	3.5	$220.00	3/96
Midsummer in the Wood	14x17	Ext	3	$50.00	11/95
Mid-May	13x15	Ext	3	$44.00	3/96
Mills at the Turn, The	18x22	Foreign	3.5	$303.00	11/94
Mills at the Turn, The	11x17	Foreign	4	$225.00	6/95
Mills at the Turn, The	18x22	Foreign	3.5	$303.00	11/94
Mills at the Turn, The	**18x22**	**Foreign**	**4**	**$385.00**	**6/95**
Mills at the Turn (untitled), The	7x9	Foreign	3.75	$72.00	4/95
Mills at the Turn (untitled), The	7x9	Foreign	4	$50.00	11/94
Mills at the Turn, The (untitled)	7x9	Foreign	3	$61.00	11/95

The following section is Miniature Exterior Scenes

(Birches & Blue Lake)	4x5	Miniature	4	$83.00	6/96
(Birches & Blue Lake)	4x5	Miniature	5	$39.00	4/94
(Birches & Country Lane)	4x5	Miniature	4	$44.00	11/94

Mary Ball Washington's Parlor

Met Half Way

129

Title	Size	Type	Rate	Amount	Date
(Birches & Country Road)	4x5	Miniature	4	$50.00	4/94
(Blossoms & Blue Pond)	4x5	Miniature	3.75	$47.00	3/96
(Blossoms & Country Lane)	4x5	Miniature	3	$39.00	3/96
(Blossoms & Rail Fence)	4x5	Miniature	4	$39.00	6/94
(Blossoms & Rocky Stream)	4x5	Miniature	5	$116.00	4/94
(Blossoms & Stone Wall)	4x5	Miniature	3.5	$72.00	6/94
(Blossoms by Country Road)	4x5	Miniature	4	$77.00	11/95
(Blossoms by Stone Wall)	4x5	Miniature	4	$33.00	4/94
(Bridge Crosses Stream)	4x5	Miniature	4	$138.00	3/96
(Calm Stream & Tall Trees)	4x5	Miniature	4	$52.00	11/95
(Colorful Leaves on Calm Stream)	4x5	Miniature	5	$61.00	4/94
(Covered Bridge)	4x5	Miniature	4	$39.00	11/95
(Fall-Colored Trees by Lake)	4x5	Miniature	3	$52.00	3/96
(Fall-Colored Trees by Stream)	4x5	Miniature	4	$39.00	11/94
(Large Rocks by Rushing Stream)	4x5	Miniature	5	$39.00	4/94
(Rocky Banks & Blue Stream)	4x5	Miniature	4	$39.00	11/95
("A Berkshire Brook")	4x5	Miniature	5	$39.00	4/94
("The Natural Bridge")	4x5	Miniature	4	$28.00	11/94
("The Natural Bridge")	4x5	Miniature	3	$52.00	11/95

The following section is Miniature Floral Scenes

Title	Size	Type	Rate	Amount	Date
(Vanity & Constancy)	4x5	Floral	5	$297.00	4/95
(A Dahlia Jar)	4x5	Floral	5	$330.00	4/95
(Above the Mahogany)	4x5	Floral	4	$99.00	4/94
(Flowers in Blue Vase)	4x5	Floral	4	$176.00	4/94
(Flowers in Golden Vase)	3x4	Floral	4	$187.00	6/95
(Fox Glove)	4x5	Floral	4	$138.00	3/96
(Full Summer)	4x5	Floral	4	$165.00	11/94
(Hollyhocks)	4x5	Floral	4	$176.00	11/95
(Mexican Zinnias)	4x5	Floral	4	$198.00	11/95
(Zinnias)	4x5	Floral	4	$165.00	11/95

The following section is Miniature Interior Scenes

Title	Size	Type	Rate	Amount	Date
(Girl Sews by Fire)	4x5	Miniature	4	$63.00	6/96
(Girl Reaches for Teapot)	4x5	Miniature	4	$94.00	6/96
(Girl Polishes Platter)	4x5	Miniature	4	$77.00	11/94
("Braiding a Rage Rug")	4x5	Miniature	4	$66.00	11/94
("Returning from a Walk")	4x5	Miniature	3	$39.00	11/94
("Tea for Two")	4x5	Miniature	3	$39.00	11/94
("The Maple Sugar Cupboard")	4x5	Miniature	4	$77.00	11/94
("The Quilting Party")	4x5	Miniature	4	$50.00	11/94
Mirror (with 2 int scenes)	13x40	Mirror	5	$440.00	11/94
Mirror (with cat scene)	7x26	Mirror	3	$193.00	3/96
Mirror (with ext scene)	9x31	Mirror	3	$88.00	11/94
Mirror (with ext scene)	6x16	Mirror	4	$66.00	6/94
Mirror (with ext scene)	16x44	Mirror	3	$165.00	4/95
Mirror (with int scene)	9x24	Mirror	4	$237.00	3/96
Mirror (with int scene)	10x23	Mirror	4	$242.00	6/94
Mirror (with int scene)	11x29	Mirror	4	$154.00	4/95
Mirror (with int scene)	14x29	Mirror	3	$275.00	6/94

The Mills at the Turn

Title	Size	Type	Rate	Amount	Date
Mirror (w/"An Old Drawing Room")	16x36	Mirror	5	$523.00	6/94
Mirror (w/"Calling at the Squire's")	8x28	Mirror	3.5	$248.00	3/96
Mirror (w/"Comfort & a Cat")	15x43	Mirror	4	$440.00	6/95
Mirror (w/"Draped in Blossoms")	12x43	Mirror	4	$468.00	6/95
Mirror (w/"Durham")	11x28	Mirror	4	$149.00	4/94
Mirror (w/"Italian Spring")	13x28	Mirror	4	$275.00	11/95
Mirror (w/"Skirmishing")	10x36	Mirror	4	$468.00	4/94
Mission Corner, A	**8x13**	**Misc Un**	**3**	**$275.00**	**6/96**
Model Picture (floral)	4x9	Misc	2	$77.00	6/95
Model Picture (large family)	7x9	Misc	2	$83.00	6/95
Mohonk Drive, A	14x18	Ext	3	$363.00	11/95
Montebello Terraces	13x16	Misc Un	4	$495.00	11/94
Monument Between Blossoms	13x16	Misc Un	4	$231.00	11/95
Morning Among the Birches	18x22	Ext	3.5	$143.00	4/95
Morning Duties	**14x17**	**Int**	**5**	**$358.00**	**4/95**
Morning Duties	10x12	Int	4	$132.00	3/96
Morning Errand, A	**13x16**	**Misc Un**	**4**	**$285.00**	**10/95**
Mosque Pitcher, A	13x16	Floral	4	$475.00	3/96
Mossy Logs	18x22	Ext	5	$330.00	11/95
Mossy Stair, A	16x20	Ext	3.5	$143.00	3/96
Mother	11x14	Child	4	$600.00	12/98
Mother of the Revolution, A	11x14	Int	4	$165.00	4/95
Mother's Day Card		Misc	4	$100.00	12/98
Mother's Day Card	4x5	Misc	4	$105.00	6/96
Mother's Day Card		Misc	4	$28.00	6/96
Mother's Day Card		Misc	4	$94.00	3/96
Mother's Day Card		Misc	4	$83.00	6/95
Mother's Day Card (framed)	4x6	Misc	4	$33.00	4/94
Mountain Born	9x11	Ext	4	$140.00	12/98
Mountain Ledges	12x16	Ext	4	$116.00	3/96
Mt. Washington Ahead	11x14	Ext	4	$140.00	1/96
Mt. Washington Base Road	9x11	Ext	2.75	$39.00	6/94
Mt. Washington in June	13x16	Ext	4	$99.00	11/95
Music of the Heart, The	13x16	Int	4	$231.00	3/96
Nan of Nantucket	**13x16**	**Misc Un**	**4**	**$235.00**	**12/94**
Nap Time Stories	13x15	Child	4	$413.00	11/94
Naptime Stories	14x17	Child	4	$1,050.00	11/94
Naptime Stories	13x16	Child	4	$605.00	6/94
Nashua Asleep, The	9x11	Ext	4	$120.00	12/98
Natural Bridge	13x17	Ext	4	$88.00	11/94
Natural Bridge, The	10x12	Misc Un	4	$121.00	6/94
Natural Bridge, The	16x20	Ext	4	$220.00	11/95
Natural Bridge, The	13x16	Misc Un	4	$160.00	6/95
Natural Bridge, The	10x12	Ext	4	$77.00	4/94
Natural Bridge, The	16x20	Misc Un	4	$275.00	7/94
Natural Bridge, The	11x14	Misc Un	3	$90.00	11/95
Natural Bridge, The	13x16	Ext	3.75	$231.00	6/96

A Mission Corner

Morning Duties

A Morning Errand

Nan of Nantucket

Title	Size	Type	Rate	Amount	Date
Nearing the Crest	11x17	Ext	4	$90.00	12/98
Neath Apple and Maple	14x17	Ext	4	$145.00	3/96
Neighbors	14x17	Int	3	$105.00	4/95
Nest, The	16x20	Foreign	4	$99.00	6/96
Nest, The	12x14	Foreign	3	$94.00	6/96
Nest, The	11x14	Foreign	4.5	$231.00	11/95
Nest, The	18x22	Foreign	4	$310.00	12/98
Nest, The	11x14	Foreign	4	$127.00	3/96
Nest, The	13x16	Foreign	4	$145.00	3/96
Nest, The	15x22	Foreign	3	$143.00	11/95
Nest, The (untitled)	7x9	Foreign	3.5	$44.00	4/95
Nesting Time	13x16	Ext	4	$85.00	12/98
Nethercote	13x17	Foreign	4	$185.00	6/95
Nethercote	13x16	Foreign	4	$165.00	6/94
Nethercote	9x11	Foreign	4	$132.00	6/94
New Birth Card	5x9	Misc	5	$220.00	6/96
New England Birches	11x14	Ext	4	$61.00	6/95
New England Birches	11x14	Ext	3	$80.00	4/96
New England Road in May, A	18x22	Ext	4	$90.00	12/98
New England Shore, The	10x16	Seascape	4	$132.00	4/94
New Hampshire Arch, A	10x16	Misc Un	4	$143.00	11/94
New Hampshire Birches	11x14	Ext	4	$150.00	5/96
New Hampshire Drive, A	11x14	Ext	3	$50.00	4/94
New Hampshire Drive, A	16x20	Ext	3.5	$94.00	11/94
New Hampshire Road, A	10x16	Ext	3	$65.00	6/95
New Hampshire Road, A	10x16	Ext	4	$105.00	6/96
New Hampshire Roadside	11x17	Ext	4	$65.00	12/98
New Hampshire Stream, A	11x14	Ext	4	$50.00	11/95
New Life	11x14	Sheep	3	$88.00	6/95
New Life	11x14	Sheep	3	$121.00	6/96
New Life	13x16	Sheep	4	$325.00	8/95
New Life	10x12	Sheep	3	$105.00	11/95
New Vineyard House, Maine, A	**12x16**	**Misc Un**	**4**	**$286.00**	**3/96**
News in Brief, The	18x22	Int	4	$145.00	12/98
News in Brief, The	14x17	Int	4	$165.00	4/95
Newton Autumn, A	12x14	Ext	3	$44.00	6/95
Newton Autumn, A	11x14	Ext	3	$60.00	8/95
Not One of the Four Hundred	14x17	Sheep	4	$363.00	6/94
Not One of the Four Hundred	13x16	Sheep	4	$225.00	1/96
Not One of the Four Hundred	15x22	Sheep	4	$425.00	7/95
Notch Mountain	13x16	Ext	4	$105.00	3/96
Nova Scotia Idyl, A	16x20	Foreign	4	$374.00	4/95
Nova Scotia Idyl, A	**9x11**	**Foreign**	**5**	**$198.00**	**6/94**
Nutting Studio Dance Card	9x14	Misc	4	$33.00	6/96
Nuttinghame Basket, A	14x17	Floral	3	$633.00	4/95
Nuttinghame Blossoms	14x16	Misc Un	3	$94.00	3/96
Nuttingholme Blossoms	14x17	Misc Un	4	$200.00	10/95
Nuttinghame Nook, A	14x17	Int	4.5	$375.00	9/94
Nuttinghame Nook, A	11x17	Int	3.5	$160.00	9/95
Nuttinghame Nook, A	10x14	Int	3	$94.00	11/94

Title	Size	Type	Rate	Amount	Date
Nutting's Expansible Catalog					
Work Copy		Misc	4	$176.00	6/96
Obstructed Brook, An	14x17	Ext	3	$60.00	4/95
Ocean Eddies	10x8	Seascape	3	$413.00	4/94
October Array, An	16x20	Ext	4.5	$176.00	6/96
October Array, An	13x16	Ext	5	$352.00	4/95
October Array, An	13x17	Ext	3	$83.00	6/96
October Array, An	9x11	Ext	4	$61.00	3/96
October Array, An	16x20	Ext	4	$145.00	12/98
October in May	11x14	Ext	3	$85.00	1/96
October on the Charles	10x16	Ext	4	$155.00	2/96
October on the River	14x17	Ext	3	$88.00	11/94
October Splenders	12x16	Ext	3	$90.00	3/96
October Waters	13x22	Ext	3.5	$94.00	3/96
Oil Painting ("Slack Water")	19x28	Misc	4	$352.00	6/94
Oil Painting ("Westfield Water")	20x26	Misc	4	$132.00	6/95
Old Back Door, An	11x14	Misc Un	4	$210.00	12/98
Old Colony Parlor, An	**13x16**	**Int**	**4**	**$230.00**	**1/96**
Old Colony Parlor, An	11x14	Int	4	$175.00	12/98
Old Drawing Room, An	10x12	Int	4	$72.00	6/96
Old Drawing Room, An	11x14	Int	4	$135.00	12/98
Old Drawing Room, An	11x14	Int	3.75	$83.00	4/95
Old Drawing Room, An	10x12	Int	4	$285.00	12/98
Old Drawing Room, An	11x17	Int	5	$160.00	6/94
Old Drawing Room, An	13x16	Int	3	$110.00	11/94
Old Fashioned Paradise, An	13x16	Misc Un	4	$185.00	10/95
Old Fashioned Paradise, An	11x14	Misc Un	4	$195.00	9/95
Old Fashioned Village	16x20	Misc Un	3	$143.00	4/94
Old Home, An	11x17	Cat	4	$297.00	6/96
Old Home, The	13x16	Cat	4	$325.00	1/96
Old Home, The	10x16	Cat	3	$110.00	3/96
Old Home, The	12x18	Cat	4	$320.00	12/98
Old Italian Arches	11x20	Foreign	3	$275.00	4/94
Old Italian Arches	12x20	Foreign	4	$413.00	4/96
Old Newbury Corner, An	13x15	Int	3	$132.00	4/94
Old Parlor Idyl, An	**14x17**	**Man**	**4**	**$475.00**	**10/95**
Old Pasture, An	9x15	Cow	3	$605.00	4/94
Old Settee, The	7x12	Child	3	$72.00	11/94
Old Time Gallant, The	11x14	Man	3.5	$715.00	4/95
Old Time Romance, An	13x16	Int	4	$210.00	12/98
Old Time Romance, An	11x14	Int	3.5	$88.00	4/95
Old Time Romance, An	11x14	Int	4	$340.00	12/98
Old Trundle Bed, The	**13x17**	**Int**	**3.5**	**$175.00**	**2/96**
Old Village Street, The	14x17	Misc Un	3.75	$303.00	3/96
Old Wentworth Days	12x14	Int	2	$121.00	6/95
Old Wentworth Days	11x14	Int	4	$155.00	12/98
Old Wentworth Days	16x20	Int	4	$375.00	5/95
Olden Time, The	11x17	Misc Un	4	$210.00	10/94
Olden Time, The	11x17	Misc Un	4	$231.00	11/94
Olden Times, The	10x16	Misc Un	4	$110.00	11/94

A New Vineyard House, Maine

A Nova Scotia Idyl

An Old Colony Parlor

133

An Old Parlor Idyl

The Old Trundle Bed

The Open Gate

Title	Size	Type	Rate	Amount	Date
On Dress Parade	13x16	Ext	4	$160.00	4/96
On Dress Parade	11x17	Ext	3	$95.00	5/96
On Either Hand	10x12	Ext	3	$72.00	11/95
On the Heights	10x16	Foreign	3.5	$413.00	6/95
On the Heights (untitled)	8x13	Foreign	3	$270.00	6/94
On the Quinnebaug	12x20	Ext	3	$100.00	7/94
On the Quinnebaug	13x16	Ext	4	$160.00	1/95
On the Quinnebaug	16x20	Ext	3	$39.00	11/94
On the Quinnebaug	15x18	Ext	4	$155.00	12/98
On the Quoile	16x20	Foreign	3	$127.00	6/94
On the Shores of the Zuyder Zee	13x16	Foreign	4	$2,970.00	6/92
On the Slope	10x16	Sheep	4	$190.00	12/98
On the Teith	11x14	Foreign	4	$209.00	6/95
Open Gate, The	13x16	Sheep	4	$275.00	7/95
Open Gate, The	**10x12**	**Sheep**	**5**	**$330.00**	**4/94**
Orange in the Toe, The	10x12	Child	3.5	$523.00	6/95
Orchard Brook, The	11x14	Ext	4	$150.00	1/96
Orchard Brook, The	13x16	Ext	3.5	$77.00	3/96
Orchard Heights	13x14	Ext	4	$65.00	12/98
Orchard Heights	14x17	Ext	3	$90.00	2/95
Orchard Shadows	11x14	Ext	4	$55.00	6/94
Original Dennison House, The	14x17	Misc Un	4	$215.00	1/96
Original Nutting Picture Studio Catalog		Misc	4	$1,012.00	6/96
Our Neighbor	12x16	Misc Un	3.5	$132.00	11/95
Out of a Garden Fair	11x14	Misc Un	3	$127.00	3/96
Out of the Garden	11x17	Misc Un	3.5	$105.00	11/94
Over the Canal	10x16	Ext	4	$150.00	3/95
Over the Crest	11x17	Ext	3	$60.00	4/95
Over the Fence	12x15	Foreign	3.75	$330.00	6/95
Over the Wall	13x15	Ext	3.5	$149.00	3/96
Overflowing Cup, An	10x12	Ext	4	$116.00	3/96
Overflowing Cup, An	7x24	Ext	4	$255.00	12/98
Ovoca, The	13x15	Foreign	4	$105.00	6/96
Pacific Coast Ledges	11x13	Seascape	3	$270.00	4/94
Palm Beach Creek	14x17	Misc Un	4	$198.00	6/94
Palmetto Grace	**14x17**	**Ext**	**4**	**$440.00**	**3/96**
Paradise Portal	13x16	Misc Un	4	$205.00	11/95
Paradise Portal	15x19	Misc Un	3	$413.00	3/96
Paradise Valley	10x16	Ext	4	$127.00	3/96
Paradise Valley	10x16	Ext	4	$110.00	6/94
Parke-Bernet Auction Catalog (1941)		Misc	3.5	$143.00	6/95
Parke-Bernet Catalog		Misc	4	$55.00	6/96
Parlor Corner, The	13x16	Int	4	$265.00	12/98
Parson's Gate, The	12x15	Misc Un	4	$185.00	2/96
Parthenon, The	13x16	Foreign	4	$210.00	1/96
Parthenon, The	**13x16**	**Foreign**	**3**	**$242.00**	**6/96**
Parting of the Ways, The	13x17	Ext	3.5	$171.00	3/96
Pasture Dell	13x16	Cow	4	$775.00	1/96
Pasture Lane, the	11x14	Ext	4	$110.00	6/96
Pasture Lane, The	12x16	Ext	4	$25.00	12/98

Title	Size	Type	Rate	Amount	Date
Pasture Lane, The	10x12	Ext	3	$39.00	4/95
Pasture Stream, A	11x17	Ext	4	$319.00	6/96
Patchwork Siesta, A	14x17	Child	3	$578.00	11/95
Patchwork Siesta, A	13x16	Child	4	$1,100.00	9/94
Patchwork Siesta, A	14x17	Child	5	$605.00	6/94
Path Among Blossoms, A	12x15	Misc Un	4	$187.00	3/96
Path of Roses, A	14x17	Foreign	4	$190.00	4/96
Path of Sweetness, A	13x17	Foreign	4	$143.00	4/95
Path of Roses, The	13x16	Foreign	4	$105.00	11/95
Patience on a Chippendale	11x14	Int	2	$61.00	4/94
Patriarch in Bloom, A	9x11	Ext	4	$125.00	12/98
Patriarch in Bloom, A	11x17	Ext	4	$72.00	6/95
Patriarch in Bloom, A	8x10	Ext	3	$55.00	4/95
Patti's Favorite Walk	11x14	Foreign	3.75	$66.00	6/96
Patti's Favorite Walk	10x12	Foreign	3	$72.00	6/96
Patti's Favorite Walk	**10x12**	**Foreign**	**4**	**$204.00**	**3/96**
Patti's Favorite Walk	13x16	Foreign	3	$468.00	6/95
Patti's Favorite Walk	14x17	Foreign	4	$72.00	6/96
Patti's Favorite Walk (untitled)	7x9	Foreign	4	$275.00	6/96
Patti's Favorite Walk (untitled)	7x9	Foreign	3.5	$105.00	6/94
Pausing for a Chat	14x17	Misc Un	4	$495.00	4/95
Peace	13x22	Ext	3	$77.00	6/94
Peaceful Stretch, A	11x17	Foreign	4	$195.00	1/96
Peaceful Stretch, A	10x16	Foreign	4	$160.00	3/96
Peaceful Stretch, A	13x19	Foreign	4	$310.00	12/98
Peep at the Hills, A	13x17	Ext	3.5	$66.00	3/96
Peep at the Hills, A	7x13	Ext	4	$85.00	12/98
Peep Down the Street, A	11x13	Misc Un	3	$105.00	11/95
Peep in the Mirror, A	11x13	Int	3.5	$61.00	6/95
Pennsylvania Hillside, a	13x16	Misc Un	4	$220.00	2/96
Pennsylvania Stream, A	13x16	Ext	4	$140.00	9/95
Pennsylvania Stream, A	**14x17**	**Ext**	**5**	**$770.00**	**6/96**
Pergola, Amlfi, The	15x17	Foreign	3	$187.00	11/95
Pergola, Amlfi, The	13x16	Foreign	4	$303.00	3/96
Pergola, Amlfi, The	14x17	Foreign	3.5	$198.00	3/96
Pergola, Amlfi, The	13x16	Foreign	4	$200.00	12/98
Pergola, Amlfi, The	13x15	Foreign	3	$55.00	6/96
Pergola, Amlfi, The	18x22	Foreign	4	$176.00	11/94
Perkiomen October, A	**13x16**	**Ext**	**4**	**$429.00**	**4/95**
Petaled	10x16	Ext	4	$39.00	4/95
Petaled	12x16	Ext	4	$88.00	6/94
Petaled Way, A	12x16	Ext	4	$80.00	12/98
Petals Above and Below	10x13	Ext	4	$75.00	12/98
Petals Above and Below	13x16	Ext	4	$175.00	2/96
Petals Above and Below	10x12	Ext	3	$61.00	3/96
Picture Catalog, 1912		Misc	5	$105.00	11/94
Picture Catalog, 1912		Misc	3	$99.00	6/94
Picture Catalog, 1912		Misc	3	$121.00	6/94
Picture Catalog, 1912		Misc	3	$110.00	6/96
Picture Catalog, 1912		Misc	4	$303.00	6/95
Picture Catalog, 1915 Expansible		Misc	4	$225.00	7/94

Palmetto Grace

The Parthenon

Patti's Favorite Walk

A Pennsylvania Stream

A Perkiomen October

A Picture Library

Title	Size	Type	Rate	Amount	Date
Picture Catalog, 1915 Expansible		Misc	4	$155.00	1/96
Picture Catalog, 1915 Expansible		Misc	3	$187.00	4/94
Picture Catalog, 1937 Recovery Edition		Misc	4	$281.00	6/94
Picture Catalog, 1937 Recovery Edition		Misc	3	$138.00	3/96
Picture Library, A	**14x17**	**Int**	**4**	**$100.00**	**12/98**
Picture Wall, The	11x14	Int	4	$210.00	8/95
Pictured Wall, The	13x15	Int	3.75	$231.00	4/95
Pilgrim Daughter, A	23x26	Int	3	$198.00	4/94
Pilgrim Prints		Misc	3.5	$6,325.00	6/95
Pine Landing	14x17	Ext	4	$88.00	6/95
Pine Landing	13x16	Ext	4	$220.00	3/96
Pine Landing	13x16	Ext	4	$165.00	4/95
Pine Landing	14x17	Ext	4	$132.00	6/95
Pine Landing	11x14	Ext	4	$120.00	12/98
Pink, Blue and Green	12x16	Ext	3	$44.00	11/95
Pink Bower, A	11x14	Ext	4	$135.00	11/95
Pink & Green	13x15	Ext	3	$66.00	6/95
Pinning the Lace	10x16	Int	4	$180.00	9/95
Pinning the Lace	10x16	Int	3	$116.00	4/94
Pirate Print	12x16	Misc	4	$25.00	6/95
Pirate Print	9x12	Misc	3	$28.00	11/95
Pirate Print ("All Smiles")	13x16	Misc	3	$14.00	4/94
Pitcher of Roses, A	8x10	Floral	4	$330.00	6/95
Pittsfield Meadow, A	11x17	Ext	4	$145.00	12/98
Plymouth Curves	12x16	Ext	4	$83.00	6/95
Plymouth Curves	10x16	Ext	3	$61.00	11/95
Plymouth Curves	13x22	Ext	3	$66.00	6/96
Plymouth Curves	10x16	Ext	4	$100.00	12/98
Plymouth Curves	13x22	Ext	4.5	$110.00	4/95
Poet's Orchard, A	10x16	Ext	4	$140.00	1/96
Poland Road, A	11x13	Ext	3	$105.00	4/95
Polishing the Pewter	11x17	Int	4	$190.00	10/95
Polishing the Sheffield	10x16	Int	4	$180.00	11/95
Pomperaug Banks	11x17	Ext	3	$99.00	6/94
Pomperaug Banks	10x16	Ext	4	$50.00	11/94
Pomperoug Banks, The	10x17	Ext	3	$154.00	4/95
Pool, The	11x14	Ext	3	$85.00	2/96
Pool at Sandwich, The	**13x16**	**Misc Un**	**4.5**	**$798.00**	**11/95**
Pool at Sandwich, A	13x16	Misc Un	4	$225.00	3/96
Pool at Sandwich, A	13x16	Misc Un	3	$66.00	6/96
Pool of Delight, A	11x14	Ext	3	$75.00	2/96
Porcelain Paint Tray		Misc	4	$33.00	6/96
Porta Della Carta	11x14	Foreign	3	$303.00	3/96
Posing (untitled)	**7x9**	**Child**	**4**	**$135.00**	**12/98**
Pouring Tea	12x15	Int	3	$110.00	11/95
Preparing an "At Home"	13x22	Int	4	$145.00	12/98
Preparing an "At Home"	13x17	Int	4	$260.00	10/95
Preparing an "At Home"	9x14	Int	4	$135.00	12/98
Present of Jewels, A	13x17	Int	4	$325.00	4/96
Presidential Range, The	7x9	Ext	3	$77.00	3/96
Pride of the Lane, The	13x16	Ext	4	$155.00	3/96

Title	Size	Type	Rate	Amount	Date
Pride of the Lane, The	14x17	Ext	4	$65.00	12/98
Pringle House Door	13x16	Misc Un	4	$275.00	6/96
Pringle Parlor	10x12	Int	3	$198.00	11/95
Priscilla Among the Heifers	13x16	Cow	4	$583.00	4/94
Private & Confidential	13x16	Int	4	$95.00	12/98
Process Prints,					
10 Laminated Place Mats	12x16	Misc	4	$47.00	6/96
Proof Sheet (framed)	10x12	Misc	4	$50.00	6/95
Proof Sheet (20 ext scenes)	11x14	Misc	4	$28.00	6/96
Proof Sheet (20 ext scenes)	11x14	Misc	4	$36.00	6/96
Proof Sheet (framed)	11x14	Misc	4	$28.00	11/94
Proof Sheet (framed)	11x14	Misc	4	$75.00	12/98
Proof Sheet (framed)	11x14	Misc	4	$50.00	3/96
Proofs-Furniture Treasury III		Misc	4	$55.00	6/96
Proud as Peacocks	13x16	Int	4	$245.00	9/95
Proud as Peacocks	14x17	Int	4	$176.00	11/95
Proud as Peacocks	16x20	Int	4	$395.00	10/95
Provincetown Hollyhocks	13x16	Misc Un	3.5	$165.00	3/96
Prudence Drawing Tea	14x17	Int	4	$220.00	6/96
Prudence Drawing Tea	14x17	Int	4	$130.00	12/98
Prudence Drawing Tea	13x22	Int	3	$94.00	11/94
Prudence Drawing Tea	16x20	Int	4	$154.00	11/94
Purity and Grace	13x16	Ext	4	$94.00	3/96
Purity and Grace	20x24	Ext	5	$264.00	6/96
Purity and Grace	16x20	Ext	3.75	$105.00	3/96
Quaint Newbury	13x16	Misc Un	3	$121.00	11/94
Question of Taste, A	10x12	Int	4.5	$253.00	11/94
Quiet Corner, A	13x16	Foreign	5	$176.00	11/94
Quilting Party, The	10x12	Int	4	$88.00	6/96
Quilting Party, The	11x14	Int	3.5	$50.00	6/96
Quilting Party, The	14x17	Int	3	$149.00	3/96
Quilting Party, The	13x15	Int	3	$155.00	1/96
Quilting Party, The	11x14	Int	4	$154.00	3/96
Quilting Party, The	11x14	Int	4	$165.00	2/96
Quilting Party, The	**14x17**	**Int**	**5**	**$325.00**	**5/95**
Quilting Party, The	15x22	Int	4	$210.00	12/98
Rag Rug Weaving	12x14	Int	3	$77.00	3/96
Ramapo Rapids	14x17	Ext	3.75	$154.00	4/95
Ranglely Shore, A	12x17	Ext	3	$66.00	11/95
Ranglely Shore, A	13x16	Ext	4	$187.00	4/95
Rangley Shore, A	10x12	Ext	4	$110.00	6/95
Rapid Transit	14x17	Misc Un	3	$688.00	11/94
Reading from Arabian Nights	13x16	Misc Un	4	$975.00	7/95
Reading from Arabian Nights (b&w)	13x16	Misc Un	4	$220.00	6/95
Ready for Callers	11x14	Int	5	$94.00	6/94
Recreation of our Foremothers	13x16	Int	4	$198.00	11/95
Red, White & Blue	13x16	Ext	4	$110.00	12/98
Red, White & Blue	11x14	Ext	4	$83.00	6/94
Red Eagle Lake	9x11	Ext	4	$105.00	3/96

The Pool at Sandwich

Posing (Untitled)

The Quilting Party

Resting at the Old Stoop

Returning from a Walk

Title	Size	Type	Rate	Amount	Date
Red Eagle Lake	9x11	Ext	4	$74.00	11/95
Red Eagle Lake	16x20	Ext	4	$132.00	3/96
Red Eagle Lake	16x20	Ext	3	$83.00	6/96
Red Eagle Lake	9x11	Ext	4	$80.00	12/98
Reeling the Yarn	14x17	Int	4	$135.00	12/98
Rest After Sewing	11x17	Int	3.75	$220.00	4/94
Rest After Sewing	13x22	Int	3	$110.00	6/94
Resting at the Old Stoop	13x15	Misc Un	3	$94.00	11/94
Resting at the Old Stoop	**13x16**	**Misc Un**	**4**	**$280.00**	**10/94**
Resting at the Old Stoop	7x9	Misc Un	4	$165.00	12/98
Restless Deep, The	10x16	Seascape	3.5	$155.00	10/95
Returning from a Walk	11x14	Int	4	$165.00	5/95
Returning from a Walk	**9x11**	**Int**	**4**	**$90.00**	**12/98**
Returning from a Walk	9x11	Int	4	$135.00	12/98
Riffle in the Stream, A	13x16	Ext	4	$132.00	6/96
Riffle in the Stream, A	13x16	Ext	3	$80.00	4/96
Riffle in the Stream, A	11x14	Ext	4	$145.00	3/96
Ripening Tints	9x11	Ext	3	$77.00	6/94
Rippling Mirror, A	13x16	Ext	4	$55.00	4/95
Rising Tide	14x20	Seascape	3.5	$154.00	3/96
River Curves	9x13	Ext	3	$39.00	4/94
River Grasses	13x16	Ext	4	$275.00	11/95
River Grasses	14x17	Ext	2	$44.00	6/96
River in Maine, A	13x16	Ext	4	$132.00	11/95
River in May, A	13x16	Ext	4	$150.00	5/96
River Meadow, The	14x17	Foreign	4	$230.00	12/98
River Valley, The	10x16	Ext	4	$94.00	11/94
Rhode Island Coast, The	12x18	Seascape	4	$375.00	2/96
Road to Far Away, The	9x15	Foreign	3	$143.00	4/95
Roadside Brook, A	11x17	Ext	4	$50.00	11/94
Roadside Brook, A	10x16	Ext	4	$160.00	3/96
Roadside Glories	9x11	Ext	3	$55.00	6/94
Roadside Glories	13x16	Ext	4	$165.00	11/95
Roadside Grace	10x14	Ext	4	$100.00	12/98
Rock Creek Banks	11x14	Ext	4	$125.00	12/98
Rock Creek in April	9x11	Ext	3.75	$198.00	4/95
Rock Creek in April	11x14	Ext	4	$135.00	7/95
Rocks Off Portland	11x14	Seascape	3	$385.00	6/96
Rocky Dell, A	11x17	Ext	4	$50.00	6/95
Romance of the Revolution, A	13x16	Int	4	$165.00	4/95
Romance of the Revolution, A	10x12	Int	4	$165.00	3/96
Rose Gate	13x16	Foreign	4	$198.00	6/95
Rose Standish (untitled)	8x12	Misc Un	3.75	$66.00	6/96
Roses and a Bud	13x16	Child	4	$220.00	6/96
Roses and a Bud	**11x14**	**Child**	**4**	**$300.00**	**12/98**
Roses and Larkspur	13x16	Floral	4	$1,210.00	6/96
Roses & Larkspur	13x16	Floral	4	$580.00	12/98
Ross on Wye (untitled)	7x9	Foreign	4	$61.00	4/95
Ross-on-Wye	10x16	Foreign	4	$265.00	12/98
Rug Maker, The	13x16	Int	5	$310.00	7/94
Rug Maker, The	16x20	Int	4	$145.00	12/98

Title	Size	Type	Rate	Amount	Date
Rug Pattern, A	13x16	Foreign	4	$200.00	5/96
Rug Pattern, A	**13x16**	**Foreign**	**4**	**$210.00**	**2/96**
Rug Pattern, The	13x16	Foreign	4	$215.00	2/96
Rural Sweetness	16x20	Ext	3	$83.00	11/94
Rural Sweetness	13x15	Ext	3	$70.00	8/95
Russet and Gold	18x22	Ext	4	$90.00	12/98
Sailing Among the Windmills	11x17	Foreign	4	$190.00	9/95
Sailing Among the Windmills	10x16	Foreign	4	$185.00	5/96
Sailing Among Windmills	10x16	Foreign	3.5	$215.00	3/96
Salem Beautiful	11x14	Misc Un	4	$95.00	12/98
Salem Dignity	12x16	Misc Un	2	$220.00	6/95
Sallying of Sally, The	13x16	Misc Un	4	$80.00	12/98
Sallying of Sally, The	14x17	Misc Un	4	$90.00	12/98
Sallying of Sally, The	14x17	Misc Un	3	$85.00	10/95
Sallying of Sally, The	14x17	Misc Un	4	$195.00	12/98
Sallying of Sally, The	13x16	Misc Un	3	$83.00	11/95
Saturday Baking	11x14	Int	5	$220.00	4/95
Scotland Beautiful	**12x15**	**Foreign**	**4**	**$285.00**	**12/98**
Scotland Forever	13x15	Foreign	4	$297.00	6/95
Sea Barriers	10x16	Seascape	4	$154.00	4/95
Sea Capn's Daughter, The	11x17	Misc Un	3	$105.00	6/96
Sea Capn's Daughter, The	12x16	Misc Un	4	$185.00	12/98
Sea Capn's Daughter, The	11x17	Misc Un	3.75	$121.00	11/95
Sea Ledges	17x21	Seascape	4	$145.00	12/98
Sea Ledges	14x17	Seascape	4	$375.00	2/95
Sea Ledges	13x19	Seascape	4	$132.00	6/95
Sea Ledges	9x14	Seascape	4	$242.00	4/95
Sea Ledges	14x17	Seascape	4	$325.00	12/98
Season of Rejoicing, The	14x17	Ext	4	$94.00	3/96
Season of Rejoicing, The	13x16	Ext	3	$66.00	4/94
Seeking the Shade	11x14	Sheep	4	$193.00	12/95
Selection, The	10x12	Int	3	$154.00	11/95
Settle Nook, A	13x16	Int	4	$175.00	1/96
Seven Bridge Road, The	12x15	Ext	4	$242.00	6/94
Sewing by the Fire	11x14	Int	4	$165.00	6/96
Sewing by the Fire	10x12	Int	4	$127.00	3/96
Sewing by the Fire	10x12	Int	3	$66.00	11/94
Sewing by the Fire, The	11x14	Int	4	$110.00	11/94
Shadowed Causeway	13x16	Ext	4	$77.00	4/94
Shadows Athwart	10x12	Ext	3.75	$44.00	4/95
Shadows Athwart	14x17	Ext	4	$35.00	12/98
Shadows Athwart	22x28	Ext	4	$83.00	11/94
Shadows Athwart	9x12	Ext	3	$50.00	11/95
Shadowy Orchard Curves	16x20	Ext	4	$225.00	5/95
Shadowy Orchard Curves	13x16	Ext	4	$155.00	4/96
Shadowy Orchard Curves	14x17	Ext	3.5	$105.00	4/95
Shadowy Orchard Curves	11x14	Ext	4	$140.00	9/95
Sheffield Basket, A	**13x16**	**Floral**	**4**	**$660.00**	**6/95**
Sheffield Basket, A (close-framed)	8x10	Floral	5	$575.00	11/94
Sheltered Road, A	13x22	Ext	3	$83.00	11/95

Roses and a Bud

A Rug Pattern

Scotland Beautiful

A Sheffield Basket

The Simple Life

A Sip of Tea

Title	Size	Type	Rate	Amount	Date
Sheltered Road, A	10x16	Ext	4	$50.00	4/95
Shore Battle, A	11x14	Seascape	4	$149.00	3/96
Shore Road, The	10x12	Ext	3	$55.00	6/96
Showered with Petals	13x16	Foreign	2	$209.00	6/96
Sign (Wallace Nutting pictures, paper, framed)	11x14	Misc	4	$39.00	11/95
Silent Shore, A	13x16	Ext	4	$140.00	12/98
Silent Shore, The	11x14	Ext	4	$75.00	12/98
Silent Shore, The	13x16	Ext	3	$83.00	4/95
Silent Shore, The	13x15	Ext	4	$160.00	12/94
Silhouette Greeting Card		Misc	4	$50.00	6/96
Silver Birches	13x16	Ext	3	$55.00	6/95
Simple Life, The	**9x11**	**Foreign**	**3**	**$110.00**	**11/95**
Sip of Tea, A	14x17	Int	3	$77.00	6/96
Sip of Tea, A	11x14	Int	4	$145.00	12/98
Sip of Tea, A	14x17	Int	3.5	$121.00	3/96
Sip of Tea, A	13x15	Int	4	$149.00	3/96
Sip of Tea, A	9x11	Int	3	$55.00	6/95
Sip of Tea, A	11x14	Int	4	$255.00	4/96
Sir William Johnson Parlor	10x13	Int	4	$230.00	12/98
Sisterly Criticism	14x17	Int	2	$154.00	6/96
Slack Water	15x22	Ext	4	$165.00	5/95
Slack Water	14x17	Ext	4	$165.00	4/95
Slack Water	10x16	Ext	3.5	$66.00	6/96
Slack Water	13x22	Ext	4	$135.00	12/98
Slack Water	13x17	Ext	3	$66.00	4/95
Slack Water (close-framed)	20x30	Ext	4	$176.00	4/95
Slow Fine, A	13x15	Int	3	$121.00	6/96
Smoke of the Evening Fires	14x20	Foreign	4.5	$297.00	11/94
Smoke of the Evening Fires	10x16	Foreign	3	$105.00	4/95
Smoke of the Evening Fires	10x16	Foreign	4	$121.00	11/95
Snow Scene	14x17	Snow	3	$550.00	6/94
Snow Scene, small close-framed	3x4	Snow	4	$72.00	6/96
Snow Scene, small close-framed	3x4	Snow	4	$72.00	6/96
Snow Scene, small close-framed	3x4	Snow	4	$44.00	6/96
Snow Scene, small close-framed	3x4	Seasow	4	$209.00	6/95
Snow Scene, small close-framed	3x4	Snow	4	$143.00	11/94
Snow Scene with House	9x11	Snow	4	$1,265.00	4/94
Snow Scene (untitled)	5x6	Snow	3	$220.00	6/96
Snow Scene (untitled)	7x9	Snow	4	$341.00	6/96
Soft Evening Lights	10x16	Ext	4	$165.00	10/95
Soft Evening Lights	10x11	Ext	4	$65.00	12/98
Soft Summer Shadows	18x22	Ext	4.5	$198.00	6/95
Soft Summer Shadows	11x14	Ext	4	$50.00	11/95
Somerset Highway, A	4x5	Misc	4	$77.00	6/94
Southbury Water	11x14	Ext	2	$36.00	6/94
Southern Charm	8x10	Misc Un	3	$72.00	6/94
Southern Colonial Room, A	**14x17**	**Int**	**4**	**$303.00**	**6/94**
Southern Puritan, A	13x15	Misc Un	4	$275.00	6/94
Southern Puritan, A	13x15	Misc Un	4	$385.00	6/95
Sparkling Blaze, The	13x16	Int	3	$72.00	4/95

Title	Size	Type	Rate	Amount	Date
Sparkling Blaze, The	10x16	Int	4	$220.00	6/96
Sparkling Blaze, The	11x14	Int	4	$290.00	4/96
Spinet Corner, The	11x14	Int	4	$121.00	6/96
Spinet Corner, The	13x16	Int	3	$110.00	6/96
Spinet Corner, The	11x14	Int	3.5	$127.00	3/96
Spinet Corner, The	14x17	Int	4	$265.00	7/95
Spinet Corner, The	10x12	Int	4	$100.00	12/98
Spires of Hope	13x16	Misc Un	5	$341.00	4/94
Spires Through Foliage	7x9	Misc	4	$209.00	6/96
Spring at the Lake	14x17	Ext	3	$50.00	11/94
Spring at the Lake	13x16	Ext	3	$83.00	11/95
Spring Basket	8x10	Floral	5	$963.00	4/94
Spring Basket	13x16	Floral	5	$633.00	6/95
Spring Bower, A	20x26	Ext	4	$121.00	11/94
Spring Colors	10x16	Ext	4	$72.00	3/96
Spring Colors	10x16	Ext	3.75	$61.00	6/95
Spring Fashion	9x15	Misc Un	4	$264.00	11/94
Spring Fashion at Old Mill	9x15	Ext	4	$193.00	6/95
Spring Fashion at the Old Home	10x16	Misc Un	4	$190.00	1/96
Spring in the Berkshires	16x20	Ext	4	$45.00	12/98
Spring in the Dell	13x16	Ext	4	$75.00	12/98
Spring in the Dell	13x16	Ext	4	$145.00	5/95
Spring in the Dell	10x12	Ext	4	$84.00	3/96
Spring in the Mountains	11x14	Foreign	3	$110.00	4/95
Spring Lane	14x17	Ext	4	$132.00	6/96
Spring Pageant, A	13x16	Ext	3	$85.00	1/96
Spring Pageant, A	11x17	Ext	4	$61.00	6/96
Spring Sweetness	11x14	Int	3	$77.00	6/95
Springfield Blossoms	14x17	Ext	3	$75.00	10/95
Springfield Lane	10x12	Ext	3.75	$61.00	11/94
Squirrel Bridge	12x16	Ext	3.75	$220.00	11/94
Squirrel Bridge	**13x16**	**Ext**	**4**	**$451.00**	**4/95**
St. Mary's in May	14x17	Foreign	4	$195.00	10/95
Stamford Roadside, A	11x14	Ext	4	$155.00	2/96
State Chamber Tea, A	12x16	Int	3	$83.00	4/95
Stately Tea Pouring, A	11x14	Int	4	$190.00	5/96
Stepping Stones at Bolton Abbey	**13x16**	**Foreign**	**4**	**$375.00**	**12/98**
Still Depths	11x14	Ext	3	$72.00	6/95
Still Depths	10x12	Ext	3.5	$138.00	3/96
Stirring Scene, A	18x22	Int	4	$198.00	11/95
Stitch in Time, A	12x15	Int	3	$193.00	3/96
Stitch in Time, A	18x22	Int	4	$90.00	12/98
Stitch in Time, A	11x14	Int	4	$155.00	12/98
Stitch in Time, A	13x16	Int	3.5	$175.00	5/95
Stitch in Time, A	10x16	Int	3	$99.00	6/96
Stokesay Castle	13x16	Misc Un	4.5	$242.00	6/95
Stone Churn, The	13x16	Seascape	4	$220.00	4/94
Stone Churn, A	**11x17**	**Seascape**	**5**	**$385.00**	**6/94**
Stream of Peace, A	12x16	Ext	4	$63.00	11/95
Street Border, A	**12x16**	**Foreign**	**4**	**$242.00**	**6/95**
Street Border, A	12x16	Foreign	4	$231.00	3/96

A Southern Colonial Room

Squirrel Bridge

Stepping Stones at Bolton Abbey

A Stone Churn

A Street Border

Title	Size	Type	Rate	Amount	Date
Street Border, A	12x16	Foreign	5	$198.00	6/94
Summer Clouds	10x16	Ext	4	$66.00	6/94
Summer Grotto	13x16	Ext	4	$110.00	11/94
Summer on the Avon	11x15	Foreign	2	$88.00	3/96
Summer Shore, A	11x14	Ext	4	$145.00	12/98
Summer Wind	15x18	Ext	4	$125.00	12/98
Summer Wind	13x22	Ext	3	$83.00	11/95
Summer Wind	12x20	Ext	4	$132.00	11/95
Summer Wind	14x20	Ext	4	$154.00	3/96
Summer Wind	14x17	Ext	3.5	$121.00	6/96
Summer Wind (close-framed)	7x9	Ext	3	$22.00	6/95
Sunday Afternoon in Old Home	12x16	Man	3	$237.00	6/96
Sunday Afternoon in Old Home	14x17	Man	3	$248.00	4/95
Sunset Fires	14x20	Ext	4	$170.00	12/98
Sunset Over the Meadows	9x14	Ext	3.75	$83.00	4/95
Sunshine and Music	13x16	Int	4	$175.00	12/98
Sunshine and Music	10x20	Int	3	$105.00	6/96
Sunshine and Music	14x17	Int	3.5	$226.00	6/94
Sunshine & Music	13x16	Int	3.5	$226.00	6/94
Swan Cove (untitled)	7x11	Snow	4	$154.00	6/96
Swan Cove (untitled)	7x11	Foreign	3	$77.00	11/94
Swimming Pool, The	15x18	Ext	4	$135.00	12/98
Swimming Pool, The	12x16	Ext	4	$77.00	6/96
Swimming Pool, The	14x17	Ext	4	$94.00	6/96
Swimming Pool, The	14x17	Ext	4	$88.00	3/96
Swimming Pool, The	18x22	Ext	4	$72.00	6/96
Swimming Pool, The	10x16	Ext	3.75	$121.00	3/96
Swimming Pool, The	18x26	Ext	4	$105.00	3/96
Swimming Pool, The	14x17	Ext	3	$44.00	6/96
Swimming Pool, The	20x40	Ext	4	$80.00	12/98
Swimming Pool, The	9x11	Ext	3	$55.00	6/96
Swimming Pool, The	11x14	Ext	3	$94.00	11/95
Swimming Pool, The (close-framed)	10x12	Ext	4	$33.00	6/95
Swirling Seas	13x16	Seascape	5	$297.00	6/94
Swirling Seas	14x20	Seascape	4	$275.00	12/98
Swirling Seas	16x20	Seascape	4	$330.00	6/95
Swirling Seas (close-framed)	16x20	Seascape	5	$523.00	3/96
Swirling Seas (close-framed)	20x30	Seascape	4	$132.00	6/95
Sylvan Dell	10x16	Ext	4	$75.00	12/98
Tap at the Squire's Door, A	11x14	Misc Un	3	$110.00	6/96
Tap at the Squire's Door, A	8x10	Misc Un	3	$55.00	6/96
Tap at the Squire's Door, A	13x16	Misc Un	4	$215.00	4/96
Tap at the Squire's Door, A	14x17	Misc Un	4	$205.00	5/96
Tea for Two	15x22	Int	4	$175.00	12/98
Tea for Two	11x14	Int	4	$75.00	12/98
Tea in Yorktown Parlor	11x17	Int	4	$190.00	12/98
Tea Maid, The	13x16	Int	4	$175.00	11/95
Tea Maid, The	13x15	Int	3	$72.00	11/94
Tea Maid, The	13x15	Int	4	$215.00	2/96

Title	Size	Type	Rate	Amount	Date
Tea Maid, The	13x15	Int	4	$155.00	12/98
Tea Maid, The	13x15	Int	3.5	$132.00	4/95
Tea Table, The	11x14	Int	4	$110.00	6/95
Thanksgiving Goodies	13x15	Int	4	$195.00	12/98
Thatched Dormers	13x16	Foreign	4	$275.00	12/95
Thatched Dormers	13x15	Foreign	4	$286.00	6/96
Thatched Dormers, Normandy	14x17	Foreign	2	$116.00	4/94
The Charles in October	12x16	Ext	3	$52.00	4/94
Three Chums	11x14	Cat	4	$248.00	11/95
Three Chums	10x12	Cat	4.5	$374.00	6/95
Three Chums	14x17	Cat	3.5	$193.00	4/95
Three Chums	11x14	Cat	4	$250.00	12/98
Thrilling Romance, A	16x20	Int	4	$195.00	9/95
Tide Marks	16x20	Foreign		$105.00	6/94
Tiger Lilies and Elder	13x16	Misc Un	4	$330.00	6/96
Time of Roses, The	10x12	Foreign	4	$265.00	12/98
Tis Rosemary	13x15	Misc Un	3	$154.00	11/95
To the End Porch	12x16	Misc Un	5	$165.00	6/94
Touching Tale, A	**11x14**	**Int**	**3**	**$154.00**	**3/96**
Touching Tale, A	11x14	Int	4	$94.00	6/95
Touching Tale, A	10x12	Int	3	$88.00	6/95
Touching Tale, A	13x17	Int	4	$105.00	6/94
Toward Purple Hills	13x16	Ext	3	$88.00	6/95
Toward Slumberland	**13x16**	**Child**	**5**	**$798.00**	**11/94**
Toward Slumberland	14x17	Child	3	$330.00	6/96
Toward the Mountains	13x16	Ext	4	$121.00	11/95
Towards the Mountains	13x16	Ext	3.75	$72.00	3/96
Tracery of May, A	14x17	Ext	2	$22.00	6/95
Tranquil Vale, The	11x17	Foreign	4	$225.00	4/96
Tranquil Vale, The	7x15	Foreign	3	$143.00	11/95
Tranquil Vale, The	15x22	Foreign	4	$138.00	4/95
Tranquil Vale, The	10x19	Foreign	3	$198.00	3/96
Tranquility Farm	13x15	Sheep	4	$374.00	6/96
Tranquility Farm	13x15	Sheep	4	$275.00	8/94
Tray, small with int scene	3x4	Misc	4	$66.00	6/96
Tray, with ext scene	12x20	Misc	3.95	$165.00	6/96
Tray (with ext scene)	9x13	Misc	4	$83.00	6/94
Tray (with ext scene)	5x7	Misc	4	$72.00	6/94
Tray (with int scene)	14x18	Misc	3	$176.00	11/95
Treasure Bag, The	13x15	Int	4	$187.00	4/94
Treasure Bag, the	10x12	Int	4	$66.00	6/96
Treasure Bag, The	11x14	Int	4.5	$215.00	7/94
Triple Int Grouping	16x33	Int	3	$468.00	6/96
Trout Brook, The	13x16	Ext	3	$90.00	4/96
True D.A.R., A	9x15	Int	4	$165.00	3/96
True D.A.R., A	11x14	Int	3.5	$314.00	6/94
Trysting Bridge, A	16x20	Foreign	3	$66.00	6/94
Tunnel of Bloom, A	14x17	Ext	3.5	$127.00	3/96
Turn of the River, A	13x16	Ext	5	$105.00	11/94
Turf Toad, The	11x17	Ext	4	$99.00	4/94
Turn of the Tide, The	9x15	Seascape	3.75	$413.00	4/95

A Touching Tale

Toward Slumberland

Uncle Sam Taking Leave

Under the Sundial

Title	Size	Type	Rate	Amount	Date
Twin Sentinels	14x17	Ext	3	$55.00	4/95
Twix't Apple and Birch	18x22	Ext	4	$149.00	3/96
Two Centuries	13x16	Misc Un	4	$358.00	4/94
Uncle Jonathan Goes to Church	12x14	Man	3	$248.00	6/94
Uncle Sam Taking Leave	9x11	Man	3	$154.00	11/95
Uncle Sam Taking Leave	13x16	Man	4.5	$165.00	6/95
Uncle Sam Taking Leave	**14x17**	**Man**	**4**	**$550.00**	**5/95**
Uncle Sam Taking Leave	12x15	Man	3	$451.00	6/96
Uncle Sam & Granny	13x15	Man	3	$55.00	3/96
Uncolored "Purity"	9x12	Ext	4	$66.00	6/95
Under Ivy Bridge	14x17	Foreign	4	$85.00	12/98
Under Ivy Bridge	18x22	Foreign	3.5	$110.00	11/94
Under Ivy Bridge (close-framed)	10x13	Foreign	4	$50.00	6/95
Under Old Apple Trees	9x15	Misc Un	5	$297.00	4/94
Under the Arches	10x12	Foreign	3.5	$99.00	11/95
Under the Blossoms	13x15	Sheep	4	$358.00	6/95
Under the Blossoms	14x17	Sheep	4	$330.00	4/94
Under the Blossoms	14x17	Sheep	3.75	$259.00	3/96
Under the Blossoms	13x16	Sheep	4	$248.00	11/95
Under the Pine	11x17	Ext	4	$94.00	3/96
Under the Sundial	**12x16**	**Foreign**	**4**	**$275.00**	**11/94**
Undulating Reflections	14x17	Misc Un	3	$165.00	4/95
Untitled Cat (cat by fire)	7x9	Cat	4	$215.00	7/94
Untitled Cat (cat by fire)	8x10	Cat	4	$175.00	8/95
Untitled Child (child in garden)	8x14	Child	3	$220.00	11/94
Untitled Child ("Posing")	7x9	Child	3.5	$105.00	11/94
Untitled Child ("Posing")	7x9	Child	3.75	$88.00	3/96
Untitled Child ("Posing")	8x10	Child	3	$33.00	11/94
Untitled Child ("Posing")	8x10	Child	4	$83.00	11/95
Untitled Child ("Posing")	7x9	Child	4	$72.00	4/95
Untitled Cow Scene	7x11	Cow	4	$154.00	11/95
Untitled Cow Scene	7x11	Cow	3	$154.00	4/95
Untitled Cow Scene	7x11	Cow	3.5	$220.00	4/94
Untitled Cow Scene	7x11	Cow	3	$121.00	3/96
Untitled Cow Scene	7x11	Cow	4	$209.00	11/95

The following section is Untitled Exterior Scenes

Title	Size	Type	Rate	Amount	Date
(Birches & Blue Lake)	7x11	Ext	4	$116.00	4/94
(Birches & Blue Lake)	7x9	Ext	3	$39.00	11/94
(Birches and Country Road)	10x12	Ext	3	$22.00	11/94
(Birches and Country Road)	8x12	Ext	4	$66.00	6/95
(Blossoms and Blue Pond)	10x12	Ext	3	$39.00	3/96
(Blossoms and Blue Pond)	7x9	Ext	4	$55.00	6/94
(Blossoms and Country Lane)	8x12	Ext	2	$14.00	4/94
(Blossoms and Country Lane)	8x10	Ext	4	$22.00	11/94
(Blossoms and Rail Fence)	10x12	Ext	4	$30.00	6/94
(Blossoms and Rail Fence)	8x12	Ext	3.75	$33.00	11/95
(Blossoms and Stone Wall)	7x9	Ext	3	$39.00	3/96
(Blossoms and Stone Wall)	8x10	Ext	3	$33.00	3/96
(Bridge Crosses Stream)	5x7	Ext	4	$44.00	3/96

Title	Size	Type	Rate	Amount	Date
(Bridge Crosses Stream)	8x12	Ext	2	$14.00	4/94
(Calm Stream and Tall Trees)	7x9	Ext	4	$66.00	11/95
(Calm Stream and Tall Trees)	10x12	Ext	4	$39.00	3/96
(Colorful Leaves on Calm Stream)	7x9	Ext	4	$17.00	4/95
(Colorful Leaves on Calm Stream)	8x12	Ext	3.75	$33.00	11/95
(Covered Bridge)	7x9	Ext	4	$22.00	6/94
(Covered Bridge)	7x11	Ext	4	$110.00	11/95
(Fall-Colored Trees by Lake)	7x9	Ext	4	$66.00	11/95
(Fall-Colored Trees by Lake)	7x9	Ext	4	$22.00	6/94
(Fall-Colored Trees by Stream)	8x10	Ext	4	$33.00	11/94
(Fall-Colored Trees by Stream)	10x12	Ext	3	$55.00	4/95
(Large Rocks by Rushing Stream)	10x12	Ext	3	$39.00	3/96
(Large Rocks by Rushing Stream)	7x9	Ext	3.5	$33.00	3/96
(Rocky Banks and Blue Stream)	8x10	Ext	3.5	$44.00	11/94
(Rocky Banks and Blue Stream)	7x9	Ext	3	$39.00	3/96
(Stone in Bridge)	10x12	Ext	4	$220.00	11/95
("A Natural Bridge")	8x10	Ext	4	$88.00	11/95
("A Pennsylvania Hillside")	8x10	Ext	3	$95.00	4/95
("A Pennsylvania Hillside")	10x12	Ext	3	$55.00	4/95
("Berkshire Pool")	11x14	Ext	3	$17.00	4/94
("Canoe Under Tall Pine Tree")	7x11	Ext	4	$36.00	3/96
("Canoe Under Tall Pine Tree")	7x9	Ext	3	$39.00	11/94
("Pine Landing")	8x12	Ext	4	$41.00	4/95
("Pine Landing")	7x11	Ext	3.5	$39.00	11/94
("Pine Landing")	10x12	Ext	3	$22.00	11/94
("The Natural Bridge")	7x9	Ext	4	$66.00	11/95
("The Natural Bridge")	8x12	Ext	4	$50.00	11/94

The following section is Untitled Floral Scenes

Title	Size	Type	Rate	Amount	Date
(Flowers in Blue Vase)	8x10	Floral	4	$286.00	11/95
(Flowers in Pink Vase)	8x10	Floral	4	$175.00	1/96
(Mexican Zinnias)	6x8	Floral	4	$165.00	11/94
(Pink & White Flowers)	8x10	Floral	4	$315.00	11/94
("Hollyhocks")	8x10	Floral	4	$275.00	10/95

The following section is Untitled Foreign Scenes

Title	Size	Type	Rate	Amount	Date
("A Garden of Larkspur")	8x10	Foreign	4	$149.00	3/96
("A Garden of Larkspur")	7x9	Foreign	4	$66.00	4/95
("A Garden of Larkspur")	6x8	Foreign	4	$72.00	4/94
("A Little Killarney Lake")	5x7	Foreign	4	$44.00	3/96
("A Little Killarney Lake")	5x7	Foreign	3.5	$83.00	11/95
("A Little Killarney Lake")	6x8	Foreign	4	$77.00	4/94
("At the Well, Sorrento")	11x14	Foreign	3	$248.00	4/95
("Durham")	7x9	Foreign	3.75	$55.00	11/95
("Dutch Maids")	10x12	Foreign	3.5	$330.00	6/95
("Evangeline Lane")	7x9	Foreign	4	$182.00	3/96
("Evangline Lane")	6x8	Foreign	4	$61.00	4/94
("Hollyhock Cottage")	7x9	Foreign	3	$61.00	11/94
("Hollyhock Cottage")	7x9	Foreign	4	$44.00	11/94
("Hollyhock Cottage")	7x9	Foreign	4	$61.00	6/94
("Joy Path")	6x8	Foreign	4	$44.00	11/94

Title	Size	Type	Rate	Amount	Date
("Joy Path")	8x10	Foreign	4	$110.00	11/94
("Larkspur")	7x9	Foreign	4	$182.00	3/96
("Larkspur")	6x8	Foreign	4	$72.00	4/94
("Larkspur")	8x10	Foreign	4	$149.00	3/96
("Larkspur")	6x8	Foreign	4	$61.00	4/94
("Larkspur")	7x9	Foreign	4	$66.00	4/95
("Litchfield Minster")	5x7	Foreign	4	$83.00	11/95
("Litchfield Minster")	5x7	Foreign	4	$44.00	3/96
("Litchfield Minster")	6x8	Foreign	4	$77.00	4/94
("Mills at the Turn")	7x9	Foreign	4	$50.00	11/94
("Mills at the Turn")	7x9	Foreign	3	$61.00	11/95
("Mills at the Turn")	7x9	Foreign	3.75	$72.00	4/95
("On the Heights")	8x13	Foreign	3	$270.00	6/94
("Patti's Favorite Walk")	7x9	Foreign	3.5	$105.00	6/94
("Ross on Wye")	7x9	Foreign	4	$61.00	4/95
("Swan Cove")	7x11	Foreign	3	$77.00	11/94
("The Nest")	7x11	Foreign	4	$61.00	4/95
("The Nest")	7x9	Foreign	3.5	$44.00	4/95

The following section is Untitled Interior Scenes

Title	Size	Type	Rate	Amount	Date
(Girl in Room with Wallpaper)	7x9	Int	3.75	$61.00	11/94
(Girl in Room with Wallpaper)	7x9	Int	3	$50.00	11/94
(Girl in Room with Wallpaper)	8x12	Int	4	$99.00	6/94
(Girl Inspects Purse)	8x12	Int	4	$110.00	4/94
(Girl Inspects Purse)	7x11	Int	4	$110.00	11/95
(Girl Inspects Purse)	7x11	Int	3.5	$55.00	11/95
(Girl Polishes Platter)	5x7	Int	4	$88.00	4/94
(Girl Polishes Platter)	7x11	Int	3	$39.00	4/94
(Girl Polishes Platter)	6x8	Int	3.5	$61.00	6/94
(Girl Reaches for Coffee Pot)	8x12	Int	4	$110.00	4/94
(Girl Reaches for Coffee Pot)	8x12	Int	4	$55.00	6/94
(Girl Reaches for Coffee Pot)	5x7	Int	4	$55.00	11/94
(Girl Reaches into Cupboard)	11x14	Int	3	$39.00	3/96
(Girl Reaches into Cupboard)	7x9	Int	4	$83.00	11/95
(Girl Reaches into Cupboard)	7x9	Int	3.5	$66.00	6/94
(Girl Sews by Fire)	5x7	Int	3	$72.00	4/95
(Girl Sews by Fire)	10x12	Int	3	$66.00	11/95
(Girl Sews by Tall Clock)	8x12	Int	4	$72.00	6/95
(Girl Sews by Tall Clock)	7x9	Int	4	$187.00	11/95
(Girl Sews by Tall Clock)	7x9	Int	4	$55.00	6/94
(Girl Sits at Piano)	8x12	Int	4	$116.00	3/96
(Girl Sits at Piano)	8x10	Int	3	$88.00	11/95
(Girl Sits at Piano)	5x7	Int	4	$50.00	6/94
(Girl Sits by Tall Clock)	7x9	Int	4	$55.00	4/95
(Girl Sits by Tall Clock)	7x9	Int	3.5	$44.00	11/95
(Girl Sits by Tall Clock)	7x9	Int	3	$66.00	11/95
(Girl with Candle in Hand)	7x11	Int	4	$61.00	11/94
(Girl with Candle in Hand)	7x9	Int	4	$99.00	4/94
(Girl with Candle in Hand)	6x9	Int	3.5	$11.00	4/95
(Two Girls by Fire)	8x12	Int	4	$88.00	11/95
(Two Girls by Fire)	8x12	Int	3	$11.00	4/95

Title	Size	Type	Rate	Amount	Date
(Two Girls by Fire)	7x11	Int	4	$72.00	11/94
(Two Girls Chat by Fire)	8x12	Int	4	$138.00	3/96
(Two Girls Chat by Fire)	7x11	Int	3	$55.00	6/95
(Two Girls Chat by Fire)	5x7	Int	3	$77.00	4/94
(Two Girls Have Tea)	7x11	Int	3.5	$110.00	4/94
(Two Girls Have Tea)	7x11	Int	4	$72.00	4/95
(Two Girls Have Tea)	7x9	Int	3	$33.00	4/95
("A Chair for John")	5x7	Int	4	$77.00	3/96
("A Chair for John")	7x9	Int	3.5	$72.00	4/94
("A Cold Day")	7x9	Int	4	$66.00	11/95
("A Cold Day")	7x9	Int	4	$39.00	11/94
("A Discovery")	8x10	Int	4	$99.00	6/94
("A Discovery")	7x9	Int	4	$72.00	11/95
("A Fleck of Sunshine")	8x10	Int	2.5	$72.00	11/95
("A Fleck of Sunshine")	8x10	Int	3.75	$94.00	3/96
("A Sip of Tea")	8x12	Int	4	$72.00	11/94
("A Sip of Tea")	7x11	Int	3	$88.00	11/95
("A Stitch in Time")	10x12	Int	4	$61.00	4/94
("A Stitch in Time")	7x9	Int	3.75	$44.00	11/95
("A Virginia Reel")	7x9	Int	4	$83.00	3/96
("A Virginia Reel")	8x12	Int	4	$83.00	4/94
("Affectionately Yours")	7x9	Int	3.5	$83.00	4/95
("Affectionately Yours")	7x9	Int	4	$94.00	3/96
("An Afternoon Tea")	7x9	Int		$72.00	6/94
("An Afternoon Tea")	10x12	Int	4	$132.00	4/94
("An Elaborate Dinner")	7x9	Int	3	$30.00	6/95
("An Elaborate Dinner")	7x9	Int	4	$66.00	11/95
("At the Fender")	7x9	Int	3	$33.00	4/94
("At the Fender")	7x9	Int	3.5	$72.00	4/94
("Braiding a Rag Rug")	7x9	Int	4	$72.00	11/95
("Braiding a Rag Rug")	5x7	Int	3	$28.00	4/94
("Christmas Jelly")	7x9	Int	4	$83.00	4/95
("Christmas Jelly")	7x9	Int	4	$44.00	11/94
("Good Night")	8x10	Int	3.5	$127.00	3/96
("Good Night")	7x11	Int	3	$50.00	4/95
("Prudence Drawing Tea")	5x7	Int	3.5	$66.00	6/95
("Prudence Drawing Tea")	7x9	Int	4	$44.00	11/94
("Returning from a Walk")	7x9	Int	4	$165.00	11/94
("Returning from a Walk")	7x9	Int	4	$50.00	6/94
("Sunshine & Music")	8x10	Int	4	$83.00	4/95
("Sunshine & Music")	6x8	Int	3	$66.00	4/95
("Tea for Two")	7x11	int	3.5	$61.00	6/94
("Tea for Two")	6x8	Int	4	$66.00	11/94
("The Maple Sugar Cupboard")	10x12	Int	3	$33.00	4/95
("The Maple Sugar Cupboard")	5x7	Int	4	$462.00	4/95
("The Quilting Party")	10x12	Int	3	$50.00	11/94
("The Quilting Party")	8x10	Int	4	$66.00	6/95

The following section is Miscellaneous Unusual Scenes

Untitled Man

(man in red coat)	5x7	Man	4	$220.00	6/95

Title	Size	Type	Rate	Amount	Date
Untitled Man					
(man & woman by fire)	13x16	Man	2	$143.00	4/95
Untitled Man					
("An Old Parlor Idyl")	13x16	Man	3	$132.00	4/95
Untitled Seascape	5x7	Seascape	3.5	$44.00	11/95
Untitled Seascape					
(waves crash against rocks)	7x9	Seascape	4	$83.00	3/96
Untitled Seascape					
(waves crash against rocks)	7x11	Seascape	3.5	$61.00	11/95
Untitled Seascape					
("Swirling Seas")	7x11	Seascape	3.5	$83.00	6/94
Untitled Seascape					
("Swirling Seas")	8x10	Seascape	3.5	$132.00	6/94
Untitled Sheep	15x17	Sheep	3	$88.00	6/94
Untitled Sheep	7x9	Sheep	4	$154.00	4/94
Untitled Sheep	7x9	Sheep	3.75	$94.00	3/96
Untitled Sheep	12x18	Sheep	3	$105.00	11/95
Untitled Snow Scene	6x8	Snow	4	$468.00	6/95
Untitled Snow Scene	10x12	Snow	4	$418.00	11/94
Untitled Snow Scene	8x10	Snow	3	$61.00	6/94
Untitled Snow Scene	6x8	Snow	4	$215.00	6/94
Untitled (cottage)	7x19	Misc Un	4	$94.00	3/96
Untitled (farm house)	8x10	Misc Un	4	$165.00	11/94
Untitled (farm house)	7x11	Misc Un	4	$105.00	3/96
Untitled (garden scene)	9x11	Misc Un	4	$77.00	4/95
Untitled (garden scene)	8x10	Misc Un	3.5	$143.00	6/94
Untitled (garden scene)	9x11	Misc Un	3	$55.00	11/95
Untitled (garden scene)	6x8	Misc Un	3	$22.00	4/94
Untitled (garden scene)	6x8	Misc Un	2.5	$50.00	3/96
Untitled (girl at doorway)	8x13	Misc Un	3	$121.00	6/94
Untitled (girl at doorway)	5x7	Misc Un	4	$44.00	11/94
Untitled					
(girl by door, close-framed)	8x10	Misc Un	4	$33.00	4/94
Untitled (girl by house)	7x11	Misc Un	3.5	$77.00	11/95
Untitled (girl by house)	8x12	Misc Un	3	$50.00	11/94
Untitled (girl by house)	7x11	Misc Un	4	$50.00	11/94
Untitled (girl by stone wall)	6x8	Misc Un	4	$72.00	11/94
Untitled (girl in red cape)	5x10	Misc Un	2	$77.00	4/95
Untitled (girl with basket0	8x12	Misc Un	3.5	$83.00	4/94
Untitled (Jungfrau)	7x9	Snow	4	$330.00	4/94
Untitled (Nantucket)	8x12	Misc Un	3	$94.00	3/96
Untitled (village)	7x11	Misc Un	3	$50.00	4/94
Untitled ("Caller's at the Squire's")	8x10	Misc Un	3	$50.00	4/95
Untitled ("Camden Mountains")	7x11	Misc Un	4	$72.00	4/95
Up the Creek	10x12	Ext	4	$145.00	2/96
Up the Hill	10x14	Ext	3	$61.00	6/95
Up the Hill	11x17	Ext	4.5	$121.00	11/95
Upper Brandon with Roses	13x16	Misc Un	5	$770.00	11/95
Upper Winooski	14x17	Ext	3	$75.00	10/95
Valley in the Pyrenees, A	13x15	Foreign	3	$94.00	3/96

Title	Size	Type	Rate	Amount	Date
Vanity & Constancy					
(close-framed)	8x10	Floral	5	$715.00	4/94
Vanity & Constancy					
(close-framed)	8x10	Floral	4	$715.00	6/94
Variety	9x11	Misc Un	5	$242.00	4/94
Vermont Curves	13x15	Ext	4	$83.00	6/95
Vermont River, A	11x14	Ext	3	$90.00	3/96
Vermont River Curve, A	10x13	Ext	3	$72.00	4/95
Vermont Road, A	10x14	Ext	4	$85.00	12/98
Vermont Road, A	13x22	Ext	3.75	$99.00	3/96
Vermont Road, A	26x30	Ext	3.5	$132.00	4/95
Vermont Spring, A	10x12	Ext	4	$83.00	4/95
Vermont Wayside, A	12x16	Ext	4	$121.00	11/95
Very Satisfactory	11x14	Int	3	$121.00	4/95
Very Satisfactory	**16x20**	**Int**	**4**	**$220.00**	**4/95**
Very Satisfactory	11x14	Int	4	$145.00	12/98
Vico Esquene	11x13	Foreign	3.5	$440.00	6/94
View from Casino, Funchal	12x16	Foreign	4.5	$1,540.00	3/96
Vilas Gorge	13x16	Ext	4	$275.00	4/94
Vilas Gorge, The	12x15	Ext	4	$160.00	5/96
Village End, The	14x20	Foreign	5	$154.00	4/94
Village Spire, The	11x14	Foreign	3	$341.00	11/95
Village Spires	13x16	Ext	4	$165.00	6/96
Village Spires	10x12	Misc Un	5	$110.00	4/94
Village Spires	10x12	Ext	4	$36.00	6/96
Village Spires	10x12	Ext	3.75	$50.00	6/95
Village Spires	10x12	Ext	4	$204.00	3/96
Village Vale, The	11x17	Ext	4	$135.00	12/98
Village Vale, The	11x17	Ext	3.75	$88.00	3/96
Village Vale, The	13x16	Misc Un	4	$220.00	2/96
Vine Gabled Mill, A	13x15	Foreign	2	$523.00	3/96
Vines and Thatch	11x14	Foreign	4	$165.00	12/98
Virginia Reel, A	14x17	Int	4	$121.00	6/95
Virginia Reel, A	16x20	Int	3	$94.00	11/94
Virginia Reel, A	16x20	Int	4	$155.00	12/98
Virginia Reel, A	16x20	Int	4.5	$297.00	6/96
Virginia Reel, A	13x16	Int	4	$154.00	11/95
Volunteer Aid	13x16	Child	3.75	$523.00	6/94
Waiting Bucket, The	9x11	Misc Un	3.75	$127.00	3/96
Waiting for Jacob	11x14	Int	4	$210.00	12/95
Waiting for Jacob	**13x15**	**Int**	**3**	**$220.00**	**4/94**
Walk Under the Buttonwood	13x16	Ext	4	$83.00	6/96
Wallace Nutting Biography		Misc	4	$61.00	6/96
Walpole Road, A	15x22	Ext	4	$160.00	4/96
Walpole Road, The	9x17	Ext	3	$105.00	3/96
Walpole Road, The	10x16	Ext	4	$140.00	9/95
Wanalancet Road, The	20x30	Ext	5	$132.00	4/95
Wanamaker Catalog		Misc	3	$110.00	6/96
Warm Spring Day, A	13x17	Sheep	3.75	$248.00	3/96
Warm Spring Day, A	14x17	Sheep	4	$285.00	12/98

Very Satisfactory

Waiting for Jacob

Warner House

Watching for Papa

The Way it Begins

Title	Size	Type	Rate	Amount	Date
Warm Spring Day, A	12x16	Sheep	4	$242.00	11/95
Warm Spring Day, A	14x21	Sheep	4	$135.00	12/98
Warm Spring Day, A	12x20	Sheep	4	$176.00	6/96
Warm Spring Day, A	18x22	Sheep	4	$248.00	4/95
Warm Spring Day, A (close-framed)	20x40	Sheep	4	$209.00	6/95
Warner Door, Portsmouth, The	11x14	Misc Un	3	$369.00	6/94
Warner House	**14x17**	**Misc Un**	**4**	**$413.00**	**3/96**
Watched Pot, A	13x15	Int	3.5	$132.00	6/94
Water Garden in Venice, A	14x17	Foreign	4	$605.00	11/94
Waterford Streamside, A	13x16	Foreign	3	$127.00	3/96
Watering Place, A	11x17	Ext	4	$83.00	4/95
Waterside Cottage, A	13x16	Foreign	3	$110.00	4/95
Warwick Castle	11x17	Foreign	4	$195.00	12/98
Washington Cherry Blossoms	9x12	Ext	3	$61.00	6/95
Washington DC Ext	8x10	Ext	3.5	$99.00	6/94
Washington DC Ext	8x10	Ext	3.5	$61.00	6/94
Washington & Jefferson Commencement Address	7x10	Misc	4	$39.00	6/95
Watching for Papa	**13x16**	**Child**	**4**	**$523.00**	**6/94**
Water Maples	13x16	Ext	4	$145.00	11/95
Water Maples	13x16	Ext	3	$75.00	8/95
Water Maples	14x17	Ext	3	$80.00	12/95
Water Maples	12x14	Ext	4	$65.00	12/98
Water Maples	14x17	Ext	4	$125.00	1/95
Water Maples	11x17	Ext	4	$135.00	12/98
Water Paths of Venice	10x14	Foreign	4	$468.00	6/94
Watersmeet	13x16	Ext	3	$95.00	1/96
Watersmeet	13x17	Ext	4	$253.00	4/95
Watersmeet	14x20	Ext	4	$60.00	12/98
Watersmeet	11x14	Ext	4	$175.00	2/98
Watersmeet	18x22	Ext	4	$165.00	12/98
Wavering Footsteps	14x17	Child	4	$350.00	12/98
Way It Begins, The	14x17	Man	3	$220.00	6/95
Way It Begins, The	**14x17**	**Man**	**4**	**$410.00**	**12/98**
Way It Begins, The	11x14	Man	3.5	$352.00	4/95
Way It Begins, The	14x17	Man	3.75	$303.00	11/95
Way It Begins, The	14x17	Man	4	$220.00	6/96
Way of the Blessed, The	18x22	Ext	4	$182.00	3/96
Way Through the Orchard, The	18x22	Ext	4	$155.00	12/95
Way Through the Orchard, The	10x12	Ext	4	$50.00	12/98
Way Through the Orchard, The	22x28	Ext	4	$154.00	6/96
Way Through the Orchard, The	11x14	Ext	4	$110.00	12/98
Wayside Inn, The	10x12	Misc Un	4	$275.00	6/95
Wayside Inn, Old Dining Room	10x12	Int	4	$336.00	4/94
Wayside Inn Approach	13x16	Misc Un	4	$280.00	12/98
Wayside Inn Approach, The	13x16	Misc Un	4	$230.00	4/96
Wayside Inn Garden	14x17	Misc Un	3	$105.00	3/96
Wayside Inn, Old Dining Room	10x12	Int	4	$336.00	4/94
Wealth of October, The	12x20	Ext	4	$72.00	6/96
Weaver, The	14x17	Int	3.5	$154.00	3/96

Title	Size	Type	Rate	Amount	Date
Weaver, the	13x16	Int	4	$495.00	6/94
Wedding Invitations	14x17	Int	3.75	$187.00	11/95
Welcome Task, A	13x17	Int	4	$253.00	4/95
Welcome Task, A	**11x14**	**Int**	**4**	**$220.00**	**11/94**
Wells from the Palace Pool	14x17	Foreign	4	$230.00	5/96
Westfield Water	10x16	Ext	4	$105.00	12/98
Westfield Water	13x16	Ext	3.75	$88.00	3/96
Westfield Water	14x17	Ext	3.5	$94.00	6/94
Westfield Water	16x20	Ext	3.5	$72.00	3/96
Westmore Drive	10x16	Ext	4	$61.00	6/95
Westmore Drive	10x12	Ext	4	$75.00	12/98
Westport Garden, A	13x16	Foreign	4	$220.00	3/96
Westport Garden, A	13x16	Foreign	3.5	$286.00	6/96
What Shall I Answer?	**10x13**	**Int**	**4**	**$225.00**	**5/95**
What Shall I Answer?	15x22	Int	4	$352.00	6/96
Where Grandma Was Born	14x17	Foreign	3	$55.00	6/95
Where Grandma Was Wed	14x17	Misc Un	3	$88.00	3/96
Where Grandma Was Wed	14x20	Misc Un	3.5	$110.00	6/96
Where Grandma Was Wed	16x20	Misc Un	3.5	$176.00	11/94
Where Grandma Was Wed	14x17	Misc Un	3	$83.00	6/96
Where Grandma Was Wed	16x20	Misc Un	4	$220.00	3/96
Where Grandma Was Wed	16x19	Misc Un	4	$145.00	12/98
Where the Stream Rests	12x16	Foreign	4	$94.00	11/95
Where Trout Lie	13x16	Ext	4	$150.00	1/96
Whirling Candlestand, A	13x16	Child	4	$410.00	12/95
Whirling Candlestand, A	14x17	Child	4	$575.00	4/96
Whirling Candlestand, A	11x14	Child	4	$303.00	4/94
Whirling Candlestand, The	12x15	Child	3.75	$330.00	6/96
Whirling Candlestand, The	13x15	Child	3	$259.00	11/95
Whirling Candlestand, The	11x14	Child	3	$121.00	4/95
White Waves	10x16	Seascape	4	$175.00	10/95
White Way	13x16	Ext	3.5	$105.00	11/95
Whitsunday	9x15	Ext	3.5	$94.00	6/95
Whitsunday	9x17	Ext	3.5	$66.00	6/95
Wig Wag Churning	13x15	Int	4	$265.00	11/95
Wig Wag Churning	14x17	Int	3	$255.00	4/95
Wild Apple and Birch	10x16	Ext	4	$94.00	11/94
Wilderness Camp, A	13x22	Ext	3	$259.00	6/94
Wilkes Barre Brook, A	13x16	Ext	4.5	$429.00	6/96
Wilkes Barre Brook, A	8x10	Ext	3	$94.00	11/95
Willow Arcade, A	13x22	Ext	3	$41.00	4/95
Winding an Old Tall Clock	9x11	Int	4	$75.00	12/98
Winding an Old Tall Clock	13x16	Int	4	$175.00	12/98
Winding an Old Tall Clock	11x14	Int	4	$175.00	8/94
Windings in Holland	13x16	Foreign	3	$198.00	6/96
Windings in Holland	**13x16**	**Foreign**	**4**	**$242.00**	**11/95**
Windings in Holland	11x14	Foreign	4	$231.00	11/95
Windings in Holland	11x14	Foreign	3.5	$72.00	4/95
Windings in Holland	11x14	Foreign	4	$175.00	12/98
Windsor Blossoms	13x16	Ext	3	$85.00	2/96
Windsor Catalog, 1918		Misc	3.5	$55.00	6/96

A Welcome Task

What Shall I Answer?

Wisteria Gate

Title	Size	Type	Rate	Amount	Date
Windsor Maid, A	14x17	Int	4	$80.00	12/98
Wine Carrier, Ravello	11x17	Foreign	3.75	$1,705.00	6/94
Winslow Water	14x17	Ext	4	$230.00	12/98
Winter Welcome Home	10x16	Snow	3	$578.00	11/94
Winter Welcome Home, The	8x12	Snow	4	$1,430.00	6/94
Winter Welcome Home, The	10x16	Snow	3	$468.00	6/95
Wissahickon Blossoms	11x14	Ext	3	$90.00	4/96
Wissachickon Decorations	11x14	Ext	4	$160.00	5/96
Wissahickon Pool, A	11x14	Ext	3	$83.00	4/95
Wisteria Gate	**11x17**	**Misc Un**	**3**	**$255.00**	**3/96**
Wisteria Lodge	**11x14**	**Misc Un**	**3**	**$275.00**	**6/94**
WNCC Newsletter (Misc. Lot)		Misc	4	$61.00	11/94
WN/Dodd Mead Contract Lot		Misc	4	$358.00	6/96
Wooden Clamps					
(from Nutting Furniture Shop)		Misc	3.5	$132.00	11/94
Woodland Cathedral	14x20	Ext	3	$50.00	11/94
Woodland Cathedral, A	13x16	Ext	3	$95.00	5/96
Woodland Cathedral, A	11x14	Ext	3.75	$77.00	6/94
Woodland Cathedral, A	16x20	Ext	3.5	$121.00	4/95
Woodland Cathedral, A	11x14	Ext	4	$94.00	4/95
Woodland Enchantment	14x17	Ext	4	$94.00	6/95
Woodland Pool, A	10x16	Ext	5	$105.00	4/95
Woodland Rest	13x16	Ext	3	$61.00	11/95
Work Basket, The	10x12	Int	4	$80.00	12/98
Work Basket, The	11x14	Int	4	$155.00	7/94
World Beautiful, The	10x12	Ext	4	$55.00	6/94
World Beautiful, The	11x14	Ext	4	$155.00	12/95
World Beautiful, The	11x14	Ext	4	$61.00	4/95
World Beautiful, The	9x11	Ext	3.5	$83.00	4/95
Xmas Card, Folding		Misc	4	$72.00	6/96
Xmas Card, Folding		Misc	4	$88.00	6/96
Xmas Card, Folding (with envelope)		Misc	4	$61.00	6/96
Xmas Card (with snow scene)		Misc	4	$198.00	6/95
Yosemite Water	10x12	Ext	3	$281.00	6/94
Youth and Spring	**11x17**	**Misc Un**	**4**	**$195.00**	**7/95**
Youth of the Saco, The	13x16	Ext	4	$143.00	6/96
Youth of the Saco, The	10x12	Ext	4	$110.00	11/94
Zinnias	13x16	Floral	4	$375.00	12/98
17th Century, The	8x10	Int	3	$83.00	4/95
18th Century, The	11x14	Int	2	$209.00	4/94

Windings in Holland

Wisteria Lodge

Youth and Spring

Glossary of Terminology Used in This Book

Backing: The protective paper backing which is glued to the back of the frame to prevent dust and other objects from getting inside the picture.

Cardboard Sleeve: A cardboard box which replaced and offered greater protection to a book than the paper dust jacket.

Close-Framed: A picture that has been framed without a mat, where the frame touches the picture.

Copyright: A copyright marking on the picture itself which Nutting applied to some, but not most, of his pictures. Copyrights are usually in the form of reversed-out block copyrights, reserved-out script copyrights, and the more common "@ WN 19xx" type of copyright.

Copyright Label: A paper label glued to the backing of pictures, typically dating from the 1930s, which confirmed that the pictures were authentic Wallace Nutting hand-colored pictures.

Dust Jacket: A protective paper covering that was on most Wallace Nutting books when originally sold. Most are now missing, having become lost or damaged.

Exterior Scene: A basic outdoor scene, usually featuring apple blossoms, birches, country lanes, streams, lakes, rivers, mountains, and other outdoor scenes without people.

Foreign Scene: A picture taken outside of the United States.

Foxing: Spotting on the matting or picture, usually caused by a high degree of acidity in the wooden or cardboard backing.

Interior Scene: A picture taken indoors, usually featuring women, and sometimes men and children, in a colonial setting with authentic antique furnishings.

Mat or Matting: The thin cardboard backing that the picture is mounted upon and which carried the signature and title.

Memorabilia: Anything associated with Wallace Nutting collecting that is not a picture, book, or furniture piece.

Miscellaneous Unusual Scene: Any Wallace Nutting picture that does not fall into the exterior, interior, or foreign categories. Usually these pictures would include men, children, animals, seascapes, architectural views, exterior scenes with people, floral arrangements, and basically anything else that doesn't fit into the other three primary categories.

Overmat: A newer, secondary matting that is placed over the original matting, sometimes for decorative purposes, but usually to cover damage to the original matting.

Picture: The actual hand-colored or black & white platinotype picture.

Platinotype: The name given to Wallace Nutting's pictures because they were printed on a special paper with a high concentration of platinum. The special platinum paper held the colors better and gave a more favorable overall appearance to the picture.

Process Print: A machine-produced print, printed in the late 1930s to 1942. There were only 12 different process print titles reproduced.

Re-Mounted: An original picture which has been removed from its original matting and placed upon a newer matting.

Re-Signed: A picture whose signature is not original, but which has been re-signed at a later date.

Stain: Damage to the original matting or picture, usually cause by water.

Untitled: A picture that has been matted and signed with either a "Wallace Nutting," "W Nutting," or "WN," but whose title has not been signed on the matting. The title was typically omitted from smaller pictures 10" x 12" or smaller because the title would have run into the signature.

Wallace Nutting

About the Author

Michael Ivankovich has been collecting Wallace Nutting pictures for more than 20 years. Buying his first picture in 1974, he started searching out Nuttings in garage sales, flea markets, antique shows, and local auctions. Shortly thereafter, he began purchasing entire collections...20...50...100...800 pictures at a time. Today he is generally considered to be the country's leading authority on Wallace Nutting pictures, books, furniture, and memorabilia.

This specialization in Wallace Nutting pictures led to his first book in 1984, *The Price Guide to Wallace Nutting Pictures* (1st Ed). Three additional editions of that book were released between 1986 – 91. He has also authored three other books relating to Wallace Nutting including: *The Alphabetical & Numerical Index to Wallace Nutting Pictures, The Guide to Wallace Nutting Furniture*, and *The Guide to Wallace Nutting-Like Photographers of the Early 20th Century*. Through his Diamond Press subsidiary company, he has also published three additional books on Wallace Nutting: *The Wallace Nutting Expansible Catalog, Wallace Nutting: A Great American Idea*, and *Wallace Nutting Windsors: Correct Windsor Furniture*.

Mr. Ivankovich conducted the first all-Wallace Nutting consignment auction in 1988, selling nearly 500 lots of Wallace Nutting pictures, books, furniture, and memorabilia in Framingham, MA. The enthusiasm generated by this auction has led to 26 more Wallace Nutting catalog auctions between 1988 – 1996, with 3 – 4 Michael Ivankovich Wallace Nutting and Nutting-like auctions taking place each year throughout the New England and Mid-Atlantic states.

These Wallace Nutting auctions have now become the national center of Wallace Nutting activity. They provide Wallace Nutting buyers with the opportunity to compete for a wide variety of Wallace Nutting items ranging from common exterior scenes to the best and rarest Wallace Nutting pictures in the country. These Wallace Nutting auctions also provide sellers of Wallace Nutting pictures with the opportunity to place their consignments in front of the country's leading and most knowledgeable collectors. And they provide all Wallace Nutting enthusiasts with the opportunity to see the largest and most diverse assortment of Wallace Nutting pictures that they will probably ever see assembled all in one place.

A frequent lecturer on Wallace Nutting, Mr. Ivankovich has written articles for most major trade papers, has appeared on various radio and television programs, and is frequently consulted by antique columnists from throughout the country. He also provides Wallace Nutting appraisal services and exhibits at select antique shows.

Mr. Ivankovich is also a licensed auctioneer, conducting various antique and collectible, household and estate, general consignment, and fund-raising auctions.

Together with his wife Susan (who has published four cookbooks, including *The Not-Strictly Vegetarian Cookbook* and *Cooking with Sundried Tomatoes*), they reside in Doylestown, PA, with their four children Jenna, Lindsey, Megan, and Nash.

COLLECTOR BOOKS

Informing Today's Collector

For over two decades we have been keeping collectors informed on trends and values in all fields of antiques and collectibles.

DOLLS, FIGURES & TEDDY BEARS

4707	A Decade of **Barbie** Dolls & Collectibles, 1981–1991, Summers	$19.95
4631	**Barbie** Doll Boom, 1986–1995, Augustyniak	$18.95
2079	**Barbie** Doll Fashion, Volume I, Eames	$24.95
4846	**Barbie** Doll Fashion, Volume II, Eames	$24.95
3957	**Barbie** Exclusives, Rana	$18.95
4632	**Barbie** Exclusives, Book II, Rana	$18.95
4557	**Barbie,** The First 30 Years, Deutsch	$24.95
4847	**Barbie** Years, 1959–1995, 2nd Ed., Olds	$17.95
3310	**Black Dolls,** 1820–1991, Perkins	$17.95
3873	**Black Dolls,** Book II, Perkins	$17.95
3810	**Chatty Cathy Dolls,** Lewis	$15.95
1529	Collector's Encyclopedia of **Barbie** Dolls, DeWein	$19.95
4882	Collector's Encyclopedia of **Barbie** Doll Exclusives and More, Augustyniak	$19.95
2211	Collector's Encyclopedia of **Madame Alexander Dolls,** Smith	$24.95
4863	Collector's Encyclopedia of **Vogue Dolls,** Izen/Stover	$29.95
3967	Collector's Guide to **Trolls,** Peterson	$19.95
4571	**Liddle Kiddles,** Identification & Value Guide, Langford	$18.95
3826	Story of **Barbie,** Westenhouser	$19.95
1513	**Teddy Bears & Steiff** Animals, Mandel	$9.95
1817	**Teddy Bears & Steiff** Animals, 2nd Series, Mandel	$19.95
2084	**Teddy Bears, Annalee's & Steiff** Animals, 3rd Series, Mandel	$19.95
1808	Wonder of **Barbie,** Manos	$9.95
1430	World of **Barbie** Dolls, Manos	$9.95
4880	World of **Raggedy Ann** Collectibles, Avery	$24.95

TOYS, MARBLES & CHRISTMAS COLLECTIBLES

3427	**Advertising Character** Collectibles, Dotz	$17.95
2333	Antique & Collector's **Marbles,** 3rd Ed., Grist	$9.95
3827	Antique & Collector's **Toys,** 1870–1950, Longest	$24.95
3956	Baby Boomer **Games,** Identification & Value Guide, Polizzi	$24.95
4934	**Breyer Animal** Collector's Guide, Identification and Values, Browell	$19.95
3717	**Christmas** Collectibles, 2nd Edition, Whitmyer	$24.95
4976	**Christmas** Ornaments, Lights & Decorations, Johnson	$24.95
4737	**Christmas** Ornaments, Lights & Decorations, Vol. II, Johnson	$24.95
4739	**Christmas** Ornaments, Lights & Decorations, Vol. III, Johnson	$24.95
4649	Classic Plastic **Model Kits,** Polizzi	$24.95
4559	Collectible **Action Figures,** 2nd Ed., Manos	$17.95
3874	Collectible Coca-Cola Toy **Trucks,** deCourtivron	$24.95
2338	Collector's Encyclopedia of **Disneyana,** Longest, Stern	$24.95
4958	Collector's Guide to **Battery Toys,** Hultzman	$19.95
4639	Collector's Guide to **Diecast Toys & Scale Models,** Johnson	$19.95
4651	Collector's Guide to **Tinker Toys,** Strange	$18.95
4566	Collector's Guide to **Tootsietoys,** 2nd Ed., Richter	$19.95
4720	The Golden Age of **Automotive Toys,** 1925–1941, Hutchison/Johnson	$24.95
3436	Grist's Big Book of **Marbles**	$19.95
3970	Grist's Machine-Made & Contemporary **Marbles,** 2nd Ed.	$9.95
4723	**Matchbox** Toys, 1947 to 1996, 2nd Ed., Johnson	$18.95
4871	**McDonald's Collectibles,** Henriques/DuVall	$19.95
1540	**Modern Toys** 1930–1980, Baker	$19.95
3888	**Motorcycle** Toys, Antique & Contemporary, Gentry/Downs	$18.95
4953	Schroeder's Collectible **Toys,** Antique to Modern Price Guide, 4th Ed.	$17.95
1886	Stern's Guide to **Disney** Collectibles	$14.95
2139	Stern's Guide to **Disney** Collectibles, 2nd Series	$14.95
3975	Stern's Guide to **Disney** Collectibles, 3rd Series	$18.95
2028	**Toys,** Antique & Collectible, Longest	$14.95
3979	**Zany Characters** of the Ad World, Lamphier	$16.95

FURNITURE

1457	American **Oak** Furniture, McNerney	$9.95
3716	American **Oak** Furniture, Book II, McNerney	$12.95
1118	Antique **Oak** Furniture, Hill	$7.95
2271	Collector's Encyclopedia of **American** Furniture, Vol. II, Swedberg	$24.95
3720	Collector's Encyclopedia of **American** Furniture, Vol. III, Swedberg	$24.95
3878	Collector's Guide to **Oak** Furniture, George	$12.95
1755	Furniture of the **Depression** Era, Swedberg	$19.95
3906	**Heywood-Wakefield** Modern Furniture, Rouland	$18.95

1885	**Victorian** Furniture, Our American Heritage, McNerney	$9.9
3829	**Victorian** Furniture, Our American Heritage, Book II, McNerney	$9.9

JEWELRY, HATPINS, WATCHES & PURSES

1712	Antique & Collector's **Thimbles** & Accessories, Mathis	$19.9
1748	Antique **Purses,** Revised Second Ed., Holiner	$19.9
1278	Art Nouveau & Art Deco **Jewelry,** Baker	$9.9
4850	Collectible **Costume Jewelry,** Simonds	$24.9
3875	Collecting Antique **Stickpins,** Kerins	$16.9
3722	Collector's Ency. of **Compacts, Carryalls & Face Powder Boxes,** Mueller	$24.9
4854	Collector's Ency. of **Compacts, Carryalls & Face Powder Boxes,** Vol. II	$24.9
4940	**Costume Jewelry,** A Practical Handbook & Value Guide, Rezazadeh	$24.9
1716	Fifty Years of Collectible **Fashion Jewelry,** 1925–1975, Baker	$19.9
1424	**Hatpins** & Hatpin Holders, Baker	$9.9
4570	Ladies' **Compacts,** Gerson	$24.9
1181	100 Years of Collectible **Jewelry,** 1850–1950, Baker	$9.9
4729	**Sewing Tools** & Trinkets, Thompson	$24.9
2348	20th Century Fashionable Plastic **Jewelry,** Baker	$19.9
4878	Vintage & Contemporary **Purse Accessories,** Gerson	$24.9
3830	Vintage **Vanity Bags & Purses,** Gerson	$24.9

INDIANS, GUNS, KNIVES, TOOLS, PRIMITIVES

1868	Antique **Tools,** Our American Heritage, McNerney	$9.9
1426	**Arrowheads** & Projectile Points, Hothem	$7.9
4943	Field Guide to **Flint Arrowheads & Knives** of the North American Indian	$14.9
2279	**Indian Artifacts** of the Midwest, Hothem	$14.9
3885	**Indian Artifacts** of the Midwest, Book II, Hothem	$16.9
4870	**Indian Artifacts** of the Midwest, Book III, Hothem	$18.9
1964	**Indian Axes** & Related Stone Artifacts, Hothem	$14.9
2023	**Keen Kutter** Collectibles, Heuring	$14.9
4724	Modern **Guns,** Identification & Values, 11th Ed., Quertermous	$12.9
2164	**Primitives,** Our American Heritage, McNerney	$9.9
1759	**Primitives,** Our American Heritage, 2nd Series, McNerney	$14.9
4730	Standard **Knife** Collector's Guide, 3rd Ed., Ritchie & Stewart	$12.9

PAPER COLLECTIBLES & BOOKS

4633	**Big Little Books,** Jacobs	$18.9
4710	Collector's Guide to **Children's Books,** Jones	$18.9
1441	Collector's Guide to **Post Cards,** Wood	$9.9
2081	Guide to Collecting **Cookbooks,** Allen	$14.9
2080	Price Guide to **Cookbooks** & Recipe Leaflets, Dickinson	$9.9
3973	**Sheet Music** Reference & Price Guide, 2nd Ed., Pafik & Guiheen	$19.9
4654	**Victorian Trade Cards,** Historical Reference & Value Guide, Cheadle	$19.9
4733	**Whitman Juvenile Books,** Brown	$17.9

GLASSWARE

4561	Collectible **Drinking Glasses,** Chase & Kelly	$17.9
4642	Collectible **Glass Shoes,** Wheatley	$19.9
4937	Coll. **Glassware** from the 40s, 50s & 60s, 4th Ed., Florence	$19.9
1810	Collector's Encyclopedia of **American Art Glass,** Shuman	$29.9
4938	Collector's Encyclopedia of **Depression Glass,** 13th Ed., Florence	$19.9
1961	Collector's Encyclopedia of **Fry Glassware,** Fry Glass Society	$24.9
1664	Collector's Encyclopedia of **Heisey Glass,** 1925–1938, Bredehoft	$24.9
3905	Collector's Encyclopedia of **Milk Glass,** Newbound	$24.9
4936	Collector's Guide to **Candy Containers,** Dezso/Poirier	$19.9
4564	**Crackle Glass,** Weitman	$19.9
4941	**Crackle Glass,** Book II, Weitman	$19.9
2275	**Czechoslovakian Glass** and Collectibles, Barta/Rose	$16.9
4714	**Czechoslovakian Glass** and Collectibles, Book II, Barta/Rose	$16.9
4716	**Elegant Glassware** of the Depression Era, 7th Ed., Florence	$19.9
1380	Encyclopedia of **Pattern Glass,** McClain	$12.9
3981	Ever's Standard **Cut Glass** Value Guide	$12.9
4659	**Fenton** Art Glass, 1907–1939, Whitmyer	$24.9
3725	**Fostoria,** Pressed, Blown & Hand Molded Shapes, Kerr	$24.9
4719	**Fostoria,** Etched, Carved & Cut Designs, Vol. II, Kerr	$24.9
3883	**Fostoria Stemware,** The Crystal for America, Long & Seate	$24.9
4644	**Imperial Carnival Glass,** Burns	$18.9
3886	**Kitchen Glassware** of the Depression Years, 5th Ed., Florence	$19.9

COLLECTOR BOOKS
Informing Today's Collector

4725	Pocket Guide to **Depression Glass,** 10th Ed., Florence	$9.95
1035	Standard Encyclopedia of **Carnival Glass,** 6th Ed., Edwards/Carwile	$24.95
4636	Standard **Carnival Glass** Price Guide, 11th Ed., Edwards/Carwile	$9.95
3375	Standard Encyclopedia of **Opalescent Glass,** 2nd ed., Edwards	$19.95
4731	**Stemware Identification,** Featuring Cordials with Values, Florence	$24.95
3326	**Very Rare Glassware** of the Depression Years, 3rd Series, Florence	$24.95
4732	**Very Rare Glassware** of the Depression Years, 5th Series, Florence	$24.95
1656	**Westmoreland Glass,** Wilson	$24.95

POTTERY

4927	**ABC Plates & Mugs,** Lindsay	$24.95
4929	**American Art Pottery,** Sigafoose	$24.95
4630	**American Limoges,** Limoges	$24.95
1312	**Blue & White Stoneware,** McNerney	$9.95
1958	So. Potteries **Blue Ridge Dinnerware,** 3rd Ed., Newbound	$14.95
1959	**Blue Willow,** 2nd Ed., Gaston	$14.95
1848	Ceramic **Coin Banks,** Stoddard	$19.95
4851	Collectible **Cups & Saucers,** Harran	$18.95
4709	Collectible **Kay Finch,** Biography, Identification & Values, Martinez/Frick	$18.95
1373	Collector's Encyclopedia of **American Dinnerware,** Cunningham	$24.95
4931	Collector's Encyclopedia of **Bauer Pottery,** Chipman	$24.95
1815	Collector's Encyclopedia of **Blue Ridge Dinnerware,** Newbound	$19.95
4932	Collector's Encyclopedia of **Blue Ridge Dinnerware,** Vol. II, Newbound	$24.95
1658	Collector's Encyclopedia of **Brush-McCoy Pottery,** Huxford	$24.95
1272	Collector's Encyclopedia of **California Pottery,** Chipman	$24.95
4811	Collector's Encyclopedia of **Colorado Pottery,** Carlton	$24.95
2133	Collector's Encyclopedia of **Cookie Jars,** Roerig	$24.95
3723	Collector's Encyclopedia of **Cookie Jars,** Book II, Roerig	$24.95
4939	Collector's Encyclopedia of **Cookie Jars,** Book III, Roerig	$24.95
4638	Collector's Encyclopedia of **Dakota Potteries,** Dommel	$24.95
5040	Collector's Encyclopedia of **Fiesta,** 8th Ed., Huxford	$19.95
4718	Collector's Encyclopedia of **Figural Planters & Vases,** Newbound	$19.95
3961	Collector's Encyclopedia of **Early Noritake,** Alden	$24.95
1439	Collector's Encyclopedia of **Flow Blue China,** Gaston	$19.95
3812	Collector's Encyclopedia of **Flow Blue China,** 2nd Ed., Gaston	$24.95
3813	Collector's Encyclopedia of **Hall China,** 2nd Ed., Whitmyer	$24.95
1431	Collector's Encyclopedia of **Homer Laughlin China,** Jasper	$24.95
1276	Collector's Encyclopedia of **Hull Pottery,** Roberts	$19.95
3962	Collector's Encyclopedia of **Lefton China,** DeLozier	$19.95
4855	Collector's Encyclopedia of **Lefton China,** Book II, DeLozier	$19.95
2210	Collector's Encyclopedia of **Limoges Porcelain,** 2nd Ed., Gaston	$24.95
1334	Collector's Encyclopedia of **Majolica Pottery,** Katz-Marks	$19.95
1358	Collector's Encyclopedia of **McCoy Pottery,** Huxford	$19.95
3963	Collector's Encyclopedia of **Metlox Potteries,** Gibbs Jr.	$24.95
1837	Collector's Encyclopedia of **Nippon Porcelain,** Van Patten	$24.95
2089	Collector's Ency. of **Nippon Porcelain,** 2nd Series, Van Patten	$24.95
1665	Collector's Ency. of **Nippon Porcelain,** 3rd Series, Van Patten	$24.95
4712	Collector's Ency. of **Nippon Porcelain,** 4th Series, Van Patten	$24.95
1447	Collector's Encyclopedia of **Noritake,** Van Patten	$19.95
1432	Collector's Encyclopedia of **Noritake,** 2nd Series, Van Patten	$24.95
2037	Collector's Encyclopedia of **Occupied Japan,** 1st Series, Florence	$14.95
2038	Collector's Encyclopedia of **Occupied Japan,** 2nd Series, Florence	$14.95
2088	Collector's Encyclopedia of **Occupied Japan,** 3rd Series, Florence	$14.95
2019	Collector's Encyclopedia of **Occupied Japan,** 4th Series, Florence	$14.95
2335	Collector's Encyclopedia of **Occupied Japan,** 5th Series, Florence	$14.95
1951	Collector's Encyclopedia of **Old Ivory China,** Hillman	$24.95
3964	Collector's Encyclopedia of **Pickard China,** Reed	$24.95
4877	Collector's Encyclopedia of **R.S. Prussia,** 4th Series, Gaston	$24.95
1034	Collector's Encyclopedia of **Roseville Pottery,** Huxford	$19.95
1035	Collector's Encyclopedia of **Roseville Pottery,** 2nd Ed., Huxford	$19.95
1856	Collector's Encyclopedia of **Russel Wright,** 2nd Ed., Kerr	$24.95
4713	Collector's Encyclopedia of **Salt Glaze Stoneware,** Taylor/Lowrance	$24.95
3314	Collector's Encyclopedia of **Van Briggle** Art Pottery, Sasicki	$24.95
1563	Collector's Encyclopedia of **Wall Pockets,** Newbound	$19.95
2111	Collector's Encyclopedia of **Weller Pottery,** Huxford	$29.95
3876	Collector's Guide to **Lu-Ray Pastels,** Meehan	$18.95
3814	Collector's Guide to **Made in Japan** Ceramics, White	$18.95
4646	Collector's Guide to **Made in Japan** Ceramics, Book II, White	$18.95
4565	Collector's Guide to **Rockingham,** The Enduring Ware, Brewer	$14.95
2339	Collector's Guide to **Shawnee Pottery,** Vanderbilt	$19.95
1425	**Cookie Jars,** Westfall	$9.95

3440	**Cookie Jars,** Book II, Westfall	$19.95
4924	Figural & Novelty **Salt & Pepper Shakers,** 2nd Series, Davern	$24.95
2379	**Lehner's** Ency. of **U.S. Marks** on Pottery, Porcelain & China	$24.95
4722	**McCoy Pottery,** Collector's Reference & Value Guide, Hanson/Nissen	$19.95
3825	**Purinton Pottery,** Morris	$24.95
4726	**Red Wing Art Pottery,** 1920s–1960s, Dollen	$19.95
1670	**Red Wing Collectibles,** DePasquale	$9.95
1440	**Red Wing Stoneware,** DePasquale	$9.95
1632	**Salt & Pepper Shakers,** Guarnaccia	$9.95
5091	**Salt & Pepper Shakers** II, Guarnaccia	$18.95
2220	**Salt & Pepper Shakers** III, Guarnaccia	$14.95
3443	**Salt & Pepper Shakers** IV, Guarnaccia	$18.95
3738	**Shawnee Pottery,** Mangus	$24.95
4629	Turn of the Century **American Dinnerware,** 1880s–1920s, Jasper	$24.95
4572	**Wall Pockets** of the Past, Perkins	$17.95
3327	**Watt Pottery** – Identification & Value Guide, Morris	$19.95

OTHER COLLECTIBLES

4704	Antique & Collectible **Buttons,** Wisniewski	$19.95
2269	Antique **Brass & Copper** Collectibles, Gaston	$16.95
1880	Antique **Iron,** McNerney	$9.95
3872	Antique **Tins,** Dodge	$24.95
4845	Antique **Typewriters & Office Collectibles,** Rehr	$19.95
1714	**Black** Collectibles, Gibbs	$19.95
1128	**Bottle** Pricing Guide, 3rd Ed., Cleveland	$7.95
4636	**Celluloid Collectibles,** Dunn	$14.95
3718	Collectible **Aluminum,** Grist	$16.95
3445	Collectible **Cats,** An Identification & Value Guide, Fyke	$18.95
4560	Collectible **Cats,** An Identification & Value Guide, Book II, Fyke	$19.95
4852	Collectible **Compact Disc** Price Guide 2, Cooper	$17.95
2018	Collector's Encyclopedia of **Granite Ware,** Greguire	$24.95
3430	Collector's Encyclopedia of **Granite Ware,** Book 2, Greguire	$24.95
4705	Collector's Guide to **Antique Radios,** 4th Ed., Bunis	$18.95
3880	Collector's Guide to **Cigarette Lighters,** Flanagan	$17.95
4637	Collector's Guide to **Cigarette Lighers,** Book II, Flanagan	$17.95
4942	Collector's Guide to **Don Winton Designs,** Ellis	$19.95
3966	Collector's Guide to **Inkwells,** Identification & Values, Badders	$18.95
4947	Collector's Guide to **Inkwells,** Book II, Badders	$19.95
4948	Collector's Guide to **Letter Openers,** Grist	$19.95
4862	Collector's Guide to **Toasters** & Accessories, Greguire	$19.95
4652	Collector's Guide to **Transistor Radios,** 2nd Ed., Bunis	$16.95
4653	Collector's Guide to **TV Memorabilia,** 1960s–1970s, Davis/Morgan	$24.95
4864	Collector's Guide to **Wallace Nutting Pictures,** Ivankovich	$18.95
1629	**Doorstops,** Identification & Values, Bertoia	$9.95
4567	Figural **Napkin Rings,** Gottschalk & Whitson	$18.95
4717	Figural **Nodders,** Includes Bobbin' Heads and Swayers, Irtz	$19.95
3968	**Fishing Lure** Collectibles, Murphy/Edmisten	$24.95
4867	**Flea Market Trader,** 11th Ed., Huxford	$9.95
4944	**Flue Covers,** Collector's Value Guide, Meckley	$12.95
4945	**G-Men and FBI Toys** and Collectibles, Whitworth	$18.95
5043	**Garage Sale & Flea Market Annual,** 6th Ed.	$19.95
3819	**General Store** Collectibles, Wilson	$24.95
4643	**Great American West** Collectibles, Wilson	$24.95
2215	**Goldstein's Coca-Cola** Collectibles	$16.95
3884	**Huxford's Collectible Advertising,** 2nd Ed.	$24.95
2216	**Kitchen Antiques,** 1790–1940, McNerney	$14.95
4950	The **Lone Ranger,** Collector's Reference & Value Guide, Felbinger	$18.95
2026	**Railroad** Collectibles, 4th Ed., Baker	$14.95
4949	**Schroeder's Antiques** Price Guide, 16th Ed., Huxford	$12.95
5007	**Silverplated Flatware,** Revised 4th Edition, Hagan	$18.95
1922	Standard **Old Bottle** Price Guide, Sellari	$14.95
4708	**Summers' Guide to Coca-Cola**	$19.95
4952	**Summers' Pocket Guide to Coca-Cola** Identifications	$9.95
3892	**Toy & Miniature Sewing Machines,** Thomas	$18.95
4876	**Toy & Miniature Sewing Machines,** Book II, Thomas	$24.95
3828	**Value Guide to Advertising Memorabilia,** Summers	$18.95
3977	**Value Guide to Gas Station** Memorabilia, Summers & Priddy	$24.95
4877	**Vintage Bar Ware,** Visakay	$24.95
4935	The **W.F. Cody Buffalo Bill** Collector's Guide with Values	$24.95
4879	**Wanted to Buy,** 6th Edition	$9.95

This is only a partial listing of the books on antiques that are available from Collector Books. All books are well illustrated and contain current values. Most of these books are available from your local bookseller, antique dealer, or public library. If you are unable to locate certain titles in your area, you may order by mail from COLLECTOR BOOKS, P.O. Box 3009, Paducah, KY 42002-3009. Customers with Visa, Discover or MasterCard may phone in orders from 7:00–5:00 CST, Monday–Friday, Toll Free 1-800-626-5420. Add $2.00 for postage for the first book ordered and $0.30 for each additional book. Include item number, title, and price when ordering. Allow 14 to 21 days for delivery.

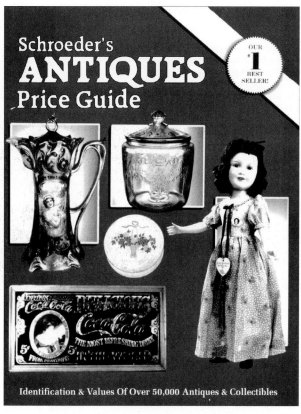